⋀ SELDOM SEEN

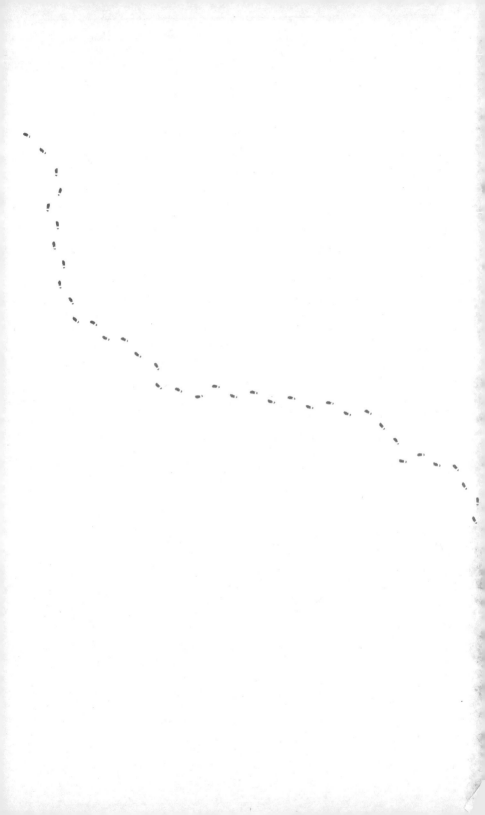

Seldom Seen

A JOURNEY INTO

THE GREAT PLAINS

Patrick Dobson

University of Nebraska Press
Lincoln and London

Manufactured in the United States of America

⊗

Library of Congress Cataloging-in-Publication Data
Dobson, Patrick.
Seldom seen : a journey into the Great Plains /
Patrick Dobson.
p. cm.
ISBN 978-0-8032-1616-7 (cloth : alk. paper)
1. Great Plains—Description and travel. 2. West
(U.S.)—Description and travel. 3. Dobson, Patrick—
Travel—Great Plains. 4. Dobson, Patrick—Travel—
West (U.S.) 5. Walking—Great Plains. 6. Automobile
travel—Great Plains. 7. Great Plains—History, Local.
8. West (U.S.)—History, Local. 9. Great Plains—
Social life and customs. 10. West (U.S.)—Social
life and customs. I. Title.
F595.3.D63 2009
917.804'33—dc22
2009004812

Set in Bulmer by Kim Essman.
Designed by Nathan Putens.

To
Virginia,
Sydney, and Nicholas.
You make all things
possible.

✦

ALLONS! the road is before us!
It is safe — I have tried it — my own feet have tried it
  well — be not detain'd! Let the paper remain on the
  desk unwritten, and the book on the shelf unopen'd!
Let the tools remain in the workshop! Let the money
  remain unearn'd!
Let the school stand! Mind not the cry of the teacher!
Let the preacher preach in his pulpit! Let the lawyer
  plead in the court, and the judge expound the law.

Camerado, I give you my hand!
I give you my love more precious than money,
I give you myself before preaching or law;
Will you give me yourself? Will you come travel with me?
Shall we stick by each other as long as we live?

WALT WHITMAN, "Song of the Open Road"

Contents

Acknowledgments

THE PEOPLE OF the Great Plains made *Seldom Seen* possible, those whose stories make up the bulk of this book and many hundreds whose stories I didn't have room here to tell. Some people stand out more than others, not because those to whom I grew close are more important than those I only knew in passing. Rather, I was fortunate to make intense friendships and meet many more people whom I wish I could have known better. It is in this spirit that I give my thanks to Craig and Jeff Bedard, Roland Bennett and Michelle Zell, Barney Buzdikian, James and Mickey Lee, Gordon Longtree, Kim and Leah Merchant, Joe Pollard, and Johnny Whisenant. Without them and the others whose names I cannot remember or never knew, I wouldn't be who I am today.

My wife, Virginia Dobson, and my daughter, Sydney Rebel, have dealt with this book for nearly seven years. Virginia has been its strongest critic. She read the manuscript repeatedly, pointing out when I had become selfish and self-serving in the text, as well as around the house. Sydney encouraged me to be the very best person and father I could. Due to this manuscript, Nicholas, our new arrival, has had to put up with having a distracted dad at home but was encouraging and supportive all the same.

My newspaper editor, Bruce Rodgers, published the first kernels of this story and made me a journalist. He thinks enough of me and my work to publish my articles, book reviews, and commentary in his Kansas City–based publications EKC and Discover Mid-America. His contributions to my life and writing are unparalleled.

Das Gemeinschaft Glas und Glaube — Udo Bethke, Ivo Rauch, Martin Streit, and Stephan Weinert; Joachim Frick, Andrea Schnellenbach, and Grahame Williams were and are ever close by, as well as Marlies and Joseph Frick, whom I love dearly. They supported me even in the darkest moments of my life and continue in that work to this day.

Martha, J. D., and Dean Hall supplied my backpack and everything in it from their store, Sticks 'n' Stones, in Raytown, Missouri. Without their support I would have been much poorer in money and spirit.

The University of Missouri–Kansas City History Department and its chair, Dr. Louis Potts, supported the writing of the final manuscript. During and after submission of the manuscript to the University of Nebraska Press, my dissertation director, Dr. John Herron, guided me through self-doubt in writing and in my doctoral studies in American environmental history. Conversations with Dr. Pellom McDaniels concerning American history and the intensely personal issues I worked through in the text were extraordinarily helpful. During our twenty-five-year acquaintance, Dr. James Falls (history) and Dr. Henry Frankel (philosophy), it seems, have believed in me and have always been sources of great encouragement. My good friends Dr. Steven John Dilks and Dr. Dan Mahala have been extraordinarily helpful and understanding in my work as a student and author. Steve took a great deal of his precious time to read and comment on the manuscript and help me through its editing.

Dr. William Neaves of the Stowers Institute for Medical Research helped me through my flawed copyediting skills and often lent heaping amounts of encouragement. I cannot say enough good things about Bill as a friend, scholar, and reader.

Heather Lundine and Bridget Barry have had faith in me and this book since the project first arrived on Heather's desk at the University of Nebraska Press. These gentle but firm editors are responsible for guiding *Seldom Seen* through the vagaries of revision, editing, and publication. Matt Bokovoy of the Oklahoma University Press gave significant encouragement as I developed this manuscript, and without him, it would never have gotten to Heather and Bridget.

Barbara Rebel and Kristi Nyberg are two brilliant, important women. They showed a great deal of patience during the trip that makes this story. I am ever indebted to them.

I owe much to the people who heard this story until they knew it as well as I did: my uncles Bill Bauer and Charles Dobson, John Biondo, Rev. David and Marie DeChant, Rob and Carol Eckhardt, Kelly Gilbert, Peter Hancock, Don Hooten, Gary Jenkins, Kevin Kinghorn, Ken Larson and Janet Ridder, Hugh O'Donnell, Patrick O'Kelley, Jeff and Kelly Rupellius, Jeph and Cherie Scanlon, Al Snodgrass, Calvin Williford, Jeff Ramsey, and Tiger Marion. Anyone would want friends such as these.

Without prodding from Conger Beasley Jr., this journey would never have made it from shoe leather to manuscript.

Finally, I am grateful to my good friend and uncle, Phil Bauer, for teaching me that any journey—including life—is just one step after another.

✶ SELDOM SEEN

1

A Leap into the Prairie Sea

IN THE SPRING of 1994, it came time to swim.

For weeks, the smell of redemption floated through windows on sweet western winds. Without my noticing it, every breeze became laced with fragrances of mown hay, cow dung, and dew on willows; perfumes of grass and rain and plowed ground. The ocean-like expanses of prairie promised baptism—a transformed life. When I slept, thunder rumbled through dreams the color of maturing wheat. I only needed a push, however slight, to jump into the grassy sea.

My existence had closed in on me, grown insular and stifling. Repairing furniture and doing general labor in an upscale hotel's engineering department rarely varied. Although I was only thirty-one, a day of adjusting thermostats or buffing chair arms for the wealthy wore me out. I spent evenings parked at the television, wondering what I'd done wrong. I was always getting off work and getting ready for work. Because of this, the Kansas City, Missouri,

I grew up in, with all its grand possibilities, looked and felt smaller at the end of every shift. As spring broke through winter, gray and brown, the city faded into grimy and sinister twilight. I became restless, critical of everything, and cynical about my own bad lot.

Two related and deeply conflicting fears kept me awake at night: Unless I changed, life would mean endless despondency and despair. Change, however, would take me into unknown territory where people like me were consumed by a mean and unforgiving world.

As a part-time single father, I used my daughter, Sydney, as an excuse to avoid taking charge of my own fortunes. Working people have to work, I told myself. I had to have a job. Bills needed to be paid whether I liked it or not: kid, rent, health insurance, and 401k contributions. My worth as a human being lies in endless files of pay stubs and records of taxes paid. Others were responsible for my misery: Sydney and her mom, my parents, my bosses and the companies they worked for, utility companies, landlords, and vast, abstracted hoards of strangers who dressed better, talked better, and lived more comfortable lives than I did. At the same time, I was petrified to think of losing time clocks, balanced checkbooks, and bragging rights based on timely payment of rent and child support. While I yearned for independence from the strictures of working life, I wanted, even needed, to be told what to do.

The contradictions became too heavy to bear. In May 1994 I was painting the floor of the engineering department the same battleship gray I painted it every month. Unmarred paint grew from the edges of the concrete-and-cinder-block room until I stood in a bare, jagged circle of dirty floor. "Nah . . . dammit," I said, feeling pretty dumb. I stared down at the paint roller, smelled the cold concrete and latex, and ran out of breath. My heart raced and pounded in my ears. A flash of lightning reflected off the door open to the loading dock and trash bins. The rumble of thunder that followed echoed in my chest. A rain-soaked breeze wafted through the steel door. The smell of mown grass and wet dirt cut through the fug of paint, cold metal, and garbage. There was a sharp ping in my chest, like the breaking of a spring wound too tightly. I had to act before getting so accustomed to gloom that I would never escape.

That afternoon I stared out my half-opened living-room window. Another thunderstorm set down on the city. Its weight and electricity, its cool, wet breezes felt good. The lightning flashes stirred memories of family vacations when I was growing up. I indulged myself in reflection.

Every year without fail, on a Friday in June or July, my mom, aggravated and harried, would herd my three siblings and me around the house and garage while she loaded our 1965 Dodge Polara station wagon with food, camping gear, and clothes. When dad arrived home from work in the evening, we'd eat a hasty dinner off paper plates and dive into the car to chase sunsets across Kansas. Besides occasionally scolding us for being kids with nothing to do, my dad was quiet and anxious to get across the Kansas plains. To him prairie was enemy of all things civilized. He would drive after sunset to avoid having to look at the expanses he reviled. Flat, ordinary, and "too damned hot," Kansas stood between him and calendar-photo backdrops of mountains, cold streams, and crisp air tinged with the sting of pine resin.

But that drive, repeated throughout my youth, was the most wonderful thing I knew. Sitting at the open window that afternoon, the memory of it haunted me and I ached for it. As we drove and evening fell, my siblings settled into somnambulant stares. Shadows lengthened across the rolling hills of eastern Kansas, giving them uncanny depth and mesmerizing color. Miles flowed by with the low hum of the Polara's V-8 and the tick-tick of rubber bumping over sections of concrete pavement. The Flint Hills' rocky-topped mesas disappeared into night, emerging again in profile against flashes of heat lightning. The stars flecked my parents' dark silhouettes in the green checks and slashes of dashboard lights reflected off the inside of the Polara's long side windows. A stillness filled the car, although the vehicle rocked and dipped and shook. Tinny voices and country music on the AM radio emerged from magical, insubstantial static. To me the voices sounded like astronauts from distant galaxies called Springfield, Illinois; Johnstown, Pennsylvania; Sedalia, Missouri.

By the time we arrived at a state park near Wilson, Kansas, my father had undergone a transformation even greater than prairie turning into night. He was free from the lonely, windowless, fluorescent-lighted room where he repaired broken cash registers. My family, as a whole, felt his relief. We children were no longer burdens to be endured with a six-pack after a day of tedium. He was jovial and loving, as he was only rarely, if ever, at home.

With happy determination, he erected our family-sized tent from confused bundles of poles, ropes, and canvas. While my dad hummed and whistled, the vacuum of night drew me past the outer ring of lantern light. Surrounded by the smells of grass wet with dew, prairie dust, and bare limestone, I stared into a clear, star-addled sky rimmed with blazes of heat lightning. Later, comfortably wrapped in my sleeping bag, I drifted to sleep, watching the tent light up with those flashes, listening to the sounds of my family sleeping and the cool wind in the grass.

Mornings on those vacations' first days, I stumbled sleepy-eyed into a blue and green and brown world of treeless, rolling hills. The sun shone brighter than at home; the land and sky were as deep and wide as I imagined the ocean to be. Windmills spiked the hills here and there. I stood or sat a little way from the tent and car, and just stared into the space. Too soon dad would scream that it was to leave and mom would herd us back into the car. Once in, my dad drove angrily, as if he couldn't sail us across the open plains and into the mountains fast enough.

I never forgot the feeling of those mornings on the prairie. Once I was old enough to drive, I made prairie journeys when restlessness and fear drove me to frustration and anger. Such trips into the endless expanses began as adventures. The gray-blue dark of a thunderstorm, a blanket of wheat or sunflowers, and the smell of dust and dry grass renewed my spirit and allowed me to imagine new possibilities when I returned to working life. But the wishful and grandiose thinking soon faded to disappointment. Fearing change, I plodded back into routine and lost the hope I'd felt on the road. For a decade and a half, I used these sojourns, long and short, as an addict uses drugs. Respite from the restlessness and fear grew ever briefer. My need to relieve these maladies pressed on me in greater measure. A short overnight or a few days in Gove County, Kansas, or Nebraska's Sandhills might let me weather a few weeks or days of old habit. But I needed more Gove Counties, more Sandhills, and more windmills atop naked hills to sate deepening depressions.

That May afternoon in 1994, I watched rain fall outside my front window and said aloud to myself without thinking, "Helena, Montana." The utterance made sense. Helena was the biggest town farthest across the Great Plains from Kansas City. Though I had only ever seen Helena as a dot on a map, I decided that in one year I would go there—on foot. Taking off across the plains struck me as the right and proper thing to do. I would inundate myself in sky and land. Kansas, Nebraska, and Wyoming, I thought, would show me a way to find a new life.

In an instant, I gained something to strive for, a real, definable goal that seemed possible. My mind raced. I realized that in all my travels, I had only ever seen the Great Plains from a car. Except for those nights between frantic drives to the mountains, I never knew what it was to be in the landscape, a part of it. What I knew of people and towns of the plains, I had gathered from rest stops and gas stations. I wanted to move slower, to feel the distance and lose myself in it. I wanted to know the plains more deeply than from conversations with strangers filling their gas tanks or coffee thermoses. With decent shoes and a backpack I would become familiar with the scenery and its people. I wouldn't hitchhike. I would need no gas stations or interstates. If offered a ride, I would take it, but no farther than the distance of a day's walk. That was enough.

After the storm, I took Sydney, who was almost three, for a walk down the green, dripping alley behind our house. I told her of my nascent plan and added, as an afterthought, that I might return on the Missouri River in a canoe.

"Why go on a trip, dad?" she said. She was holding my hand, watching cardinals flitter from puddles to trees and back again.

"It makes sense."

"Why?" she said. We stopped to pick a few violets out of the gravel next to the pavement.

"To change things up a little, I guess."

She smiled, cocked her head, and raised her hands, palms up. "I'm happy for you, Dad. When we get home, can I have some candy?"

I felt guilty. She was too young to understand. I would be leaving her for several months. But my desire to escape my self-centered trap outweighed what seemed to be a self-serving expedition. I'd been nudged and had jumped. The journey was already underway.

For the next year, I served banquets at the hotel in the evening after working in the engineering department. I wheedled as much overtime as I could out of my bosses. I calculated how each hour would contribute toward paying child support, day care, rent, and expenses for the five months I thought the trip might take.

Slowly and cautiously, I let my workmates in on my plan. Some discounted the idea outright. Others' eyes lit up when I spoke of what I wanted to do. Without fail, however, they asked questions that filled me with dread. What will you eat? Where will you sleep? What will you do when it rains?

My friend Zaid asked me one day as we were rolling round banquet tables into the ballroom, "So, mister, are you taking a gun on your trip?"

"What for?" The thought hadn't occurred to me.

"For protection, you know. There's all kinds of people out there. What happens if you run into someone who wants you or your stuff?" He wrinkled his eyebrows, pursed his lips, and nodded his head. "Oh, yeah; you'll want to take a gun."

His question and advice caught me off guard.

"Zaid," I said finally, "I want to meet people, not shoot them."

"That's idiotic," he said, as he snapped the metal table legs into place and hefted his table upright. He shook his head as he walked away, leaving me alone in the cavernous ballroom.

Zaid was only the first to ask if I would take a gun. Soon it was the first question people asked and the most frequent—before inquiries about why I wanted to go. Abstract criminal hordes, lone stranglers, and sex fiends came to my friends' minds before wild nature, wild weather, or wildlife. Frankly, I was scared of people *and* nature, but shooting at them didn't strike me as a way to change life for the better. I would have to deal with my deep-seated fears the same way I would deal with the unknown path I had chosen. I would just have to meet it and see what happened.

From the day the gray paint revealed a sad future if I did not alter its course, I climbed through thick curtains of dread and doubt. Many times only two things kept me going: the fear of not taking the trip and never being able to, and the work of getting things together for the trip. Paying for simple equipment, such as a pack stove, shelter, and boots, demanded more labor at the hotel than just what was needed to cover five months of bills. I arranged through a local retail store and a canoe maker in Maine to get the most expensive items gratis—and suffered uneasy feelings of having asked for others' charity. I queried hundreds of publications around the country about writing a column or story about the trip. I received only two letters of interest. One was from the editor of a local alternative newspaper who wanted a story and a picture from the road every two weeks. The other was from a national magazine that never returned my reply.

Meanwhile I tried to get in shape to make the trip, but failed. After long hours at work I lacked the energy to do much else than watch TV and sleep. I decided to get in shape along the way—the dumbest resolution I ever made. Hands down.

Exactly one year after the gray paint, the thunderstorms, and the walk in the alley, I pulled on my backpack and stepped off my front porch, without a gun, into an unknown world.

2

"I'm going to Helena, Montana"

MY TRIP STARTED late in the morning on May 1, 1995. It also ended that day and almost didn't begin again. A year of working, saving, and daydreaming had not readied me for the actual experience of walking away from home. Misgiving and anxiety hounded me across the park in front of my house and on across the city. Montana, if there was such a place, seemed impossibly far away. How long was it going to take, really? What would I do if, as Zaid said, someone wanted me or my stuff? Where would I sleep?

After five anxiety-ridden miles, I turned toward home. Ashamed, I spun around to continue west. Just as quickly I whirled around again. I paced the same block in a suburban neighborhood for over an hour. I finally convinced myself that it was too late in the day to continue and that it was time to go home. In the early evening I climbed my porch steps, embarrassed, isolated, and afraid.

I moped through the front door, and dropped my pack and boots in the middle of the living-room floor. They looked pathetically inadequate for exploring a world that had existed largely in my head for the previous decades. Feeling cowardly, I chided myself for being—myself. What was I trying to prove? Why couldn't I just go to work and raise a kid like everybody else? Why couldn't I follow through on one courageous change? One minute I was determined to leave early the next day; the next, I resolved to stay home for good. But no excuse seemed sufficient for abandoning the trip—not after all the work and effort. And regardless of courage, I couldn't return to work and face people I had told a hundred times I was leaving. I had to go. I was frightened. I wanted to disappear.

After a few hours I surrendered, if only out of exhaustion. It's natural to be frightened, I said. Anyone would be. It's all right to have a rough beginning. Take a deep breath, try again. I went out and flopped into the porch swing. Venus fell behind the oak trees and apartment buildings silhouetted against the sunset's last pale light. Morning would bring a new day and a fresh start. Knowing it might take time to muster the courage to make such a big leap, I gave myself permission to fall short and felt the tension ease in my chest. I called my uncle Phil, at whose house I had planned to spend the night, and told him that I would see him the next day.

When the alarm went off in the morning, I was staring at the ceiling, conjuring the guts to put my feet to the floor. I talked myself through putting boots on, eating, pulling on the pack. When off the front porch, I was determined to get across the park. The noonday sun was warm on my face. Kids played on the fountain, and their screams and shouts were reassuring—children were playing in fountains and swimming pools the same way all the way across the plains. I'd cross town to Uncle Phil's place. Then I'd decide if I wanted to go further. In the meantime, I'd take my time and just walk. Walking's good.

By the time I made it to my father's childhood home, just two blocks from my front door, a reflective calm had settled in. Flecks of light fell through the elm and walnut trees and wandered over the grass. Parti-colored impatiens seemed to whirl in window boxes. In this house, when I was a kid, my dad pulled me away from holiday dinners into the mildewed basement. He pulled two three-legged stools up to shelves stacked with steamer trunks. From these he lifted flaking, black-and-white photographs and crumbling newspapers. He held them to the bare bulb with a gentleness and reverence he reserved only for these moments. He didn't know who the people in the pictures were; only that imagining them in their time helped him escape his tormented life for a moment. Down there in the basement he didn't complain. He was not angry or disappointed. He was solemn, calm. He even smiled.

As I grew into my teens I often snuck downstairs to the shelves alone. Amid slick, black seeps and stands of broken furniture, the vagaries of growing up disappeared in memories of moments when my father was gentle, relaxed, and attentive. Dusty air and the smell of mothballs wafted from the trunks when I lifted their lids. I climbed up on a stool and made up my own stories about the dour Germans and pugnacious Irish peering from the photos, their backs straight, collars stiff. They were so disconnected from my Technicolor world, they intrigued and frightened me. They had my physical features. Their serious and unsmiling faces were set on broad shoulders and thick necks. They all had my small eyes and broad chin. Their hands, set one on the other or gently folded, were like my father's, his father's, and mine—rough and wide with knuckles like knots in rope.

Now I looked up into the trees and took a deep breath. Fear and excitement jostled deep in my chest. I laughed at how silly and embarrassed I had felt the day before. The air tasted of walnut leaves and cut grass. The sun flashed through the leaves. As I walked away from the house, I felt the ground rising under my boots. My world, once so small and close, had suddenly become startlingly large and uncertain—and exciting because of it. Without walls and fences, everything was possible. With no shades to pull, no doors to lock, nothing to hide behind, the world was as exposed to me as I was to it. There was good in that.

I walked tree-lined streets into the neighborhood where my uncles Phil and Chris had grown up. Phil was my age and Chris four years older. We knew the neighborhood's broad sweeps and tiny corners as only kids allowed to wander can. The old houses inspired stories—monsters in basements, crazy sisters chained in attics, Russian spies hiding in garden sheds. Imagining villains in the shadows and gunfighters around corners, we played hide-and-seek among neighbors' houses and in the shade of huge, ancient trees. We meandered through yards and alleys to the nearby shopping district to play pinball or roller skate down the sidewalks. We avoided neighbors we knew would scold us and made sure those who would fix us lemonade knew we were around. Evenings, when we were supposed to be at home (or close to it), the three of us played in the street in front of my uncles' house while neighbors sat on their porches drinking coffee and watching evening turn to night. After dark we swung in the glider on the porch and watched people walking their dogs and chatting with neighbors.

Phil and Chris's neighborhood was a stark contrast to my own. My family lived in a newer part of town. Chain-link fences cordoned yards and linked identical houses together. There were no porches, only garages and nondescript front doors. My mom often chased my siblings and me from the house to "do something outside." But there was rarely anything to do. There were no alleys, odd corners, or empty lots, no parks or playgrounds. Neighbor kids stayed in their yards and rarely invited us in. My siblings and I tried to make up tales of monsters and Russian spies. But such stories attached to interchangeable houses were never scary, just contrived and empty. I spent endless hours moping around the rusty swing set in my back-yard, looking forward to weekly visits with my uncles in a world wider, brighter, and more human than my own.

In the early 1980s, when I was twenty, I fled home for the urban neighborhoods where Phil, Chris, and I had wandered as kids. Except for two years working as a vineyard apprentice in Germany and two years in grad school at the University of Wyoming in Laramie, I had lived in the inner city ever since. Now, as I walked streets that had been part of my life for so long, I began to understand how time had changed the old neighborhood. The yards were uniformly trimmed, and many were fenced. The once shabby alleys were treeless. Cars lined every inch of curb. In the shopping district, upscale and boutique shops and department stores replaced dime and drug stores. Kids on roller skates had disappeared. Still, the architecture varied and was pleasing to the eye. And while life here had changed over the years and with generations, streets were still alive with pedestrians.

I crossed the indistinct state boundary into Kansas. The road ran down through the bluffs into the Kansas River valley, between rows of new apartments and ramshackle houses. The day had grown hot. Just a few hours into the trip, my feet were searing and raw, and my hips and knees ached. My mood had become heavy. I took a break in the narrow shadow of a First World War artillery cannon in the scrubby square of a park. I didn't know how the downward swing in my disposition had begun—whether from dodging bottles thrown from passing cars or from the heat of the day and the weight of the pack. To distract myself, I read and reread the American Legion's bronze plaque commemorating the dedication of the cannon. I looked out over the industrial haze blanketing the valley floor. Tentacles of railroad and pavement roped together grain elevators and shabby neighborhoods. My thoughts raced between doubt and determination. I looked for a sign. The muzzle of the cannon pointed at a McDonald's across the street.

A cold drink in the air-conditioned restaurant eased the anxiety and renewed my purpose. The rhythm of walking soon elevated my mood. I cut along the top of the north side of bluffs overlooking the Kansas River. The houses near downtown Kansas City, Kansas, were dilapidated but full of life. The air smelled of fried rice and enchiladas. Porch-swing conversations bubbled in Spanish, Haitian French, and Vietnamese. An old man in a bowler and dusty suit, walking an ancient and bloated dog, asked me where I was headed and shook my hand when I told him. Firefighters waved at me from lawn chairs in front of their firehouses. Shouts in Spanish and Vietnamese echoed in the dark interiors of auto repair shops. At bus stops, old people, working men, and young mothers talked and read newspapers. A pretty young girl walked out of the sun with two children behind her and one in her arms. The sidewalk was cracked, the buildings around her crumbling. A door squeaked and banged in the breeze. "Buenos dias," she said, and smiled. The ache in my shoulders and feet eased.

Soon this liveliness faded into ranch and split-level neighborhoods, and strip malls and shopping centers. Then the sidewalk ran out; it just ended in the middle of someone's yard. The houses seemed empty and lifeless on their groomed squares of grass. Although there were no people on the street, I began to feel self-conscious, like I had the day before—as if all eyes were on me. I found myself making sure that my shirt was tucked in and my socks were even. I felt ridiculous.

My feet began to burn again as I crossed hundreds of acres of blazing parking lots. I was shuffling past a tire store in one of those lots when my uncle Phil pulled his small pickup next to me.

"Hey, bud, you're walking kinda funny," he said. He puffed a cigarette and tugged the brim of his ball cap.

"My feet hurt." I shifted from one foot to the other, like I was dancing on hot coals.

"Wanna ride the rest of the way?" He looked out the window at my boots. I looked with him.

"No. I'll make it to your place," I said to the ground.

"Have it your way. How're you feeling?" He draped his hand

with the cigarette over the wheel and squinted out over the expanse of yellow-striped pavement. Heat shimmered in mirages.

"Excited," I said. "Scared."

"What of?"

"I don't know. Of everything." I put my hand on his door; the hot metal shot a molten bolt into my chest and up my neck. It felt good.

"Thought so." He puffed his cigarette, blowing the smoke into the sky. "Don't worry. You're just going to my place, two more miles. I'll meet you there. I'm running an errand and'll be back in an hour or so. Call if things get hard."

He pulled his cap lower and shifted his truck into gear. He pulled across six lanes and headed east. I stumbled on. The malls and stacks of apartments soon broke into isolated developments. The sky yellowed and the sun ducked behind jagged lines of cedar and scrubby oak.

In front of Phil's apartment building I eased onto the warm cement of the stoop and took off my boots. I pulled off my socks and considered my feet. Fifteen miles had wrecked them. Blisters covered the backs and bottoms of both heels and most of my toes. As I sat trying to banish the thought of fourteen hundred more miles, a rusting Cadillac convertible with Texas plates pulled to the curb and coughed into silence. The driver, a tall and lanky man, clicked to the apartment door on the heels of his cowboy boots and stood with his hand on the knob. His short-sleeve print shirt flapped open, exposing tufts of gray hair on his bony chest.

"Whurya from?" he said. He squinted and his face wrinkled like a wadded towel.

"Well, I left early this afternoon from Gillham Park in Midtown." I said. Suddenly, I wasn't sure I was going to make it much farther.

"No shee-it. Them feet of yours look bad." With boots cocked beneath bowlegs, looking like a marionette, he pulled a cigarette from his shirt pocket and hung it on his lower lip.

"They are," I said.

"Whoya waitin' for?"

"My uncle, Phil Bauer. He lives here on the basement floor. He'll be back soon."

"Whurya goin'?" He touched a lighter to his smoke and then reached inside his shirt and scratched.

"I'm going to Helena, Montana."

"With nothin' but that pack?"

"Yeah. That's what I want to do," I said.

"Ooooh, mah Gawd, you crazy bastard sombitch," he growled. He slung himself through the door and slammed it, cleaving the blue balloon of cigarette smoke.

Later, after Phil and I had eaten, we turned off the lights and settled into the couch to watch a video. A storm blew in from the west, heavy and loud.

"You going be all right?" Phil asked when the movie was over. We listened to the thunder as we sat in the glow of the TV.

"Hell, I don't know" I said. "One minute I'm bouncing along, happy to be on my way and feeling great; the next I'm down in the dumps and scared shitless."

"Anxiety, I think they call it," he said with a nod. "I feel like that a lot. Mornings mostly. But don't worry. You've only done one day. Things're going to get better. I can almost guarantee it."

When Phil went to bed, I lay on the couch, listening to the rain. Thunder shook the apartment. Rain splattered from a downspout outside the little window. The wind whipped the curtains and lightning set specters dancing against the wall. The sharp tang of ozone hung in the air. By morning the rain had turned to steady drizzle.

Phil asked through the steam of his coffee if I wanted a ride. After months of wanting to get underway, to get out of town, I said yes. A few minutes later, the windshield wipers beat melancholy rhythms against the foggy morning. Junkyards and shuttered antique shops along the banks of the Kansas River gave way to fading red-and-white farmhouses and dilapidated barns. We entered a stretch of fog that narrowed the world to the road and shoulder. Phil pulled into a parking lot on a dreary business strip outside Bonner Springs, a small town on the edge of Kansas City, Kansas.

"It's always going be just one thing, you know," Phil said. He looked over a cigarette and smiled. "You do just one thing, anything, and then you do another. That's what'll get you down the road."

I looked into the fog through the drops on the windshield. The places I had seen while walking to Phil's had been familiar, but they had seemed fresh and filled with both beauty and a delicious ugliness that I had never seen from a car. The next thing, the thing in front of me, wasn't so frightening. I wasn't going to Montana today, I thought, just to Lawrence, Kansas. I pulled on my nylon rain gear and stepped from the truck.

"You know my number," Phil said. He pulled his hood up against the rain. He gave me a hug, stepped back, and lit another cigarette, his hands trembling in the cold. He handed me a small stone from his pocket, his lucky stone, and told me to keep it. "Wherever you are, just call. I can't drive out to get you from Bumfuck but we can make sure you get back somehow." He shoved his hands in his armpits and gazed out over the trees toward the river.

3

"Don't worry, kid, you'll be all right"

THE WATERPROOF NYLON pants I'd put on at the back of Phil's truck shed rain into my boots. But one step after another, the first mile into Bonner Springs eased a bone-deep chill that had come from more things than the cold air.

The rhythm of walking worked up through my body, anesthetized joints and feet, and began to clear the fog of worry. Thoughts began to bump along with strides and footfalls, cracks in the shoulder, and guardrail posts. Soon I felt as if I was blending into and flowing along the ribbon of pavement. Human and nature merged. Bud-filigreed trees scratched against the melancholy dimness of the day. Spears of new grass poked through narrow strips of winter-dead weeds in parking lots and along road shoulders. Beyond the town, the road fell into a grassy valley rimmed with oak and hickory. The aroma of cow dung, new asphalt pavement, and cut grass floated on the air. A creek sloshed and splattered under the hum of a factory and the sound of rain. A yellow lab, square across the breast and head high, loped down a long drive from a faded chartreuse split-level set on an incline above a weed-choked pond. Behind the house, a lone pair of jeans ran in the wind on a clothesline. Backhoes and tractors sat cow-like in blue-green carpets of wheat sweeping the horizon.

Ten miles from Bonner Springs the wind picked up and turned cold. A steel curtain closed off the sky, cloaking everything in dark, electric blue-gray. Wet and shivering, I took refuge in a convenience store under cottonwoods next to the Kansas River. The place smelled of microwave burritos and hot dogs sweating under heat lamps.

Dripping, I stood at the window a minute and watched the rain beat down on the road and the fields beyond. This kind of weather had been my favorite my whole life. Any storm that rendered the day into something new brought a certain kind of danger and relief with it. Thunder and lightning released long-built, hidden tensions in my chest and neck. The sound of rain, light or pounding, soothed me, as if the chaotic rattle put some angry, caged animal inside to sleep. Dark, wet days stirred melancholy and put me into moods rife with memory and introspection. Watching the storm through the window of the store and knowing I would be out in it again, I felt excitement bred of contentment, nostalgia for other days, and fear.

After I changed clothes in the store's bathroom, the woman under an imposing pile of hair behind the register invited me to the stools at a long counter. She cupped an elbow in one hand and a cigarette in the other. I sat down with a cup of coffee. A man seated at the counter said he had been the area's mail carrier his entire career. He looked at my boots bubbling at the seams.

"Yeah, I gave up my job 'cause of days like today," he said, laughing. Leaning forward on the counter, he twisted his head up to look at me. "Really. I'm retired. I looked forward to retirement my whole life. It was going to be different, you know. Something new every day. Only once I was retired I didn't know what to do. I sometimes walk, just for the hell of it, just to get some of that feeling of the old days. At least I know how to walk."

"Don't let him kid you," the woman under the hair scoffed. She leaned between the register and a rack of lighters and Slim Jims. "Every day he walks from that house over there," she pointed to a house across the street, "to here." She pointed at the counter. "Bugs me to death 'cause he keeps winning that damn keno and rubs my nose in it." A new number came up on the video screen above the counter where we sat. Both took up pencils and checked their cards.

"I hope you're slow enough to miss the snow," the woman said, not looking up from her card. "Blizzard blew through Nebraska yesterday. Big news."

"It'll be better when I get there," I said, trying not to reveal the uncertainty her statement had put into me.

"It'll be cold and wet," the mailman said, looking serious and doubtful. Then his eyes lit up and his face broke into a smile. He giggled and slapped me on the back. With a new number up on the video screen, he checked his keno card.

"Don't worry, kid," he said, blackening a circle with his pencil. "You'll be all right. I walked in cold and wet my whole life. Look at me." He leaned back and grabbed his ample paunch with both hands. "I turned out all right."

"Ha," the cashier sneered. She looked over her glasses at me with a grin.

I headed out when the rain stopped. Cold wind whipped and stung my face until after a few miles the cloud cover began to break. Occasional streaks of sunlight played across the road and fields. I rested on guardrails where stands of trees swayed over creeks. I lit out from those pauses bouncing the pack against my butt. I felt I had the entire world to myself and began to hum to the sound and feel of my feet on the pavement. At first I looked to make sure that no one was around to hear. But within four or five miles, I lost every shred of self-consciousness and began to talk to myself openly, making jokes, singing, and yelling as loud as I could. I whistled long-forgotten tunes, made up silly walking-rhythm melodies, and laughed at my own jokes. A lost thought or forgotten lyrics halted the yakking and singing. The sudden silence produced a buzz in my ears broken only by the sound of wind in the grass. After a while I took up talking to pigs and chickens, which seemed not to notice. Herds of cattle, however, swung their heads to follow me as I walked by them. They reminded me of senators listening to a speech or hoards of serious opera patrons. I addressed one of these cow congresses: "No, no. I'm not going to Montana today, no sir. I'm gonna save Lawrence from Quantrill." I lectured to another: "Ladies and gentlemen, some would try to tell you that money is the object of life. They are wrong. The object of life is repeated conjugation—verbal, physical, and microbial." To another I shouted, "I'm the new sheriff in this town! I make the law, and you do as I say!" And to yet another, "Texas John Slaughter made 'em do what they oughter. They didn't. Zip. They died." Harebrained aphorisms chugged through my head and mouth to the cadence of my stride: "An apple a day keeps the girlies at bay." "Red eye in fright puts you out for the night." "Cold hands, hot weenie; cold hands, hot weenie; cold hands, hot weenie."

The highway dropped out of wooded hills to the floor of the Kansas River Valley, an expanse of black fields and squares of wheat, level as standing water. A few knots of trees around farmhouses and a serpentine line of cottonwoods along a creek broke the valley's uniformity. Traffic grew heavier. The shoulder shrunk to a narrow rattle of pavement and then to an anemic strip of rock and sand. Drivers seemed to creep closer as they approached. I moved off the shoulder. My once-jovial banter grew courser in vocabulary and intent, as blistered feet tripped over knotted tufts of grass. "Shit, shit, shit," I said to myself. "Torture, one step at a time."

Just north of Lawrence, a concrete tepee stood in a small grove of oaks near a crossroad. Massachusetts Street wound past a motel, gas station, and auto body shop—all named "Jayhawk" after the pro-Union guerillas that populated the country around the town during the Civil War. The Kansas University athletic teams were Jayhawks, their fans Jayhawkers. The word has grown into a collective identity signified by the University's mascot, a red-and-blue cartoon bird.

I spent a few days in Lawrence at the home of a friend of a friend. My feet were in bad shape after the walk to Uncle Phil's. But the thirty-five miles from Bonner Springs had turned them into tenderized meat. They stung and throbbed. Blisters covered my heels and most of my toes. Hiking boots, I decided, were intended for dirt paths and rocky terrain, not for hard, flat pavement. The stiff soles provided little cushion. The leather uppers hindered a good stride.

A couple of days off my feet healed them enough to continue on with new shoes. I bounced out of town on a road that rolled between forested hilltops and flowing wheat. Powder-puff clouds sent shadows across verdant landscape. In tiny, tree-shaded Lecompton, the puffy clouds gathered into a thunderstorm. Darkness settled on long windbreaks. Gusts rife with ozone and the smell of snow sent fluttering creases across expanses of blue-green wheat. The pretty, narrow lane out of Lecompton ended at a neatly tended park crowded with pin oaks. A creek gurgled at the bottom of a small draw. Cold wind blew rain through the little brick-and-wood shelter and over the concrete picnic table in the middle. I shivered, wet and sitting still. After a while the wind let up and rain came straight down. My breath hung in the tiny shelter like balloons. I changed my clothes and put my bare feet up, despite the chill, to dry them and air still-healing blisters before heading west again.

The weather swung low and sputtered. The highway, U.S. 40, wound through narrow valleys and small stands of woods. The shoulder, a muddy dribble of gravel, disappeared at road cuts. Walking turned from pleasant striding into jagged stumbling. Facing another shoulder-less road cut, I reluctantly turned and stuck out my thumb, and felt a brief blitz of guilt. Before I left on the trip,

I had vowed not to hitchhike. But after five or six miles of dodging trucks and sliding around on loose gravel, the declaration was easy to turn back on. A young kid in a pickup dropped me where the road widened outside of Topeka. There prairie broke into suburbs, and suburbs into tumbledown urban landscape.

My mood brightened. I have always liked the fracture and chaos of the urban landscape, and the people who carve their livings out of what others want to forget. Makeshift businesses, used-car lots, and storefront churches slouched next to abandoned and broken buildings, recycling and junk businesses, empty lots, and broken cars along potholed streets. Men stood outside barbershops and in the dark holes of garages. Kids on bikes streaked by on wet sidewalks. The smells of grilled ribs, enchiladas, and stir-fry mingled in the air.

After a while, however, rain began again in earnest. My feet stung once more and my joints ached in pounding thuds. I suddenly missed my daughter very much. She was eating ice cream when I called her from a stand-alone payphone perched atop a metal pole in a grocery-store parking lot.

"Why're you crying, Dad?" she asked.

"Well, I love you, Honey." Self-consciously, I bent down and dug my face into the telephone's tiny blue-and-white box. The phone was one someone would use from a car window. I must have looked like a turtle.

"I love you too." She licked ice cream with a slurp. "But why're you crying?"

"Because I miss you, Sydney, I miss you a lot." My voice reverberated in the metal box.

"I miss you too, Dad, but I'm not crying."

I laughed and sobbed. I missed her, but not because I had not seen her—it had only been a few days. But talking to her made me realize the distance growing between me and the misery I had become accustomed to at home. It felt good but sad. I wanted and needed to release myself from past and future. But the ground was uncertain. I had no idea what I was headed into. When our conversation ended, I turned down the road, trying to hide my sobs and square myself with the grief and joy fighting in my chest.

By the time I made downtown Topeka, walking had taken away tears. But there was no resolution of the conflict of past and future gnawing at my insides, no end of the up-and-down moods the clash produced. The emotions and the work of the day had worn on me. I was exhausted. I checked into a motel, glad to get in from the wind and wet and cold. The desk clerk discounted the room because I had no car. The smell of fried food and mold hung heavy in the hotel's halls but the room was warm and incandescent and had a pleasant scent of lavender. Shorts, shirt, underpants, and socks drying on sconces soon filled the room with the smell of wet cotton. I cooked dinner on the pack stove set on the sidewalk. I sat on the end of the bed, ate rice and beans, and watched television, which in just a few days had become foreign and strange. The hotel's chlorine-laced hot tub induced deep sleep.

The sky had cleared the next morning. Clean, empty streets. Fresh, crisp, clear air. Silver Lake Road headed west from the Topeka rail yards, flat and straight and empty. Along the banks of the Kansas River, trains filled with grain, freight, and coal snaked into and out of rows of towering cottonwoods and behind batteries of grain elevators. The country was green and sodden. Clapboard farmhouses in mounds of cedar and oak sprung from plowed, dark fields spread over the wide valley. In the distance, radio masts and an occasional house spiked the top of scantily forested hills. The day grew hot and the blue sky hazy. Slight breezes gathered into wind, coarse against my lips and eyes. Frogs burped, squawked, and squealed in every ditch and glittering puddle.

Ten miles on, at Kiro, I doffed my pack and leaned against a stop sign near a house with a fenced yard. I felt tired and good. I drank deeply of sun-warmed water, which was beginning to be a pleasant sensation. Sweat had dried gritty on my skin. My legs ached and my feet stung in ways that made me feel alive.

A Bassett hound appeared from a little door on the screened porch and lumbered across the yard. It stopped under a catalpa growing near the fence. Shaking its head, it moaned and howled and threw slobber in wide arcs. Soon, however, it grew bored and retreated to the porch. Then it seemed to remember a man wasn't supposed to be sitting against the stop sign, and it returned to moan again. Finally it gave up and lay with its nose and floppy ears hanging out of the doggie door.

The owner came out and introduced himself as Mike. He was tall. His red hair sprayed from beneath a yellow ball cap. When he smiled, his freckled face broadened and crows' feet tightened around bright blue eyes. The dog howled again. Mike leaned on the chain-link fence.

"Flash thinks he's a lotta dog," he said. "But he's just a pushover. You come outta Topeka?"

"Yeah. Really, Kansas City. I'm hoping to make Saint Marys today." I stood from the stop sign.

"Well, you're ambitious." He shook my hand. "Kiro's just a spot. Useta be a waterin' station for coal-fired trains. It's a nice place, middla nowhere."

He invited me into his house through a small mudroom hung with garden implements and lined with boots. The kitchen was worn but spotless. Frilled, cream-colored curtains covered the windows. Mike filled my water bottles from the tap and topped them off with ice cubes. We sat at a small Formica-topped table, where he spread a road atlas. His wife walked in.

"I reeled in somebody," he said over his shoulder. "We're just gonna look at the map a minute."

"You boys'll like some tea." She put glasses, already sweaty in the heat, in front of us on the flowered tablecloth. "Don't mind the kitchen. Me and Mike just had lunch." I glanced around and saw the dishes stacked neatly in a drainer by the sink. Otherwise, the place was perfect.

"Silver Lake's further on," Mike said. "The road you're on useta lead outta Topeka to Silver Lake, but that was a long time ago, before the highway." He traced his finger along the map, seeing things there I couldn't. "You'll wanna take the highway. It ain't bad walkin'. Shoulder's wide and traffic ain't bad.

"I hadda walk that stretch into town a few times when my car broke down." He looked up, his ice-blue eyes focused on my hat. "Now that I'm thinkin' about it, seems like the only times I walked was when the car broke down—and I haven't walked it since I got a decent car. Problems of prosperity, you know." He picked up his tea and took a long pull.

"A guy I asked directions from in Topeka told me the road was a nightmare," I said. The man had had nothing but awful things to say about the highway. The prospect of dodging traffic for twenty or more miles had scared the crap out of me.

"'Parently that man you asked doesn't know what he's talking about," Mike laughed, and his eyes squinted in a cheerful way. "Frankly, I think people's pretty much afraid of being uncomfortable," he went on. "They'll do just about anything to avoid gettin' into what they think is prickly. But I've found once I get into situations I'm afraid of, none of them are nearly as bad as I thought they were gonna be."

It made sense to me. My fears of trespassing in a field, having to sleep in the dirt between rows of corn, and being awoken and chased by dogs in the middle of the night were rooted in not wanting to be uncomfortable. I wanted to be confident about my surroundings. But I didn't say it. Instead I told Mike of my trip and the things I'd seen so far. We had a good laugh about my twirling around and around and then heading home on my first day out.

When we were done with iced tea and maps, Mike walked me to the fence gate. Flash waddled along next to him, sedate but still slobbery. "You come by anytime you're out this way," Mike said. As I walked away, he tipped up his cap; tufts of his red hair flittered in the breeze.

The seventeen miles into Saint Marys led across undulating fields of hay and wheat and into tree-lined valleys. The time passed pleasantly as I strode through the tiny towns of Silver Lake and Rossville. I was cheered at the thought that my anxiety and fear was abating with experience and acquaintance with the road.

Saint Marys was a pretty and well-kept place. It was just becoming a bedroom community for Topeka and had the feel of new money and care. The uniformity of franchise fast food and convenience-store plazas that inevitably come with a certain degree of prosperity, however, had not yet arrived. The streets formed a perfect grid on the face of the prairie, with a park and a little business strip along the highway.

I had been anxious to see what I would find in Saint Marys. People had been unfriendly and standoffish every time I had been through before. I soon found that nothing had changed. The convenience-store clerk laughed when asked about a motel or rooming house and walked away from the counter. I called St. Mary's College, housed in a group of brick buildings that had been, in the distant past, an Indian mission for which the town was named. The man who answered said he was a priest and gave me the home number for the school secretary. A woman answered guardedly at first, then became frantic when I told her who I was.

"Who gave you this number?" she said, her voice shrill and edged with fear. "Who are you? What are you doing here?"

"I'm walking through and need a place to stay," I said. "I wanted to see if I could rent a dorm room since summer's begun and the students are out. A lot of colleges rent empty dorm rooms. I'd thought I check and see."

"I see," she said and paused. Complete silence. "Well, we don't do that," she said finally with some urgency. "No, I don't think we do that. You'll have to call or go see Mr. Cain." She gave me the man's address, told me to look up the number in the phone book, and hung up.

Even if the woman had been put out by my call, maybe Mr. Cain wouldn't. Besides, the prospect of settling into a comfy room in a house was inviting. I walked through the quiet, tree-lined streets to Mr. Cain's one-story clapboard on the edge of town. No one answered. Inside was dark. Age had settled in and around ornate furniture and yellowed chintz drapes. Plants withered in the window next to the door.

Next door a man working in his yard looked up from his rake and smiled.

"I was trying to catch Mr. Cain," I said.

"Well, he was just out working on his shrubs. He didn't answer?" A breeze ruffled the leaves and grass in the pile at the end of the rake.

"No," I said. "There doesn't appear to be anyone home."

"He's there," he said, throwing the rake up over his shoulder. "Come inside and use the phone."

I looked up Cain's number in the phone book. An old man answered, suspicion in his voice. I was struck with a sudden sense of déjà vu.

"Mr. Cain, this is Patrick Dobson. The secretary at the school gave me your name and said you might rent me a room for the night." The man with the rake who'd welcomed me into his house put a cold glass of lemonade next to the phone.

"Yes," Cain said, a little warmer. "You say the secretary gave you my name? What exactly are you doing here?" I imagined a tall, skinny man bent over the phone. I could hear him breathe.

"Well, I'm walking through. Since there're no motels in town, I called the school to see about a student room."

"And she gave you my name?" Cain's voice tightened again. I

heard him slide something across a wooden table. "Who are you with?"

"Well, just myself." A swallow of lemonade felt like it had splashed cold and fresh over the inside of my rib cage.

"I mean, what group are you with?" I thought I could hear the ticking of a wall clock over the phone.

"No group, Mr. Cain. I'm on my own."

"Well," he said with a rasp. "I'm not a hotel you know. You'll just have to look somewhere else." He was nervous and angry. "No grace without God! No salvation without the true church!" He slammed the phone down—I heard isolated clicks and snaps.

I was tired. My feet hurt. I was thinking of sleeping in the bushes. But these strange people had piqued my curiosity. The secretary was disturbed and frightened when I called back.

"You mean Cain didn't have a room?" she asked.

"Not that he'd let me stay in."

"Oh my God!" the woman growled. "Hold on."

She talked to someone a minute. I heard only muffled sounds through a hand.

"You'll take a ride to Wamego," she snapped. Wamego was fifteen miles west.

"Well, no, that's not necessary." I finished the last of the lemonade; ice cubes rattled in the glass.

"Yes, it is," she insisted. "It is. So don't you move. We'll get you out of town. Meet my husband at the gas station." She hung up.

This was interesting. I didn't like being told what to do, but I had never been ridden out of town before. I didn't have the courage to sleep next to the road or walk up to a house and ask if I could stay in a field. I had never done that before, and in that moment I didn't feel it was time to start. It never occurred to me to ask the man in whose home I sat about taking up a corner of his back yard.

A rusting Chevy van sputtered up to the gas pumps of the convenience store where the clerk had been so rude before. A bandy-legged driver in faded jeans jumped to the pavement. His cowboy boots were so worn they curled up at the toes. His ragged cowboy hat, festooned with Texas and Confederate flag pins, looked like the one Slim Pickens wore as Major T. J. "King" Kong in *Dr. Strangelove.* The odd man hooked the pump nozzle into the van's tank and clicked over. He shifted his weight to one hip and offered his hand but didn't introduce himself.

"You the fella walkin' cross the country?" he said. He tipped up his hat and smiled. "Lemme get a little gas here and we'll head out."

After he had paid and climbed behind the wheel, he didn't speak. He leaned forward and drove with both hands on the top of the steering wheel. He adjusted his hat and wiped his mouth with the back of his hand. Then he began to pray out loud. I figured that was his way, but it set me on edge and made me wonder why I was putting myself into this situation.

"We thank the Lord an' Savior Jesus Christ for all the greatness of the land an' of this day," he said in a voice that approached rage, eyes dead level at the road. "We pray for the redemption of sinners an' guidance to those that'd harm us."

While he called on patron saints of travel, roads, weather, and crops, I sought my inner motivation for taking this ride. Did I just want to get west faster? Was I looking for an easier way?

The man cut my thoughts short when he invited me to say the "Our Father" with him. I wasn't religious or even a believer. But I wanted to keep the peace, so I did. At the same time, I looked around to make sure I could grab my pack and get out in a hurry, just in case.

"You Catholic?" he said at the end of the prayer. The sun cast yellow and red over the wheat fields. The swollen Kansas River eased by the overgrown grass next to the highway.

"I went to Catholic grade school and high school," I said. I *didn't* tell him that I hadn't been to church except to look at art or to see a concert for fifteen years, or that despite my parents' desperate attempt to mold a conservative Catholic, I had abandoned the faith and become an agnostic, somewhat pagan, unmarried father. None of that was his business. But to tell him so might have produced consequences I didn't want to deal with. The path to salvation, I figured, would be more easily tread with my godless hide than without.

He turned suddenly, and, with a mean-spirited grimace, spit Latin as if through a cheese grater. I tried to look sincere when I shrugged my shoulders.

"You don't know what that means, do ya'?" He squinted his eyes and cocked his head.

I shook my head. "I never studied Latin."

"So, yer a *New* Catholic." He squinted, tightened his lips, and nodded, as if he had just found me out.

"New Catholic?" I never knew there were old and new Catholics.

"Yeah, a Catholic raised up in the apostasy of Vatican Two."

"What?" I said as if I had no clue what he was talking about.

He wanted a fight. But I was determined to be easy to live with. I sat bumping along in a van with a right-wing Catholic dissenter, a familiar type. My father (a one-time John Bircher) had taken up with some zealous Catholics when I was a kid. The Second Vatican Council (1962—65) had relieved some of the strictures of the practice of Catholic faith. But some conservatives, of whom my father was one, understood the vast forces of modernization and social fragmentation of the 1960s as being the advent of demon rule. Vatican II, they maintained, weakened the faith from within, leading Catholics to comfort within the secular state and moral relativism. Because of this the faithful were less likely to enjoy eternal life at the right hand of God. Some went so far as to call Vatican II's religious tolerance a violation of Catholicism as the one, true faith—a form of heresy. Others held that Vatican II represented the church's complete abandonment of Catholic faith to serve the ends of evil-minded power mongers.

Believers across this tilted spectrum tended to mix theology with old-time laissez faire capitalism, conspiracy, patriotic paranoia, and reactionary antisocialism. To them, social and political movements that interfered with their struggle to shape the world according to a nostalgic and imagined past were secular plots to bring about the apocalyptic rule of Satan. Everything from the Civil Rights movement to feminism and from United Nations internationalism and industrial globalization to new perspectives on sexual morality was part of Satan's plan.

⨍ I found it all to be, at base, reactionary and irrational, not to mention antidemocratic and wildly suspicious of human beings doing what they saw fit in a fractured and confusing world. After all, I figured, if the prophecies of Revelations were true, what's to worry about? God wins. But, not having the gift of prophecy, I kept my thoughts to myself. There was no way of telling what this righteous Texan might do if I told him what I thought.

Facing forward, he cocked his head and squinted again. His hands tightened on the wheel. I put one hand near my pack, which was behind my seat, and the other on the door handle.

He lowered his voice. "Vatican II, *in case you don't know*," he said, his voice increasing in volume and intensity, "is part of the international Jewish conspiracy to destroy the One True Church and rob the faithful of salvation here and in the hereafter. Jews, atheism, commonists, an' their *fellow travelers* in the gov'ment know weakenin' the church and convincin' people it is right to do so is the first step in takin' over!"

"No kiddin'?" I said. "Taking over what?"

"Why, the United States. Bringin' on the reign of Satan." His voice rose again and he assumed the homiletic cadence of a fiery preacher. "Inundatin' the world in vice an' avarice an' evil. Everyone should know about it but they can't. The media—the *media*—they're part of it. An agent of Satan, all of 'em." Spit flew from his lips. His face shook. He pounded the steering wheel. "The press and gov'ment, the bureaucracy and politicians and lawyers are plottin' to destroy the one, true Catholic faith and deprive human bein's of their rightful salvation. It's everywhere, all over. De-nial of school prayer, the rise of the sec'lar state, separation of church and state, gov'ment regulations, envIRNmentalism, abortion—FEMINISM! All part of Satan's method and plan."

His voice lowered again, only to rise to a fiery crescendo. "But Jesus' time an' the Way of the Cross'll return the supremacy of the One True Church again, an' soon. SINNERS WILL BE DRIVEN THROUGH THE GATES OF HELL!"

My guide took quite a bit of pleasure in knowing that all of us sinners would suffer eternal fire. I looked out the window at the wheat. I wished Jesus had a less full plate and that Wamego was closer.

After my driver's diatribe, we rode in uncomfortable silence. Outside choruses of frogs sang. The sun squeezed into the horizon like a magician's egg. Every now and then the organic fug of river mud and field dust blew through the window. The bandy-legged man pulled into a convenience-store parking lot in Wamego and was suddenly calm and friendly, almost self-conscious and apologetic after his outburst. I felt sorry for the guy but really wanted out of his van.

"Here you got yer motel," he said, gesturing. "An' over there is yer Taco Bell an' yer McDonald's." I said thanks and was glad to see the sunset reflect off the mirrored surface of the van's tinted windows as he drove away.

Inside the store, the coffee was fresh and the clerk friendly. The place smelled of people, coffee, and ice cream. Small children and adolescents with cups of soda pop crowded around video games and pinball machines. Furrow-faced farmers with calloused and stained hands sat drinking coffee at molded plastic tables and benches. In the twilight, highway travelers pulled up to gas pumps. They all stopped and reared their heads back when the bright mercury lamps under the canopy clunked on. I sipped my coffee at one of the tables and listened to kids' banter and the farmers' low-pitched, sonorous voices. After all the apostasy and gov'ment conspiracy, I found people and their secular activities calming. I rather liked being a heathen.

A cop in the store had started looking me over as soon as I had walked in. The backpack, I guessed, stuck out in the crowd. After a while, the cop came over and introduced himself with a strong but soft-skinned hand. William Moore held his broad shoulders back, a smile flashing under his moustache. He hooked his thumbs into his gun belt when he talked. When he figured I wasn't into mischief, he offered to call the town's two motels and disappeared behind the counter.

"Well, they're full," he said when he came back. He sat down and slid a fresh cup of coffee across the table to me. "I hope it's good. They got cream and sugar over there." He looked out at the fields across the street. He had been raised in Kansas, he said, and decided to return after a stint in the army in Vietnam. He was glad he had come back. He had raised his family in Wamego. He smiled at the story of what had happened in Saint Marys.

"Well, they're strange birds," he said. "Some say those people at the school have been excommunicated or something for rejecting Vatican II and the pope. But you know rumors are what they are. That doesn't matter much to me. I say believe what you want." He looked into his coffee cup.

"Usually they keep to themselves," he said after a pause. "But the bombing of the federal building in Oklahoma City three weeks ago has got feds all over central Kansas. There's been talk of militia groups, heavy arms, radical activity around Rossville, Saint Marys, and Herrington. I thought they might be jumpy in Saint Marys but they must have it pretty bad. They didn't know if you were press or FBI, or whatever. I bet that's why they wanted you out of town."

A patrol car pulled up in front of the store. The officer on duty waved. Moore had radioed him after finding no vacancy at the motels. Moore wiped the table with a napkin and we threw our coffee cups into the trash.

"Hello, Nick Flores," said the officer, introducing himself and offering a hand the size of a baseball mitt out the car window.

"What do you think about putting this guy up in the park?" Moore said.

"Sure, I don't see why not. You just can't put up a tent. Do you mind?"

Both officers looked self-conscious, as if they were sorry they could not find anything better.

"Well, no," I said, "not at all."

Moore hefted my backpack into the back seat of the patrol car, wished me well, and walked back to the store. Flores pulled the cruiser into the evening. We drove slowly down tree-lined streets, the light of sunset flashing through the leaves. He waved at pedestrians and stopped to joke with a woman about her errant husband. He spoke to a man about the man's sick dog. At the end of a strange day, it felt good and safe to be with a man like Flores.

"You know," I offered, "this is the first time I've ever been in a patrol car and not been under arrest."

"Some people never get so lucky," he laughed. We pulled up to the park. "I know it's not much." He draped his hand over the wheel. "But there's a bathroom where you can freshen up. And water. Call from the park phone if you need anything. I'll be around all night."

I walked up to a picnic shelter near the park pond. The last twilight skittered through oak and sycamore leaves. A Dutch-style windmill stood on a mound to one side of the small park. Geese drifted in the hourglass-shaped pond. A fountain flowed from beneath a statue of Venus on four sea-shell-flanked columns on a little island. A few kids fished for bluegill, their bobbers twirling in the bubbles from the fountain. Tracks for a small-scale train, put away for the night, bent around the lake and through the park under a green canopy. The vanes of the windmill creaked in the breeze.

After dark, sodium lamps in the shelter bathed the concrete floor and tables with orange light. The geese splashed and their honks echoed under the picnic-shelter roof. Every time I fell asleep, geese honked, startling me awake and leaving me with my thoughts. Over the last days, feelings of despair had lain alongside knowledge that life was never going to be the same for me, for good or ill. No amount of sadness or fear would change that. I tried to imagine going back, what I would do or say when faced with people who set such hope in me in the days before I had left. I took a deep breath. I had committed myself to this journey. How it would change things was not clear yet. Anything could happen.

Long after a church bell rang midnight, I had given up trying to get to sleep and settled with just being as relaxed as I could make myself. With cats chasing after goslings, this was not a night to sleep.

4

MANHATTAN, RANDOLPH,
MARYSVILLE

"It's the best you're gonna find here"

A LITTLE GIRL with a big smile peered over edge of the picnic table, her face framed in the shelter's rafters. The light of late morning reflected off the concrete onto her face.

"I'm Janna," she said. "Whatcha doin'?"

"Just waking up. How 'bout you?"

"I been watchin' ya sleep."

She was about eight years old. Her shirt and shorts barely fit her; her belly stuck out in a big smile. Her feet were bare. She was alone. As I pulled myself out of my bag and put on my shoes, she kept close and asked a hundred questions, most of which barely penetrated my lack-of-sleep haze. I struck the pack stove to make tea. We sat at the table and shared some granola bars. I rubbed sleep from my eyes.

"Where are your parents?" I asked after a while. We were alone in the park.

"They're at home, sleepin'." Granola bar crumbs rained down her shirt.

Some kids came down to the pond with fishing poles. They affixed worms to hooks and plunked bobbers into the water.

"Do your mom and dad know you're here?" I said.

"Sure, where else would I be?"

We ate dried apricots. The day was cloudless. A hot breeze blew in under the shelter. Janna said when school was out she spent nearly every morning in the park. I liked her. She reminded me of Sydney—self-assured, innocent, offhanded. After I finished my tea, I went about the business of getting packed and ready to leave.

"When ya get where you're going, will you remember me?" she said. We walked across the park. She took my hand and steered me past the choo-choo shed to the main road.

"I'm sure I will."

"When ya tell people about me, tell them my parents are the greatest parents ever."

"I will if you promise me not to talk to strangers, and especially not to hold their hands," I said.

"But you're no stranger," she said. "Everyone knows you're here."

I had not been alone in Wamego that night; that was comforting. At the same time, it made me uneasy to know that eyes were on me, to understand how little anonymity a stranger could enjoy in a small town. How many Saint Maryans knew I'd been run out of town because some zealots were uncertain of my pursuit of a place to sleep for the night? What would they have thought of me if Mr. Cain had let me overnight in his musty house? I only knew that after the holy hootenanny in the Texan's van, I had been a sight more comfortable amid the flock of geese than I would have been waiting with Mr. Cain and his flock for the Second Coming to rescue us from "commonists." As it was, they delivered me to a beautiful place and the comfortable guidance of a child.

Janna let go of my hand at the edge of the park. She wanted to walk further. I told her I didn't think it was a good idea, and left her waving and saying good-bye over and over.

Soon the rhythm of footsteps worked up through my legs and back. The events of the previous day had set me askew. Walking breathing deeply, and thinking of a little girl watching me sleep straightened me right up. I lost myself again in the landscape.

Smooth hills spread out west of Wamego. With every mile the heat increased until it shimmered off the pavement. Rocky mesa tops of the Flint Hills in the distance became more prominent. Corn and wheat spread out from the road into the tiny scrub-choked ravines. Houses next to the road sat in neat, trimmed yards. Here and there, play-set swings creaked in the breeze. After the wind died toward the middle of the day, laundry that had flapped and rioted on clotheslines now hung motionless. The entire morning only one or two cars passed.

In the warmth, what started as a vague thought of soda pop grew to a craving. I walked into the first convenience store I came upon, one hacked into the side of a hill halfway between Wamego and Manhattan. The frigid air inside the store stunned me. I bought a pop and screwed the top off while standing at the counter. Sharp bubbles and cold stung my throat. I drank the entire bottle in one tip and fetched another to take outside and tipple more slowly. After almost thirty miles, my feet stung and bled. I was ready to get off them. On the front walk, as I worked over my damaged toes with tape, gauze, and scissors, a skinny man with thick glasses and a bright smile walked up. "Where're you going?" he said. "Where did you come from?" The man's name was Dan Karamanski. He said he worked in Kansas City as a gardener and part time in a bookstore, that he had a little free time and was taking a few days to drive around Kansas. I told him that I understood the impulse.

Dan and I decided to camp at Tuttle Creek Reservoir, north of Manhattan. Once my pack was in the trunk of his car, we drove the lonely highway into town. Our conversation about seeing Kansas went off on tangents that included past travels in general.

"I've been across the nation once myself," he said. Mailboxes at the end of driveways waved red flags. "Two years ago, I cycled from Seattle to Bar Harbor, Maine. I met many good people along the way. They taught me a few things. The greatest was that people like to meet travelers. They aren't scared of them. Most aren't, anyway. Before that trip, I would never have talked to a stranger, much less invited them along for a ride. I had to think about why I was afraid to meet people on the road. And then it occurred to me I really didn't have a reason. I realized the people who had told me to be wary of strangers were really telling me about what they were afraid of."

The last thought intrigued me. Mike in Kiro had said that people were afraid of being uncomfortable. Maybe people telling me to take a gun to protect myself were frightened themselves of being around people they did not know, in places unfamiliar to them. They were mostly playing it safe, I supposed. I was not—and was either lucky or stupid. For most of my life, my interest in people had trumped my innate fear of them and led me into questionable relationships more times than I liked to remember—the encounter I'd had with the zealot of Saint Marys was a prime example. Anxiety about winding up in uncomfortable situations did not stunt curiosity about what lay around the bend, which sometimes left me dancing in brambles. Despite the occasional setback, I was always willing to believe that a stranger such as Dan had good to give to the world.

We arrived at the reservoir in the late afternoon and stood on asphalt with the toes of our boots in the water: the campground we wanted to use was flooded. The tops of picnic tables and signs rippled the surface of the lake hundreds of feet from its shore.

"It's been in the news, you know, all this rain," Dan said, looking out over the water. "If it rains much more, the Corps of Engineers is going to evacuate the campground below the Tuttle Creek dam. But we're safe here, I'd think." Water lapped the asphalt. Dan pushed a stick in the ground at the water's edge and we soon found that the lake was still rising.

We sat a long while atop a picnic table that was still on dry land,

and stared out over the water. There was no breeze. The lake's surface lifted in slight swells but otherwise was glass smooth, iridescent blue and pink under the prairie sky. The slight scent of sodden grass and fishy mud came from the water. An even carpet of blond grass with hints of green spread up from the lake to the hilltops and rises above. But for gulls yelping in the distance it was perfectly silent. This was something to live for, this quiet, this place where I could hear my heart beat.

Dan pitched a satisfied sigh into the silence and said it was time to think of dinner. The sound of his feet in the grass made the stillness and space even more perceptible. He lifted my pack from the trunk to get to his food and cooking utensils.

"Your pack's too heavy," he said. "Before we eat, let's see what we can do to take care of this."

He lifted the pack up on the picnic table with his knee, unfastened the buckles, and untied the cords. I didn't know what he was up to, and it was strange seeing someone breach the one thing I held most sacred. It was like watching an operation. But somehow I trusted him. I knew my pack had been too heavy. My hip and knee joints stung. My feet blistered. Some pain, I thought, was from walking on hard pavement. Now, as I watched Dan, I began to suspect that much of it came from the weight of the pack.

Like a magician pulling handkerchiefs from a pocket, Dan pulled things out of the pack. He stacked my life as I knew it into three piles on the table.

"This," he said, pointing to a stack of goods that included some clothes, a pocketknife, and the pack stove, "is the 'need' pile. This one is 'don't need.' And this one, 'maybe.'"

After my first two or three days of walking, particularly after dealing with feet that blistered and re-blistered, I had considered lightening my load. But every time I thought of taking something out and sending it home, I was afraid I'd desperately need it as soon as it was gone (frightened of being uncomfortable, as Mike had said when we sat at his kitchen table in Kiro). Now, as Dan went through my things, he didn't give me time to second guess or protest. Instead a sense of relief settled into my chest. A complete stranger was deciding what to send home and what to carry. I trusted him not out of some heartfelt impulse but because I had worn myself out.

"Now, you can put the 'need' stuff back into the pack." As I did, to my surprise, Dan picked up the "don't need" and "maybe" piles and stowed them in the trunk of his car.

"I'll drop these things off at your house," he said.

I didn't know what to say. I had backpacked remote areas of Missouri, Colorado, and Wyoming. No picnic tables. No fire rings. Just a compass, map, and maybe a trail. It had never occurred to me that a two- or three-month trip by foot along highways demanded less equipment than did a weekend in the woods. Dan had removed heavier items: tent, rope, extra boots, my gloves and sweaters, and all but two days of clothes. He left me with a knife, spoon, small cooking pot, and cup. He took away all my books except the one I was reading. He emptied out all the dried food and gave me a few dollars for it, because, as he put it, there were grocery stores everywhere.

"I didn't need any of this stuff when I was cycling," he said, as he looked into the truck. "And you won't either. You'll find lighter is better, even without things you think you can't live without."

The pack's new weight made me smile. It was some twenty pounds lighter and had a lot less to fiddle with. I had essential clothes, the stove, half a cook set, a small candle lantern, flashlight, compass, pocketknife, a book, and a notebook. I considered my aching feet, pounding hips and knees, and my back. This leap of faith was easy to make.

"You might miss a couple of things," he said, adjusting the pack on my back. "But what I'm taking you haven't used and probably won't. Anything you need, you can buy."

Even books, I thought. We shook hands on it.

And my heart broke. Inner ties to place—manifest in material goods—were becoming undone. I had built the contents of the pack on what I had known. But that knowledge had weight, and that weight had done me harm. Having a new life meant coming un-cleaved from the things I thought bound me to place. Dan was right: whatever I needed I could get, and I could live without the rest. I understood, finally, how to move from one place to another, from one life to another, without looking back. Material goods left behind were to be found on the road ahead. New relationships would be found there. And I'd find myself there, too.

We built a fire with driftwood, talked, and listened to gulls and meadowlarks until dusk. After dark I walked up to use the camp-ground phone. Cottonwoods towered over the shower house where the phone was located. A warm wind rattled the leaves. The sound of tires whining on pavement miles distant rose up over the lake, and coyotes yipped and sang. Down at the lake our small fire radiated a yellow swatch around Dan. Later, I fell asleep later to the sound of whip-poor-wills echoing over the water.

Before Dan headed out the next morning we went to a camping store in town to replace my tent with a lightweight, waterproof nylon tarp. With a couple of sticks and tent stakes, the tarp would make a fine lean-to or small tent, depending on the weather. The new outfit of twelve or fourteen ounces replaced five pounds of tent now in Dan's trunk.

"Don't worry about your stuff," he said before he drove away. "You're going to be all right."

I overnighted under my new tarp at the campground under the Tuttle Creek Dam. The place was mostly empty; paved spaces for RVs looked like ribs off the spine of a long-dead animal. The man attending the park entrance let me through without paying. "You ain't got a car," he said, "you ain't gotta pay. At least in my book." I set up in a picnic shelter and pulled the tarp over me. Wind sprayed rain through the shelter and flapped the tarp in loud fits. Thunder erupted. I fell into fractured sleep, making believe the tarp would save me when the dam broke.

The sky still hung low and dark the next morning. I headed north. The Flint Hills broadened to wide plateaus above the Blue River Valley. Farther on, expanses of corn and wheat washed into brush- and tree-studded hills that tumbled down to the reservoir tossing under the stormy sky. Twenty miles of long rolling hills fell behind quickly, almost without effort.

Near Randolph, a tiny town at the edge of the Flint Hills, the sky grew steel-gray. Evening darkened quickly as the storm grew heavier. The air became cold and filled with ozone. Randolph's town park was next to the highway and exposed to the houses around it. The shelters were set on tiny squares of water-puddled concrete. Rain draining from the leaky shelters splattered on the picnic tables. Up the highway a few blocks, a crumbling cinder-block building sat like a bunker, marked with a sign: "Randolph Motel." The advertised price was attractive, and the bleak bunker was refuge from the cold and wind.

A gravel parking lot spread between the cinder-block walls of the U-shaped building. Lightning flashes illuminated a few cars and a semi. Closed curtains cloaked the windows of all the rooms whether there was a car in front or not. My room let out a musty sigh when I opened the door. It was spare and dim, lit by a single lamp on a nightstand. The brown leavings of a hundred trucker dinners covered an old gas range next to the door. The cold, still air smelled faintly of natural gas. But the closeness and light of the room was good for me.

After a dribbling shower in a rusty stall, I eased my aches into the lumpy mattress. The vent in the room's ceiling squealed. The smell of meat grease mingled with odors of natural gas and carpet mold.

I blinked and suddenly it was another rainy morning. On foot again, I stopped at an old gas station at the corner for a cup of coffee out of the rain. More than a service station, it was a compact store, crowded with all the essentials for farm and small-town life. Shelves held groceries, boots, bait (some of it live), fishing tackle, toys, and watches. I bought a few supplies from the proprietors, David and Roxie Sharp, and took a deep breath before leaning out into the sheets of rain.

"I'll give you a ride up the road if you'll help me pump out the cellar," David said to my back. "It's been raining for weeks, it seems. We'll probably need lifejackets soon if I don't get to the water down there. Fortunately, we sell 'em."

A minute later, I was holding the end of a sputtering garden hose over a toilet. David ran a pump on the other end in the basement. Roxie stood in the bathroom door holding a price gun. She wore a red sweater and blue jeans, and her brown hair curled in tussled locks around her squarish face and wire-rimmed glasses. We anticipated a full stream of water and listened to the hose gasp and cough in the toilet. Water began to run steadily after a long series of jerks and more coughs. I asked if the store kept them afloat.

"When the basement's not flooded, you mean?" She leaned against the door jamb. "Well, I run the place, which pays for itself. David's a full-time firefighter in Manhattan. That pays the bills. We also farm a hundred ten acres of wheat and raise about forty head of cattle."

She peeled off to help a customer and stock shelves. When she came back, she held out a little stuffed pig.

"You can send this to your daughter," she said. "It'll be good for her to know her dad's thinking of her."

When the water sputtered to a stop, David, now in rubber boots, flopped into the bathroom and asked if I'd help him pump out the basement of his farmhouse. I thanked Roxie and went with David to his rusting Ford LTD. The wind had picked up and blew sheets of rain horizontal. We drove farm roads across evening-dark prairie. Windbreaks of squat oak, thorny locust, and hedge apple soldiered by. Clumps of taller trees in the distance marked farmyards. David had one hand on the wheel, the other under the bib of his overalls. He occasionally rubbed his friendly, shaggy-dog face as if he were remembering things he had to do and then rehung his hand in his overalls.

"Firefighting's a good profession," David said when I asked him about his living. He turned and smiled. His eyes were sparkling-water blue. "Service to others and a steady paycheck. That lets me farm, which is what I really want to do."

"How about the store?"

"Well, Randolph's a tiny place, you know, sort of nowhere from nothing. We use to have a regular store in town years ago. But Wal-mart's sort of taken it and everything else off the map. When the gas station owner closed the place, that was it for Randolph. Roxie didn't like farming much and had this idea we could make a go with a little store. Things people needed between going shopping, that sort of thing. It's a tough business, but so far it's been good to us, and we make it go by putting in the time and energy. Plus we listen to what people need, put it in stock, and keep changing things. What-ever the market is, really. It seems to work."

The rain slowed to a stop and the wind eased, but the sky remained deep blue-gray, almost black in places. David and Roxie's farmstead was a lonely place in a stand of cedar. The house, hedge, garden, silo, and outbuildings sat in a dooryard not much bigger than a few acres. Beyond lay flatness and wheat and sky. It was one of the most starkly beautiful scenes I had ever witnessed.

"Boy," I said, stepping from the car, "you're right out here in the middle of it, aren't ya?"

David looked toward the sky. "Well," he said, shifting his gaze toward the horizon, "you don't get any closer than this." A smile liv-ened his sagging face. He turned his strong hands over and rubbed the legs of his overalls. His eyes were intense. "It's farming. It's in my blood."

The house looked like it belonged to a man who worked too hard at too many things. The roof sagged and the clapboard was naked of paint in wide swaths. Cows grazed at a hay pile next to a toppled concrete silo. From behind the rubble of a spare-parts pile, a little dog growled across the yard. By the time he got to me, though, he was wagging his tail so hard that his butt shook from side to side.

David had bought the place in 1980 and was promptly mired in the farm depression. It was something he said he had "never gotten up from. I plan to paint the house and clean up the yard every spring but never find the time. Important thing is," he said, peering through the cellar door, one hand on the back of his little dog, "the basement's dry."

We drove back out to the highway on soggy gravel roads by fence lines dressed in tall grass and stringy vines. "Randolph's a small town, and people know each other's business," David said. "Sometimes it helps. Sometimes it's confining. But with the store and the farm I get a sense of contributing to the place I grew up." He wanted to know what I planned to do and laughed when I said I wanted to write. "The first thing I ever wrote was in college," he told me with a smile. "That's when I found out I'm just no good with language. I'm lucky to finish a sentence."

The jagged ridges and ravines of the Flint Hills grew more narrow, the hills gentler. Technology and finance were emptying prairie towns that the eighties farm crisis had left in tatters. John Steinbeck wrote in *The Grapes of Wrath*, "A man can hold land if he can just eat and pay taxes; he can do that . . . until his crops fail one day." It was as true in the 1990s as during the 1980s and 1930s. Market and finance favored consolidation. When a farmer grew tired, as David would someday, he could sell his land to a neighbor, lease it to another farmer in a crop-sharing venture, or buy his neighbor's land. But it all led to the same result: fewer and fewer farmers like David.

"The price of wheat hovers at seventy-five percent of what it was in 1980 when I started," David said. His voice was comfortable, a steady cadence rife with central Kansas twang. He didn't seem bitter, only honest about his prospects.

"Corn isn't worth planting anymore," he said. "I only lose money on corn. The price is the same as it was in 1949. Our money's worth less now than then. When the price I get for growing corn remains the same year after year . . . well, I can only get so efficient to make any kind of margin—one man and his land.

"Hell, I don't even keep pigs or chickens anymore, like you think of farmers doing. Plowing land and raising livestock just isn't something you can do anymore. You just can't keep enough of them unless you devote everything to them."

We drove the line of an old railroad grade, one of dozens of closed lines and failed railroads that crisscrossed the plains. He looked out the driver-side window at the empty fields and sighed.

"My costs have gone up plenty," he said. "But I've tightened up as I've gone along. After a while, enough is enough, and you need to get bigger or get out. I just want to farm my bit, get a fair price, and take care of my family. But growth, that's what's demanded. So the Sharps are growing in a different way. Since we're so far from a Walmart or any grocery, we opened our store and found our niche."

The blanket of clouds ended abruptly in a straight line up ahead, and David smiled when we drove into the sun. We wound our way into Marysville and David dropped me off at the Riley County Courthouse, a native-limestone building nearly a hundred years old. He refused to take money for the ride. "It's just something you do," he said, shifting the car into gear. "Besides, the pleasure's been all mine."

I walked down to the public library to get some information about the town. When I told the library volunteer, Ms. Lyhane, what I wanted, she said that her husband Mike was involved in the preservation of a local Oregon Trail ford of the Blue River, called Marshall's Ferry, and that he would love to show it to me.

Mike soon arrived in a pickup. He was a big man with a bushy beard, useful boots, and a powerful, if paunchy, physique. We drove out to the ford. At the river he showed me the swale that wagon wheels had worn into the riverbank. Mike had a booming voice, and I could tell from his tone that he felt connected to this place. He saw things among the cottonwoods and tangles of grapevines that made history as he knew it live here. It allowed him escape from his work in highway construction yet bound him irrevocably to the place of his birth. His goal of making a park at the ford would give something back to the town he loved and, quite likely, give his name a lasting legacy.

"Hundreds of thousands of white settlers, following what used to be an Otoe trade route, crossed this shallow point on the Blue on their way to the North Platte River and then to Oregon," he said, his eyes focused on scenes only he could see. "Over time, the Mormon and California trails also crossed the river here. Entrepreneurs, mostly people who had once been emigrants themselves, opened ferries. Ferry passage was too expensive for most people, as much as twenty dollars for a wagon and oxen. But many still found a ferry worth the money over putting family and possessions at risk."

Mike grew animated when he explained that Colonel Frank Marshall had arrived in 1852 and established a trading post and tavern near his ferry. "He charged less than the competition—five dollars a wagon and twenty-five cents per head of livestock. Marshall drove the other ferrymen out of business and built trade at his hotel, livery, and hardware store," Mike said, sounding envious. "When competition built in the ferry and outfitting business, he moved into land speculation. The town that sprung up on land he owned around the ford, he named after his wife, Mary." Later, the Pony Express established a station in the town, and in 1860 a small railroad, the Elwood and Marysville, laid tracks to take advantage of the increasing grain and commercial trade.

Back at the truck, we shucked river mud from our shoes and drove back into town to visit Mike's friend, Ken Martin. He was a slight man under a cowboy hat. His thick glasses, beard, and moustache made his face seem crowded and inaccessible. But he was a friendly and open sort who had been president of the National Pony Express Association. Ken turned on the light in a stand-alone garage behind his house, illuminating his collection of Pony Express memorabilia. He stood like a proud kid, reliving his cowboys-and-Indians summer fun. In dozens of glass cases and home-built exhibits, he had everything from authentic Pony Express saddles, rider uniforms, handkerchiefs, and gloves, to Chinese-manufactured shot glasses, pins, snow globes, and posters featuring a wind-blown Pony Express rider.

I knew the Pony Express as a blip in American history, lasting from 1860 till the telegraph put it out of business a year and a half later. Its myth outstripped its historical import, inspiring the logo for the U.S. Post Office Department (until 1972), as well as generations of pulp novels, histories, and movies. But Ken was obsessed by the idealized lone rider crossing the plains in all weather on his speedy steed, fleeing hostile Indians and bandits. He had subsumed the fabled legacy of the Pony Express into his identity, much the same way Mike had equated Marysville's beginnings with his own character. The Pony Express gave Ken's home meaning and importance in the larger sweep of American history, preserving him a place in Marysville's future.

"We ride ponies in an annual reenactment of the mail express from St. Joseph, Missouri, to Sacramento, California," Ken said. "Everything is authentic: our dress, our gear, and the route. We do stay the nights in hotels or in camps. But we try to give people the feel of how it was."

I was thinking of the experience that living history produced in me and in people around me. At state and national parks, where I had seen living history exhibits and interpretations, people found the material interesting in a way that educated them about the past, but also made them feel good about their lives in the present. On the other hand, the actors always seemed more interested in the minutiae of authenticity than the tourists. It struck me that Ken and his pals sought to give themselves a feel of what it was to be in a time they believed was rawer and more pure than the one they lived in. Such was Ken's passion that in the late eighties he had helped groups of Europeans fascinated with the American West start their own Pony Express associations. He and his friends had ridden through the streets of Paris and Prague, dressed in their full historical garb.

Later Ken took me to meet Sharon and Howard Kessinger, who had offered a bed for the night. As opposed to connecting past to present through history as Mike and Ken had, Sharon and Howard made a living in the more recent past. They owned and edited the town newspaper, the *Marysville Advocate*. The Kessingers were strong-willed people—Howard, a shy but determined man, Sharon more outgoing. They had written for the Abilene and Oberlin papers before buying the *Advocate* in 1970. They believed most people were good, or could be, but both lamented the recent, spiteful turn in American politics, often based on a past as mythologized and idealized as that viewed by Mike and Ken. This fixation threatened, the Kessingers thought, the foundations of community sanity.

"Moderation and understanding," Howard said, "have become rare leaves in our political winds. The newspaper matters. It's more than sound bites and rumors bantered about on radio or by TV talking heads. It doesn't just tell people about their town as it is, rather than as it should be, it tells them about each other. When you know your neighbors, you tend not to fear them. They are real people, not abstract 'thems' and 'usses.'"

Rain had begun again in earnest and fell on the house in a steady, soothing thrum. Sitting in the warm, incandescent living room, we talked over cups of spicy tea about politics and cultural trends until we became sleepy and slow. They showed me to an immaculate room with a neatly made bed. I stared out a large bay window netted with rain, thinking of the people I had met so far. They seemed to have a strong sense of where they were and what their lives were about. William Moore and Dan Flores liked where they lived and related what they did to the people they did it for. David and Roxie Sharp refused to abandon their town and instead tried to breathe life back into it. In a mythic West, Mike Lyhane and Ken Martin found identity and purpose. Sharon and Howard defined their lives by digging into the tiny corners of Marysville and bringing that world to their neighbors. They all had what I wanted: contentment and purpose. They had made their own way, and, in doing so, determined their place in this world. I fell asleep envious of them.

5

BEATRICE, NEBRASKA;
WILBER

"You'll find everything you need there"

THE PEOPLE I had met in the previous days had shown what it was like to be tethered to a place without feeling they had to know what came next. I needed to do the same. I looked down the Pony Express Highway, U.S. 36. The road bolted straight west over grassland and between cornfields past a statue of the legendary Express rider at the edge of Marysville. I was now walking along northbound on U.S. 77, which climbed out of the Blue River Valley into imposing, clear sky. Rolling hills, wooded in their creases, curled up to the Kansas-Nebraska border. There the land leveled into naked, sodden fields of black soil; many farmers hadn't had a chance to plow and plant before rain had turned the ground into soup.

This day, however, was warm and clear, the wind coarse and dry. The onset of a hard sweat felt good. I had taken to setting out each day with a gallon milk jug of water. Having that container in hand was a whole lot easier than fishing water bottles out of my backpack every fifteen minutes. Besides, the pack was heavy enough without the eight pounds a full gallon of water weighed. The jug also kept my hands busy. I filled it as often as I remembered. On a hot day, walking twenty-five or thirty miles, I went through three to five gallons of water and another couple after settling in for the evening. Having enough water was essential. Dehydration made me cranky. I walked faster, obsessed about nothing and everything. I fell into a sort of tunnel vision where I noticed only pavement and horizon. A slug of water in those moments sharpened the world and made eyesight and hearing more acute. I had more energy and my mood brightened.

I had also learned how to apportion the day's walking to my advantage. My pace was about three miles per hour. I consistently put twenty miles behind me in about six hours. I found early on that walking that distance straight through was not the fastest way to get where I wanted to on a particular day. Breaks on guardrails, rocks, or in roadside parks every five miles or so for a gulp of water and a few bites of candy bar made the miles fly by. I discovered that I liked myself a lot better if I took breaks. During a pause I was able to focus on things that might be bothering me. I might not get them worked out, but I was able to identify inner turmoil that might boil to the surface later as anxiety and anger.

Breaks in the day also made me more aware of the world around me. I made long lists of birds, bugs, and plants in my head and repeated them so I could write them down later. Over the distances, I noticed subtle changes in flora lining the ditches and right-of-ways between the road and the fences. At the Kansas-Nebraska border I perceived for the first time in my life the physical differences between the states. A person blowing through the landscape in a car might never notice that Nebraska farmers planted more corn and less wheat and soybeans than Kansans. Another might drive these county roads their whole lives and not notice that fence lines on one side of the state line didn't quite match up to those on the other side. The corners and curves they took as they drove north or south at the border were due to adjustments in survey grids. At the state line, the asphalt I had walked for most of the way from Kansas City turned into evenly divided concrete rectangles—the kind that make car tires bounce in rhythmic *b-bump* . . . *b-bump* . . . *b-bump*. From car windows, they might never understand, as I hadn't until then, that imaginary lines on maps had come, over time, to have physical manifestations.

I counted sections of concrete pavement and sang silly renditions of the national anthem. "Oh, say can you see / grass and wheat like ocean waves / like in all the God-Bless-America films / they made us watch in Catholic school / and Boy Scouts and dumbass children's films." I daydreamed of my daughter and made up names for the old, rusted cars Nebraskans drove: Chevy Imrustia, Toyota Corodna, Ford Insurance Agent. I wondered briefly where I would sleep that night and decided that I would stop at Wymore, twenty-six miles north of Marysville, and see if the town had a little park. The thought didn't develop much before meadowlarks perched on a succession of metal fence posts snagged it away from me.

I walked up a long rise toward the edge of Wymore. The grass between the road and fences turned from gold and green to silver as the wind laid it over. The sky turned a hazy, baby-blue shade in the midday heat. A behemoth Chevrolet rocketed by and pulled onto an easement at the top of the rise. As the driver backed the car back onto the concrete to turn around, he grazed another car traveling toward me. The Chevy stove in the rear taillight and bumper of the other car. Shiny splinters sprayed across the pavement. A hubcap pitched into the ditch. The drivers got out of their cars and were talking as I passed. I gave the hubcap to a tall, older man dressed in a long-sleeve western shirt and bolo tie. He was surveying the damage to the bumper of his Chevrolet.

"Anybody hurt?" I asked.

"Naw, everything's all right," he said. He took the hubcap with one hand and adjusted his horn-rimmed glasses with the other. Under his papery skin his wrists and hands were mere bone and tendon. He had run his full-sized Chevy into a smallish, beat-up Chrysler, driven by a man who was short and stocky. He smiled shyly and tugged the bill of his dirty ball cap. I moved on. A while later, the big Chevrolet rolled by and the tall man waved. He drove ahead about a mile and then turned onto another easement and backed out just as before, this time safely, and pulled up in front of me.

"Say, son, let me take you up the road," the man said from behind the wheel through the passenger-side window. "Me and my missus're headed into Beatrice." *Be-AT-riss*, he pronounced it. He pointed to the woman in the passenger seat. "I think it's a hell of a thing for a man to walk a road like this. Whadya say?"

"Well, thanks. But I'd like to walk."

"Come on, son. Let us take you up the road a piece. The missus'd like it." He again indicated the woman, who sat passively and staring forward. I didn't sense friendliness in his voice but what person who had just smashed up his car could really sound friendly? It occurred to me that he had been turning his car around to offer me a ride when he had crashed with into the Chrysler. I climbed in the back seat behind "the missus." The tall stranger looked ahead, both hands on top of the steering wheel, pulled back on the road, and started talking. He told me that he had retired from the oil business in Wyoming and become a missionary. As a younger man, he had hitchhiked from San Francisco to Kansas City, and from Malta, Montana, to Juarez, Mexico. His starched collar rubbed against his leathery neck. He adjusted his bolo tie from time to time.

"Poor hayseed," he said after a few minutes, referring to the man in the Chrysler. "I talked him outta calling the cops for fifty bucks. Beatrice is filled with 'em, hayseeds just like that one. But it's better than being in a big town filled with culluds and spics."

The taste of metal and electricity filled my mouth. My head spun. I felt I was floating in a dream; the car and scenery became two-dimensional, as if on a postcard. I didn't know what to say. Having grown up in a white suburb, I was glad to escape undercurrents of racial prejudice that suffused my family home and the place we lived when I moved out on my own. Since that time, over a decade previous, I had lived in Midtown Kansas City, a checkerboard of urban neighborhoods where race was less important than class and income. My neighborhood was a place where whites, blacks, and Hispanics called each other by name. Certainly race mattered, but it didn't constitute separation and otherness the way it did to the old missionary. It hurt now, after so many years of having to fight through the racism I grew up with, to hear the man talk this way.

"Not that I got anything against 'em, you know," he said over his shoulder. "Just feel better with my own kind."

"What kind is that?" My face was hot—and, I supposed, red.

"You know, like us." He was calm, matter of fact, assuming I felt the same as he. My hands were shaking. I turned and watched fences and rows of corn shift in wide arcs as they marched toward the horizon. The world outside was suddenly as strange, lonely, and depressing as the interior of that car. Once in a while a clapboard house and a couple of silos popped out of the landscape, and a broken fence marked an old property line. I wanted to tell the man to stop the car and let me out. There was nowhere for me to go.

"Where was you going to stay?" he said.

"Wymore." I kept my face to the window to hide angry tears welling up in my eyes.

"What the hell's in Wymore? There ain't nothing there."

"Well, it's a dot on the map," I said as calmly as I could. "A dot usually has a park I can bed down in."

We drove by Wymore. The stranger rolled his eyes. "I'll get you to Beatrice," he said.

Religious articles and tracts lay on the back seat. A *Book of Mormon* and a *Holy Bible* were on top of a stack of official-looking books and spiral notebooks. I tried to separate the man from his spiritual faith. The tall stranger didn't say much more, contenting himself to drive. He looked grandfatherly—neatly dressed and well-kept, with a straight back. His wife, a matronly and quiet woman, said nothing and never moved. She could have been a corpse. The contradictions and stereotypes were too hard to sort through, and I slumped against the back seat, my face to the window.

At the edge of Beatrice I bid the man and his wife good-bye, glad to be rid of them. The sun was setting. My pack, at first, felt too heavy to lift. Once I started walking, I felt better. The bump-a-bump rhythm of my steps rose up through my legs and back and settled into my shoulders. I sought some understanding of the old mission-ary. Perhaps, I said to myself, he had never really been able to see others except through the lens of race. He had not had reason to examine the miserable order underneath the generations-old oppres-sion that produced utterances like "culluds and spics."

The missionary's attitude reminded me of what I had grown up with. Parents, relatives, and strangers had conversations over when "those Negroes" were going to start moving into the neighborhood. Among the kids in our all-white Catholic school, there were con-stant jokes about doormen, janitors, and elevator operators. One time when I was little, Fred, a man who lived across the street, had his car broken into. He and my dad loved guns. Fred came over and asked my dad what kind of gun he would use if he were to go on a "nigger hunt." I asked my dad what it was. It sounded fun and I wanted to go. My dad told Fred that he wasn't going hunting, but that he would keep his eye out for them. He then turned to me and told me that the whole thing was nothing I needed to know about.

The most hurtful racial incident of my life was of my own making, however. One autumn, after a game of Cub Scout hardball against a team of black Scouts, I threw the ball back and forth with a friendly kid from the other team. After a while my team captain asked me what I was doing with the "nigger." I was stunned, and other kid looked confused. I desperately wanted my teammates to leave so I could say I was sorry to the kid and go back to playing catch. But I was the fat kid, eager for approval, and I wanted my teammates to · like me.

"Chillen, that's what their mommas call them, chillen and chillens," another of my teammates said. "Niggers can't even talk right. 'Ol' Man River,' and all that, with lots of chillens and stuff."

My teammates laughed the kind of jeering laughter that cuts deep. I fought back tears. Suddenly, I wanted that kid, with whom I was having so much fun, to hurt.

I turned on the kid. "Yeah, chile," I screamed suddenly. "What do you want for Christmas, chile? What are you gonna get for Christmas, chile? Black dollies? Huh, chile?"

I said it over and over, poking the kid in the side with my ball glove. He sat stoically on a park bench, immovable and unexpressive, which prompted me to work all the harder on him. Saying things I had heard my friends say would, I hoped, make me feel whole and bring me admiration. But my throat hurt; there were gravel and razor blades in my voice. Through the ringing in my ears, I heard cicadas buzzing in the trees. Yellow and orange sunset rays fell across the park. I kept it up, with my teammates behind me, until that kid started to cry. My friends began laughing at me. I jeered even harder. I never felt so empty.

I never made fun of anyone like that again. But having been inundated by racism—explicit and implicit—for decades, I knew and understood the beliefs and feelings of the racist. Being sensitive to the pain of others, I had to face the confusion of hating and fearing someone because of their race or ethnicity and understanding them as human. It was a painful process, as any leap toward rejecting what one has spent a lifetime learning must be. I had to have faith in my human intuition when everything in my history cried out against it. I had to stand up for what I thought was right at the risk of rejection and ridicule from those I loved. That meant, of course, accepting the missionary for who he was and praying, in my own way, that his attitudes would never hurt anyone other than him.

Then I did my best to put the old man and his wife from my head. I counted mature oaks in the yards of little bungalows and cottages. I kept track of how many dogs and cats I saw behind the fences. I counted the dogwood trees but somehow got them confused with redbuds. Soon the old missionary and his wife drifted away and thoughts of a cup of tea and a bowl of rice bumped around in my head. I walked to a convenience store to get some hot food and directions to the town park. I made myself a cup of tea. The woman behind the counter, whose nametag said "Peg," was short, round-faced, and talkative. I asked her where I could find the police station so I could see if I could stay in the park. She disappeared behind the cigarettes and half-pints of liquor. When she reappeared, she handed me the keys to her house.

"It's up this street here," she said pointing. "There, at the second corner."

I looked at the keys in my hand. I was stunned. My feet hurt. I could still feel the tension in my neck and chest from dealing with the missionary. My face tightened as sweat dried in the air-conditioned store. I asked myself: What do you do when a complete stranger hands you the keys to her house as an invitation to overnight? How do you take it? What do you say? I felt stupid.

"You know," she said with a laugh, "you don't have anything to worry about. I trust you. You'll find everything you need at my house. Take a shower and put your feet up. Remote's in the drawer in the coffee table and food's in the refrigerator."

Peg's house was a simple single-story, porch-less wood frame on a street lined with the same kind of houses, all painted hues of green and blue. The interior was simple, worn but clean. Hand-sewn curtains covered the windows. A simple, hand-embroidered cloth covered the small dining table in the living room. Family photos and children's drawings hung on the walls. Soon after I arrived, a local newspaper reporter knocked on the door and said Peg had called him. The kid was just out of journalism school. He smiled a comfortable and self-contented smile and took notes like mad.

After he left, the place was quiet except for the sound of a lawnmower filtering in through the walls. I had found the remote control but television made the place seem like everywhere else and I turned it off and listened to the street outside. Children screamed and chattered. Every now and then, a dog went into a barking fit. Giving up trying to sort through the conflicts of the day and the wonder of such a generous stranger, I sat back with my feet up and drifted into sleep over my notebook and book of sea stories. In late evening a babysitter brought home Peg's kids, John and Jessica (aged six and eight), to get them cleaned up before their bedtime. We had a long chat in which they revealed themselves to be smart, curious, and gentle. After they went off to sleep, I lay myself down in a firm, warm bed, looking at Peg's family pictures in the light of a small lamp on the dresser. I kept thinking of my daughter, how she would look when she was Peg's age, and how she might treat strangers. I never did hear Peg come in from work, nor did I see her gather blankets from around me to make herself a bed on the couch.

Pickup trucks without mufflers began driving by Peg's place about 5:00 a.m. and never quit. I faded in and out of sleep until I rose from bed a couple of hours later. Peg had already been up for quite a while. We talked at the dining table over coffee. She'd lost a son to leukemia fifteen years earlier. At that time she was a caseworker at a local mental-health agency and had suffered a breakdown that nearly killed her.

"The doctor told me to quit," she said. She looked into her coffee cup. "Years later, my marriage went sour. I've worked at the Quik-Stop ever since and somehow make ends meet. It's not bad. The kids are taken care of, and they seem all right. Work's close. I'm pretty happy." She lifted her coffee cup and smiled.

"You kind of make the life you want for yourself," she continued, "even when the rest of the world is forcing you into things, I think. It hasn't been easy, but we have a nice little house here."

"The kids seem pretty well adjusted," I said. Another pickup clattered by.

"Oh, they are," she said. "They are doing very well. They have good attitudes about things. Some people are like that."

"I suspect they're getting it from their mom."

"Nice of you to say so," she said. Her face brightened. "There're nights I used to cry about how hard it all was. Then I looked around and realized just how much I have to be grateful for. Once that happened, I haven't really been down about much since. When I do get a little tired or *ungrateful* and worried about how we'll make it, I just stop and take a deep breath, think about the kids, this little house. It's all pretty good after that."

Whether she was grateful to a god or just in general, she did not say; in not saying it, she showed faith evangelizers cannot touch. I stood to make ready to go.

"Listen, I've already called my friend, Linda," she said as I put on my boots. "We're gonna take you to Wilber this morning, if you don't mind. Linda and I need a girl's day. After we drop you off, we'll do a little shopping."

"Really, that's not—" But she cut me off, telling me that everything had already been arranged.

We spent the morning sailing down tiny two-lane roads through little towns hunkered between farm fields. Peg and Linda laughed and told me stories they both knew well. In the early afternoon we arrived in a checkerboard of wheat and bare fields that enveloped Wilber. Peg handed me a small piece of flint. She called it her lucky stone and told me to use it when I needed it. I put it in my pocket with others I'd been given for the same purpose.

Signs proclaimed Wilber "the Czech Capital of the U.S.A." Sycamores lined the streets. Lawn mowers and weed whackers slashed and hummed. I walked up to the Hotel Wilber and set my pack on the front porch. The hotel was a two-story wooden structure with a red-shingled roof. No one was in the place. I wanted just to take in the pretty bowl of fields that spread out before the town, and finding and walking to a park seemed too much work. Sharp squirts of lawnmower-engine sounds echoed under the wooden roof. Clouds arced slowly over the bowl of sky. After a while, a spirited woman in her late thirties walked out to the porch and introduced herself as "Frances, the manager." Frances was petite, sturdy, and energetic. She had a deep voice, and her hands were rough and strong. She handed me a glass of lemonade and we sat in wicker chairs under the awning. We talked through the late afternoon.

"I was born in Wilber and lived here until I was twenty-two," she said. "Then, after my marriage went bad, I packed the car and headed west with my baby. I lived in a couple of California cities and in Seattle, Washington. Five years ago, I decided to come back to get my son set up in high school here. I needed a job and wound up running the bed-and-breakfast."

The hotel, built in 1895, had languished in the early 1970s. Later that decade, townspeople picked up hammers and saved the place. Without anyone to run it, or even a good idea about what to do with a renovated hotel, the town council began to lease the place to independent managers. In the early 1990s, they made a deal with Frances. She would run the place as a bed-and-breakfast and build the business. The result was a beautiful place with good food, a large and inviting lobby, and dining room with hardwood floors and oak trim. Each of the twelve rooms Frances showed me was comfortable and individually decorated in cutesy, but comfortable bric-a-brac. Every bed had a thick quilt and was filled with stuffed animals. The whole place reminded me of a make-believe grandma's house.

Business had been brisk, Frances said, but she was bored. Except for a few travelers, she knew her customers, even if she had never seen them before. They were "mostly people who know what they want when they arrive. A fairy-tale night in a place that's clean, feeds their need for nostalgia, and smells nice. They are good people, and I like being in the hotel business. It's fun. But year after year, it's goose and deer hunters in the winter, people visiting their families in town in the spring and fall, and summer tourists."

Frances wrote my name in a large ledger at an oak counter. Next to the cash register were Chamber of Commerce pamphlets and tourist guides, most emphasizing Wilber's Czech-ness. I took a long walk after setting my pack in one of those frilly rooms. On Main Street, Czech folk music played over speakers mounted on telephone poles, Czech flags flew from building facades, and Czech phrases and colors were painted on the sides of buildings. All this could not disguise the fact that Wilber was a Midwestern farm town, and, like most of those towns, afraid to be like the rest. All the Czech music and decoration struck me as contrived and mawkish, though. Wilber was more honest along its side streets. A canopy of cottonwood and walnut trees covered neat bungalows and trim yards. Toward the edges of town, shabbier houses and trailers gave way to open farm country. A row of silos lined the railroad tracks near a fertilizer and agricultural chemical depot. Grain trucks and pickups rumbled along the streets. Semis honked through on Nebraska Route 41, and trains rumbled past the silos. Very American-looking white kids lifted fingers from their steering wheels as they drove by.

Arriving back at the hotel, I walked into a troupe of preteen and teenaged dancers, dressed in garish Czech garb, dancing to recorded music. Members of the Nebraska Division of Tourism and travel agents stood smiling and sipping iced tea. Bureaucratic-looking people took notes and stood behind a small group of tourists in a square of white lattice fence covered with vines. Everyone applauded when the music stopped, and the dancers bowed. Another song started and the dancers seemed to take up where they left off. A couple of men in red vests and black pants danced into the group, escorting women in white-aproned black skirts and blouses with puffy, crinoline sleeves. None of the dancers, adults or children, looked like they were having fun. Instead they looked worried about getting the steps right for their coaches or teachers who mingled with the official types. Another round of soft applause puttered around the crowd at the end of the dance. Then everyone lined up at a table for Czech pastries and more iced tea.

Despite the activity, I was the hotel's only guest. That night Frances and I sat up in her room in the back of the second story of the hotel. It was sparsely appointed, with enough personal possessions to make it her own. Some exercise equipment stood against one wall. A small television perched on a chest of drawers next to a boom box. We sat on an open sleeping bag on the floor, drank fragrant, hot tea, and talked. After her son graduated high school in a year, she said, she planned to sell the business and leave Wilber again. She didn't know what she would do, but she felt she had to leave. The town was too small and close.

"So, why did *you* leave? What do you hope to find?" she said after a long pause.

"Oh, well, I got scared that my life was always going to be the same but was afraid to do anything about it," I said. "I suppose it got to be too much after a while. Funny how it worked out, once I had it in my head. I had a goal, and work and life didn't seem so bad. Once I had my mind set on the trip, I had to go or face never being able to go. You know, live with having missed the *one* opportunity in life to do something bold. I want to provide a good life for my daughter. She's a great kid and I hope that I can be a different father to her than the dad I had."

"What was so bad about your father?"

"It wasn't that he was awful," I said. "For thirty-five years, he worked hard at a job he hated during the day and drank too much at night. He was never happy."

"But don't you think that he was just trying to do what was best?" she sat up and crossed her legs, hands on her knees.

"Sure, but I think that if you're unhappy and frustrated all the time, you can't help but take that out on the people around you. I don't want to do that."

She asked what my being "in the middle of all that space" had to do with being a better dad.

"It's not just about being a dad, really," I said. "I'm tired of defining myself as a good person just because I have a job and pay rent on time. I know I'm selfish. But I wish my dad had been so selfish, you know, shown me that some risks are worth taking."

I asked her what she wanted to do.

She lay down on her back and looked up at the ceiling. "Underneath, Wilber's just a small town," she said. "Everyone knows everybody else's business even if what they think and hear is imaginary and just mean rumor. We once had a black family here. I knew them pretty well. They had some kids my son's age. After a while, being on the outside of everything and having everyone in their business was too much for them. The father got another job out of town so they could leave."

The Czech-ness of the town, she said, "is fading, if it's not gone already. The Czech stuff you see is all for tourists. That will be around as long as someone's making money, and it's drawing people into what's just a farm town. All the Czech this town has is made up. I'm not sure anyone really knows what it was to be Czech in Europe in, say, 1880. What we have isn't old country Czech, or whatever. I don't think you can really know what 'Czech' was like unless you fix it in time and space. And I can't believe most Czechs lived like we think they did. What we have is a carnival we put on for the tourists."

She sat up and sipped her tea. "After my son gets out of high school, I'll go someplace. Maybe back to California, where I used to live; or maybe east. I don't know. All I know is that Wilber's not the place I'll be in five years."

Frances turned on her side and propped herself up on an elbow. Sometimes when we shifted in our places, I could smell her hair—

earthy and pleasant. We were alone, her son at the rodeo and planning to stay overnight at a friend's house. I wanted to be close to her, to kiss her. But I was afraid of ruining the time we were having, putting something in the mix that I only imagined was there, afraid of breaking what may have been a trust. At the same time, the notion that she might have wanted that closeness made me indecisive and nervous. I desperately wanted to ask if she wanted something more than company. I certainly did—to be warm and close and lost in companionship and affection. But I didn't ask, and went down the hall to bed feeling lonely.

6

FRIEND, HASTINGS,
HANSEN, MINDEN

The Jims

THE LANDSCAPE WAS hard, sharp-edged, cheerless. The highway, U.S. 6, cut flat and straight as a knife across endless plowed ground. Cows sloshed around in mud, their hind ends turned into the wind. Clumps of trees, black against the gray mist, indicated lonely farmsteads. Telephone poles like skeletal snake spines disappeared into the drizzle. I could still smell Frances's hair and see the lithe curve of her neck. I could imagine the warmth and softness of her skin. I cursed myself for being afraid to touch her and silly at presuming she had wanted to be touched. Ego-dented and embarrassed, I imagined what she might be thinking of me now.

At the intersection of Nebraska highways 103 and 33, someone had spray-painted the opening lines of Dr. Seuss's *Green Eggs and Ham* across a whitewashed billboard behind an abandoned gas station. The next lines of the book were scrawled on the pavement at my feet. The entire text of *Green Eggs and Ham*, it turned out, was painted across two miles of pavement—in the same hand, and, except for the opening lines, all in white paint.

That crazy Sam-I-Am broke my hard, selfish mood, and I was grateful to the person who had stolen Seuss's work and displayed it so imaginatively. Being with Frances had been something of a dream. I had not known that kind of acquaintance with another person for ages. For the first time in almost two weeks on the road, I had broken my defensive outer shell and watched a woman open hers. I had revealed things that were important, if only for me to hear and understand. Had I been greedy? Taken a stranger hostage? I don't know. But as I ended my reading of *Green Eggs and Ham*, I sensed that it was reasonable while transitioning into a new and unimaginable future to feel vulnerable and unsure, to have doubt—and to want to be liked and held dear as a result. I was content, in that moment, to have had the blessing of Frances's gentle and understanding company.

My heartbeats soon fell in time with my footfalls; my breaths floated visibly in the chill air. A new excitement pulsed in my veins. The rain-washed air smelled fresh.

The grain elevators of the tiny town of Dorchester (population 610) rose from the mist from thickets of cedars, poked into the foggy sky like fingers. At first the buildings reminded me of those in Fritz Lang's *Metropolis*, then like the black-and-white Emerald City in *The Wizard of Oz*. The town soon appeared beyond those machine-age structures, and it was apparently devoid of human beings—despite pretty houses, tended yards, and newly paved streets. Even the gas station was unpeopled. It was automatic—"VISA, MASTERCARD, OR CO-OP CREDIT CARDS ONLY".

By the time I walked into the next town, Friend, twenty-seven miles of pavement had fallen easily behind me that day. I felt tired but was tempted to keep going right on past the town. A dismal row of ramshackle houses, and liquor stores and motels with broken and sagging awnings stretched along the highway. Then, in a line of implement dealers and machine shops, a bright light shone in the cold: the town's combined pizzeria, video rental outlet, convenience store, coffee shop, and gas station. I wanted coffee, steaming and syrupy with sugar and cream.

The place was bustling. As in Wamego, the store was more of a community center than a gas station. Kids played video games, and more sat at molded plastic tables drinking pop. A couple of young boys in oversized sleeveless shirts and ball caps were trying to talk the clerk into letting them buy cigarettes. "Just what're your moms gonna think?" the clerk said as she shooed them away. "Now get outta here before I tell 'em." Families ate hot dogs and drank from giant plastic cups. Married couples sat drinking coffee, visiting with others across the tables and shelves of convenience-food items. With nods and waves, people walking in acknowledged those already settled. News and gossip whipped around the soda fountain and coffee machine.

I drew coffee from an industrial metal urn and sat down with the town weekly, the *Friend Sentinel*. I sat in the swirl of conversations and read through names in the *Sentinel* birth and wedding announcements. The names were good and strong: Brutus, De Haus, Indermark, Jessop, Kerzner, Ketchum, Kraus, Kidwell, Mack, Rasch, and Yokel. My favorite was Devilbiss—a derivation of the German Teufelbiss, Devil's Bite.

The park was across town, away from the highway. Beyond the swimming pool, swings, and picnic shelters, baseball diamonds fanned into plowed fields broken now and then by clusters of trees. The west wind had grown stiff and cold, and the sky had slammed shut again. In a tiny shelter I fixed some tea and rice on the pack stove and then walked around the park to keep off the chill. Fifteen small marble slabs planted at the base of trees commemorated events and institutions: The tenth anniversary of the United Nations, 1955; Friend Centennial, 1871–1971; Members of Grange Local 390. While I was talking to my daughter on a pay phone behind a small park building, a woman came out and asked if I wanted ice cream. A minute later a tall kid with strong, broad shoulders set a paper plate with cake, nuts, pretzels, and a fork on top of the phone box.

I dug into the cake with a smile and shortly afterward entered the building. Inside was warm and bright. It turned out that the kid who had given me the cake was having high-school graduation party. Tabletops were piled with hamburgers, hot dogs, chips, pickles, and pop. People were dressed in heavy sweaters, jeans, and party hats. Many had already seen me at the convenience store—the stranger with a backpack—and wanted to know where I was going, what I did when it rained, and if I missed my family. In turn they told me about *their* travels and families. It was an unexpected pleasure to find people who needed someone to listen to them as much as I needed someone to listen to me. When the party broke up, a woman asked if I had a place to stay. I pointed to the picnic shelter with my things, and she shook her head.

"Well, that just ain't gonna do," she said. "Not on a night like tonight." She adjusted her thick glasses and pulled a lock of graying blond hair back from her round face. For over a half hour the rain had been spattering the windows and hail ticked against the roof.

"I'll be all right. Really. I have everything I need," I said. A plan for how I would build a dry shelter was coming together in my head. I was ready to put theory into practice.

"Maybe," she said. "But that's no reason we can't offer you a place on our couch." A lanky and strong man sidled up to her. He had dark hair and the sallow eyes of the chronic insomniac. Charlotte and Jim were born-again Christians. Both wore jeans and sweatshirts with Christian logos and Bible quotes. They had a modest home, they said, and strict morals. They smoked liked factories.

"We're old hippies," Charlotte said. "We like what you're doing. We want to have a hand in that."

In my experience people who identified themselves as hippies really weren't. Self-confessed hippies often confused their reactionary establishmentarianism with alternative approaches to living and production in a capitalist society. But I liked these people. They smiled a lot. They struck me as honest and generous.

It took half a minute to put my things into the back of their pickup and another thirty seconds to drive to their house. Vines and bushes grew up around a small porch and up the dingy siding. Water stains ran down the ceiling corners of the pale-blue living room. Jim and I sat in a couple of armchairs covered with fuggy homemade afghans. Charlotte went to the kitchen to make coffee. Jim surfed TV channels while he told me of the town's problems, farming problems, the nation's problems—most of which originated in people failing God and God's punishment for that failure.

Jim didn't believe in a lot of things. He did not believe in homosexuality. "It's unnatural," he said. He did not believe in abortion, which he called "killing a human being, a defenseless baby human being." He didn't believe in voting for a Democrat, "unless he were saved and pledged to fulfill a Christian agenda." Even so he did not believe there were many Democrats he could vote for, certainly not Bill Clinton. He didn't believe in welfare but would support some government programs, he said, "if the money were disbursed in a good and Christian way, with Christian goals in mind."

"Doesn't all that kind of go against the separation of church and state in the First Amendment?" I could think of nothing else to say to a man who believed in the Lord and little else.

"Just because I don't want my tax money spent on abortions," Jim said, "doesn't mean I want to tell anyone who to worship or what to write." He lit another cigarette with a lighter he always seemed to have in his hand. He sat in a comfortable recliner, an ashtray on the arm filled with butts. "I am devoted, however, to righting society's sinfulness with Christian principles."

He went on until he ran out of steam, continuing with the remote control, stopping from time to time to let a talking head finish a sentence. I liked Jim. Despite the fire of his rhetoric, he struck me as a good, well-meaning guy. Perhaps, like me, he had mired himself in too few challenges, too many responsibilities, and too much fear. His thumb working the remote, his eyes drooped after a while. Before he and Charlotte went to bed, Jim asked if I would stay a few days. He had some business near Hastings, where I was headed, and wanted to take me up the road.

"It'll give you a chance to get to know the town a little, rather than having to travel off right away," he said.

"I tell you what," I said. "I'd like to take you up on that, 'cause it doesn't sound like a bad idea. Let's see what the weather is tomorrow, how things go."

"We'd love to have you," Charlotte said.

Sunday morning was rainy, windy, and cold. Instead of church Jim attended endless reruns of Rush Limbaugh's television program, moving from one satellite channel to another to catch various episodes. When this show ran out, he tuned his satellite system to other conservative talk programs. He watched Jerry Falwell's *Old Time Gospel Hour*. He skipped the *700 Club*, however—"Robertson's erratic and unpredictable," he said. He tuned to evangelical church hours, prophecy theologians, and reactionary ranters. Cigarette smoke flowed from Jim's nose and mouth as he talked at me. People would be judged by their faith in the Lord and Savior Jesus Christ, he explained. "Lack of faith condemns a person to hell, regardless of good thoughts, actions, or intents." We went into the kitchen for more coffee and stood next to a greasy range from which he lit cigarettes over a burner. During that hour, he never provoked or elicited my opinion. He didn't ask me what I believed. He didn't condemn or judge or try to convert me. It was as if he was talking to himself.

Then Charlotte told me of other strangers they had taken in: bums, Christians, and travelers, as well as a duo of "feminists" and the only black vagrant they'd ever seen in Friend. They had put up families in trouble, folks they called poor Christians, and sinners.

Most had been well-behaved. But some had stayed too long or stolen goods and money from them.

"Why do you do it?" I said. "Most people would stop taking in strangers after they get their good nature violated a few times."

"Because we have to," Jim said. "I've never given it much thought. It's just something you're supposed to do without asking, I guess."

"But don't you worry about getting hurt or having more stuff stolen?"

"Sure," he said. He leaned against the 1970s-green refrigerator. "It's always there. The worry, I mean. But if you're truly generous, you take the risk. If you get burned and stop, you have to wonder if you were generous in the first place. Or had some misplaced expectations anyway. But if you put your trust in others, you can't go wrong most of the time."

Jim asked if I was any relation to James Dobson. Since leaving Kansas City, people frequently asked me about my relationship to the Christian thinker and moralist. His Focus on the Family organization, radio shows, and frequent appearances on cable television had built a following among people like Jim who needed affirmation of their brands of protestant Christianity (or who needed to believe the nation was falling apart). When people asked me about Dobson, it was hard to tell whether they were trying to assay my political leaning, figure out my religious inclination, or start a conversation. From the way Jim beamed, I could tell he wanted conversation.

"No. No relation," I said. "I've heard of him, though."

"Well, we listen to Jim Dobson on the radio," he said. "He's a good man. You should listen to his show sometime."

"I will. Thanks." The truth was that I most admired the devoted and zealous when they kept to themselves. This high regard diminished to complete distrust when it came to those who made my spirituality their business. I hadn't lied to Jim. In fact, I had heard James Dobson on the radio and seen him on television. I just didn't tell Jim that Dobson's message didn't impress me.

The next day, I walked to Jim's shop where he repaired video games. Dirty storefronts in the center of town were bereft of business, except for a photography studio that had placed portraits in the windows. Jim worked on Friend's main street. His shop had been an arcade and recreation hall for kids. It was no bigger than an average living room and was lined with movie and NASCAR posters. Christian versions of comic-book superheroes flew about the walls doing the work of the Lord. Bible verses were hand-lettered beneath them in garish colors. Jim had been in the arcade business for about a year before deciding that the place was too much work, the kids more interested in the shoot-'em-up video games than in his godly message.

His shop was filled with video games in various stages of being recycled. Empty video-game cabinets stood randomly about the floor. Between them were picture tubes, nests of wires, and guts of video games. It was a hard-scrabble living, delivering and servicing the machines, constantly dickering with business owners over placement and percentages. His margin was small or nonexistent. Taxes and licenses notched his meager income—he was busy, not prosperous.

I watched Jim as he flipped metal levers, adjusted apertures on coin devices, and soldered circuit boards. "I hate the way people cheat these things," he said over his shoulder. "It wouldn't be so bad . . . a couple of lost games. But cheating breaks a machine."

People had kicked and tilted, banged and pounded, and the cabinets holding the video chassis looked like it. Players had spilled pop and beer into the electronics. Games had burned patterns into the screens of the picture tubes lying around the floor. But it seemed Jim never bought a new machine to replace the ones the sinners ruined.

Jim unplugged a smoking soldering iron, and packed it and few tools into a briefcase for the ride to Hastings. It was a dark day; storms and wind shook the truck. He stopped at a commercial campground next to the interstate, a square of ground bare but for a small copse of trees and a few buildings. He hailed a woman from a doublewide behind the campground store. She waved at us before climbing into her truck and driving to the campground store less than fifty yards from her door. The place was dark and smelled of musty liquor and dust. I mooned around the bar, trying not to be bored or notice the smell much. Jim worked for an hour on circuit boards in the guts of a video trivia game. The woman talked on and on about newer, more lucrative games, intimating that she wanted those machines without ever saying it. But I could see in Jim's face that he was hanging on here, trying to make do with what he had and could afford.

Back in the truck Jim talked again about abortion and the evils of the federal government. I tried to listen but wound up trying to *look* like I was listening. I stared out the windshield and the side window. The land looked grim and hard. Black, unplowed fields stretched into the mist. Between sentences Jim searched the radio dial for Limbaugh's next show and somehow got stuck ranting about the Federal Reserve System and international trade. The whole antimodern rant sounded the same no matter who it came from—Jim, "Jim" Dobson, Rush, the numerous conservative talk-radio and cable programs. These people seemed to have given up, found excuses to stand still and dream of a time that never was. They sounded as if they believed they were powerless and that everyone except them was wrong. All they could do was sit back and sneer. And to make matters worse, the religious icons Jim so admired had turned religion and visceral reaction into a tool of power and capital gain. Jim, hard as his life was, had become their servant.

In the end Jim's talking wore me out and I was glad to climb from his truck about three miles outside of Hastings. The road stretched over a rise and into the dark sky.

"Sorry I've been inattentive," I said, hefting my pack from the back of his truck. "I just have a couple of things on my mind." "Aw, that's all right," he said. "I know how I can be. It's just I don't get to talk about these things much." He winked and shook my hand.

Jim smiled as he put the truck in gear. I watched him disappear into the drizzle. Plowed fields flowed over the horizon to the edge of the road. The feeling of being lost grew strong. I stood and looked at my feet. Jim was a lonely guy, and I felt for him. He had grown frustrated and angry about being in a world he could not control. Feeling powerless, he fought everything and nothing. He had become a man without a goal or purpose, who wandered from one fight to the next—even if most of those conflicts were in his own head. Still he was truly generous by anyone's standards, and therein, I hoped, was salvation from the irritants he made for himself.

As I walked I had to laugh. I had met a hundred guys like Jim, people who were obsessed and filled with contradiction, and who created their own challenges. One of them was me.

I took deep breaths and felt my mood lift with the fresh air. Being out in the open made me uncertain and anxious, but free again. I didn't envy Jim. Besides being smoky, his world had been airless and taut. I understood its complexities and knew its safety, certainty, and discomfort. I was beginning to find that risk had its own advantages, not the least of which was a different kind of pain than that of sitting still, waiting for something, anything, to happen. And I wondered if I hung on to fear, any fear, because it was familiar and comfortable.

The plain dropped into the wide, board-flat Platte River Valley. Lines of cottonwoods grew snakelike along the river. Billboards and gas stations brought me to the outskirts of Hastings. Soon brick, one- and two-story shops and restaurants gave the town a familiar charm. Soon the rain started again. The few trees along the road whipped in the wind. The sky brightened with flashes of lightning. At a motel at the edge of town, I stood under the awning outside the office and listened to hail pop the sheet metal. The rain sprayed up in a fog under the awning and blurred the day into a vast gray cloud.

The man behind the register in the office seemed bothered to have a customer. He was tall and thin, with a leathery face and tiny, squinted eyes. He snorted and quit hugging the register long enough to snatch the money out of my hand with his long, bony fingers.

The room was big, comfortable, and immaculately clean. Lightning flashed; hail sounded like applause. When the rain let up, I walked in big circles around Hastings. With a good appetite and craving for hot coffee, I stopped in at a coffee shop near the center of town. Pieces of pie sat in neat rows in a glass-fronted stainless-steel case. The waitresses wore identical uniforms, white dresses and orange aprons that came up in a bib. I had taken a stool at the long Formica counter next to a man with a sweeper moustache, who was wearing a ball cap and overalls. His big hands enveloped a coffee cup.

"How do. I've never seen you in here before," he said.

"I haven't ever been here," I said. "I'm on a little trip. My name's Patrick."

"I'm Jim Wach," he said. Another Jim! I thought. The Great Plains was lousy with Jims.

The new Jim looked like a farmer in a television program. But he wasn't a farmer. He had been a lineman with Lincoln Telephone for twenty years.

"Every phone in town is a Lincoln telephone," he said. "Pay phones, business phones, and private phones. And I'm a part of everyone having a phone."

We took our cups and sat at one of the booths under a bright light.

"It's my day off . . . the day I get to cat around town," Jim said. "I usually do some grocery shopping and stop off for coffee before heading home to Hansen. That's a little place outside of Hastings where my wife and I live."

His face brightened. "Hey, listen, I'm gonna call my wife and tell her to put a plate out for you. If she doesn't mind, and you don't either, I wanta have you over for dinner."

The sky had broken into puffy clouds. The late afternoon sun tapped the plain in radiant wands. The newly washed air was clear for miles. Jim's town, Hansen, was a knot of houses under towering oaks and cottonwoods in the otherwise treeless farmland. His house was a small, one-story, clapboard-and-shingle set among others like it along a gravel street. In the side yard, a deer fence squared off a vegetable garden. A few grapevines grew on a picket trellis. Sprays of flowers lined the walk. A small statue of Jesus with upraised hands stood in an island of daffodils on one side of the driveway.

Jim's home was simple and warm. Flaky gray-and-black photos hung in oval frames on the walls. We sat at a dinette table in the kitchen. A small light fixture hung from the high ceiling down close to the table. Jim's wife, Evelyn, served pork chops smothered in steaming corn chowder. She hardly said a word as she spooned au gratin potatoes and green salad onto the plates. Jim, however, talked a streak, telling about his family, his job, and his garden. The smell of the food made me ache inside, it was so fine. Jim and Evelyn's house was safe. Jim was a good man, with a good family. Evelyn had cooked an excellent dinner.

After we ate, Evelyn read a novel at the cleared table; her book took a bite out of the circle of light from the bulb above. Food had calmed Jim. He talked slower, with a more determined cadence. He was like a boy, willing and able, even eager, to open up to a stranger. And I liked being around him. After a time we went in the living room where he showed off more family pictures. His daughters were grown and off to college. He could hardly restrain his enthusiasm.

After a while he grew quiet again.

"I couldn't go to college, not right off," he said, as we sat down in comfortable armchairs. "I still want to take some courses someday, but with job and family, especially since the girls are in school, I just can't."

He turned and smiled under his big moustache. "But there's always retirement."

Dark had fallen by the time we drove back into Hastings. We splashed into the motel parking lot, and he pulled his pickup to the office and turned off the ignition. Rain pattered on the truck's roof.

"Do you know what you're looking for?" he said. "Exactly, I mean."

"Not really," I said, watching rivulets jumble and dance down the windshield. "Only that life will be different. That home might mean something other than working a job."

"Some of us are lucky," he said, turning his head. His eyes sparkled in the light seeping through the rain on the windshield. "We go to work because they give it meaning, those people at home. That's enough. There's nothing wrong with that not being enough, and I understand what you're talking about. But I've been fortunate. I'm glad I know that. I hope you find your place someday too."

I felt tired and good as I stepped from the truck. The wind was crisp and getting cooler. A lone light shone in the office. The leathery man stood behind the cash register with his arms around it, staring out at the vacancy sign. He was still hugging the register the next morning when I went to check out. Windows surrounded the office, and men in overalls sat at a Formica table under them. They were locals in for what looked to be a routine cup of coffee.

"Fine day," I said to Leatherman, who was irritated. The sky and the air were crystal clear. "How far it is to Minden?"

"About thirty. Ya git there by puttin' one foot in front of the other."

"No kiddin'," I said, refusing to be insulted.

"I used to walk," one of the men at the table said, pointing to my backpack. "I use to walk a long way when I was a young man. We had a truck, but I liked to walk. Everywhere. To the grocery store. To work. To go visiting. I don't do it much anymore."

"Don't let him bullshit you, boy," said the man next to the first. "He hasn't walked anywhere in three decades."

"Yeah," first man said. "The car just kind of takes over all by itself if you let it, then you never come away."

I walked away wondering how such a distasteful man could run such comfortable motel. A freight train roared down the tracks next to the road and swept the air away. Walking that close to the train, I had the vertiginous feeling of being pulled into it. At Heartwell, I sat on a bridge over the tracks and stared down into coal cars as they blurred by. Besides a grain elevator at the foot of the bridge, nothing between the bridge and the horizon was higher. One of the four storage silos grouped together in a little square had a gaping hole that ran from about fifteen feet above the ground nearly to the top. It looked as if Godzilla had taken a bite out of it. Machine sheds next to the broken silo were twisted and bent. Men with bulldozers pushed debris around the empty lot. Clouds soon moved in and cloaked the road, which made walking the rest of the way into Minden pleasant and cool. The day was over all too soon.

I wanted to go through Minden so I could see the town's prominent tourist attraction, Pioneer Village. While I was in grad school at the University of Wyoming in the early 1990s, I commuted on holidays and long weekends from Laramie to see my daughter in Kansas City. I had read and reread billboards along I-80 advertising Harold Warp's Pioneer Village in Minden, "where history comes alive." Warp's Village had become a thing of my imagination; a complex of images and thoughts that enlivened lonely miles of grueling interstate and wakeful nights camped under the stars where the sound of train whistles washed over new-planted corn. In my mind it promised something simple, good, and whole that I had never known but was willing to believe might exist.

With a sense of excitement I paid for my camping spot and set up my square on the sodden turf of the empty tent campground. The RV "village" on the other side of a hedge was crowded and loud with generators, children screaming, and parents yelling. Music of all kinds rose up out of that oddly urban place, along with the sound of a hundred air conditioners and television channels. After dark the sound began to fade, almost as if controlled by a dial. Shortly after ten the place fell quiet. I lit my candle lamp to read by, and covered myself with my waterproof tarp in case of rain. The heavy, cool haze that wasn't quite fog gave streetlights over the campground halos. Trains busted by every twenty minutes, emphasizing the silence between. Frogs sang in the hedge.

The next morning I toured Pioneer Village. In the 1920s, Harold Warp had invented Flex-o-glass, a thick plastic film to cover greenhouses. With this and a dozen other plastic marvels he became fabulously wealthy after World War II—not only from manufacture of his inventions but from the sale of licenses to his patents. With his money he bought yachts, cars, and houses. When he'd sated his desires for personal comfort, he created an attraction commemorating his childhood in Minden. In 1953 Pioneer Village opened to the public as the nation's largest privately funded collection of Americana. Warp stocked it with a schoolhouse that reminded him of the one he'd attended as a child. He trucked in buildings—houses and outbuildings—that reminded him of the good old days. Then he began to create a collection of cars, trucks, motorcycles, and home appliances. Display barns held airplanes, engines, farm implements, and tractors. The collections idealized and memorialized nostalgic ideals of family, hard work, and wealth. Catch phrases that were allegedly signature Warp—"Warpisms"—hung on little plaques and placards randomly placed on piles of machinery and knickknacks: "Success is the accumulation of remembered mistakes." "An idea and courage make ambition. Ambition and hard work make success." Ultimately these were the platitudes the wealthy say to people who stay poor.

The imaginary Pioneer Village that had for years kept me such company on the highway turned out to be an expensive collection of attic sweepings. The disappointment reminded me of seeing the mechanical works beneath the displays at Disneyland when I was a kid, being frightened by a locally famous television clown at a Laundromat promotion, and watching my plastic, secret-spy submarine fizz and sink in the bathtub. I tried to think what I had expected—perhaps something more real? Then it struck me. Pioneer Village *was* real. Illusion was the product, and the illusion was as real as the ground I stood on. Pioneer Village was an artifact of a mythical and nostalgic history detached from reality. It was what Americans wanted to believe: we are a simple and good people who solve problems, get rich, and show the world the wonder of our God, our families, and our nation. The rich were rich because of their genius and the brilliance of their system. For the wealthy, there was no luck, advantage of inheritance, or reliance on others, only successful individual initiative. If the poor were poor, it was their own damn fault. No one exploited or bullied anyone else.

The Warp past was easily swallowed, digested, and regurgitated. I had wanted Pioneer Village to show me something other than how history had been used to insulate rich from poor, to justify economic power and political and social hierarchy, and to make those who supported the tiers above them satisfied with their duty and position. I wanted to see how ordinary people could win and to know how they could gain advantage in global systems increasingly aligned against them. Basically I wanted Warp and Pioneer Village to be everything they could not be. My expectations were as artificial and contrived as any of Warp's silly sayings. This didn't make the dream I dreamed during all those highway miles any less real. It only made the reality disappointing.

Later I spread my sleeping bag in a picnic shelter at Fort Kearny State Recreation Area. Sitting cross-legged on a picnic table, I watched the haze rising from the fields turn orange in the sunset. Rain clouds turned the dusk quickly into night. A strange calm had settled in me. Realizing that Warp's Pioneer Village could be so disappointing, I tried to determine what I hoped to find on the trip, what my expectations were, and how they could lead to more disappointment. Ultimately I wanted to be free of what made me an unhappy, maladjusted person. But if things were different, I wondered, would they be better or just different? Would the restlessness and irritableness disappear, remain, or take unexpected and unrecognizable form? Having to live with the consequences of the trip lay in a future too distant and abstract for me to imagine. It was better to meet each day without a notion of what I wanted to happen, and instead live with what did. I realized that short conversations with my daughter every other day or every few days had slowly, inevitably, ceased to cause me pain and insecurity. I missed her but knew I would be back, I just didn't know who I'd be or how my view of the world would change. I had become comfortable being on my own and with strangers who came to seem so close so quickly. What lay in the future was not really my business. My business was to deal with things as they came. My ambition should be to be without ambition: I would seek to know more about the land that had so absorbed me for so long. I would meet more people and see more of their lives. More than that would be gravy.

The rain began to fall. The mercury lamps made blue pools of light in the inky night. Now and then lightning flashed across the horizon. I crawled into my sleeping bag and thought of Frances again, and the Jims. The shelter smelled of wet concrete and sodden grass. The rain came and went, beating soothing rhythms on the roof of the shelter and bubbling through the downspouts. There was a long way to go. I had become comfortable with that and had begun to un-Warp myself.

7

LEXINGTON, COZAD,

NORTH PLATTE

"It's better to try something and apologize later"

MAY WAS DEPENDABLE only in its variability. Weather since my departure had been as often wet and cold as it had been pleasant or searing hot. One day might erupt in startling, bright colors, the sun lighting flowing fields of wheat and multi-hued flowers. Then the land would darken, deepening hues of green to blue or even black. Mornings the sky might open and warm hedgerow and prairie, raising expectations for a great day. But within an hour those same signs of life could be lost in nearly impenetrable cold rain. Most surprising, however, was when the weather cleared suddenly in the late evening to reveal stunning sunsets that faded into veils of stars.

Without a car to limit the view, these aspects of land and sky were nakedly apparent. Far from being boring expanses, Kansas and Nebraska were complexly clad spaces. Lines of cottonwoods wandered among hay fields and irrigated row crops. Willows and Russian olives crowded river banks like endless green boas tossed carelessly on the valley floor. Wheat and grass, bare soil, and ribbons of pavement supported endless sky, clouded or clear. The colors revealed in the play of light and shadow were overwhelming, sometimes too much to bear. At times I felt cheated. High speeds and automobile glass had filtered out the nuances of land and sky, sunlight and time of day, plant and animal. I had missed out all these years.

I was also an outsider. Having grown up on the edge of the Great Plains, I only had the barest notion of its importance—and the depths of my ignorance were becoming obvious. In the past its people and places were always fresh and different to me. My vision had not suffered the fatigue of life and work in what, despite physical expanses, could be close economic and social quarters. I was oblivious to the politics of relationships in small towns and the problems associated with small-town and rural life. I knew nothing of people's ambitions, thwarted or fulfilled. Resentments festered here as they did anywhere else. As I discovered how little I knew, boundaries between city and country, and separating human and nature, grew more indistinct and blurred. Regardless of the cultural oppositions between rural and urban life, my personal narrative was bound to this land and the people that supported me. My city and its streets depended on the plains, globalization's promises of freedom from geographical constraint notwithstanding. I was becoming a speck in deep and complicated relationships that I'd previously not known existed. The smaller I felt, the more relieved I was of the responsibility and folly of being significant. Oddly, being neither lost nor found was not so frightening anymore.

My morning cup of tea had gone cold in my hand. I had been standing for who knows how long just outside a picnic shelter. Clouds filled the sky to the horizon, spilling onto the carpet of grass and farm field that flowed to my feet. Windmills, farmsteads, towns, and lone cars on the highway were mere spots. I stood and stared, mesmerized, until the time came to walk the ten miles to Kearney. Then I did.

I was becoming anxious. A friend, June, was to join me for the weekend. We had just started dating shortly before I left. The occasional telephone conversations we had in the intervening weeks had been pleasant and upbeat. She had been encouraging in difficult moments. My mind ran wild in the long periods of solitude. At the end of a day of travel, I dreamed up romantic scenarios and conversations that lovers might enjoy after a long absence, particularly after my extraordinary time with Frances at the Hotel Wilber.

Downtown Kearney was quiet but alive. Three- and four-story buildings lined the main streets. Big awnings hung over storefronts and the front doors of lawyers' and doctors' offices, apartments, and shops. I sat on benches downtown, watching people, walking when I got cold. I gave up thinking that there was something I had to do— because I was doing it. The town came to life after 7:00 p.m., when retail commerce shifted to restaurant and bar traffic. People moved singly and in groups, finding warmth behind neon lights.

When June showed up the next evening she was sedate. Having driven three hundred fifty miles from Kansas City after a day's work, she was not in a mood for the energy I possessed, nor for my affections. We sat in the motel room I had checked into earlier in the day, with little to say. I had come to believe through solitude and imagination that she had thought of me as much as I had thought of her. But here was emptiness and longing where I had expected joy and fulfillment. In solitude I had created impossible notions of our relationship and inordinate expectations for our rendezvous. Unease and doubt grew as I realized how little we knew each other. In fact we were barely acquainted. Our time together in Kansas City had been short and intense but had ended as abruptly as it had begun. The journey intensified physical and psychic distance between unfamiliar people. Since I had left, our lives had taken wildly different directions. My foundations were crumbling. Her day-to-day existence had not changed.

When the silence finally broke, she said she was far less enthusiastic about our meeting than I was. She needed to get to know who I was becoming and the time was again too short. I asked her why she had come all the way to meet me. She said she had wanted to make the trip in the way that she might drive across town to meet an old colleague in whom she had once been romantically interested. Would I be different, she wondered? Would I have a beard and longer hair? What would I have learned? Would I have met other women? Slept with them? My heart sank.

After dinner in town, we tuned to cable channels in the motel room. Intimacy was an affair that was as melancholy as it was joyful and invigorating. With little to say, we settled in bed and listened to traffic on the strip until we fell into restless sleep.

The next day we checked into a motel near Lexington, a town whose main business was an IBP slaughterhouse and meat-processing plant. June and I walked around town, mostly silent. I fell to thinking of the slaughterhouse. Its shape and appearance was little different from a car factory, where raw materials streamed in one end and emerged as finished products on the other. Cattle and pork producers provided the factory with genetically refined items. Beefs matured on tiny plots of earth, eating a half-digested mush of catfish, silage, and fermented corn. Employees injected herds—assets representing cash and market advantage—with hormones and antibiotics to increase the efficiency of energy input. At the processing plant, workers packaged those ciphers into identical shrink-wrapped packages for store shelves. Ultimately this means of producing food had no heart in it. It was no wonder that David Sharp couldn't keep livestock anymore, or that he would have to give up farming one day and stick to his store and job in town.

But the processing plant produced some benefit for Lexington. IBP needed hands to run their meat factory. Increasingly those hands belonged to immigrants who had reconstituted Lexington, where, for decades before the plant opened, farm consolidation had forced an exodus of white farmers and their children. Lexington's five thousand immigrants, most Hispanic and many undocumented, filled pews and revived once-deteriorating churches. They had transformed what had become a dour, defensive, self-conscious place into a living organism of unbelievable complexity and color.

June and I drove south across the Platte River to Johnson Lake, a vacation and weekend spot. Cottonwoods, sandy beaches, and weekend houses ringed the lake. At one of those beaches of fine, beige sand, we sat on slabs of sandstone, staring across the water. Carpets of ladybugs crawled over the beach and on the long, uncut grass along the shore. They dripped from the cottonwoods into our hair and onto our arms and shirts. They covered pieces of driftwood along the edge of the water and crawled over our shoes and up our legs. The sun set behind orange and purple clouds, and the quiet hush of the treeless plains beyond the lake crept in with the cool evening breeze. Whip-poor-wills began to call over the water.

We were contemplative, melancholy. Over the last two days, our expectations of each other had neither been satisfied nor crushed. Reality had turned out to be much different than what we had imagined. News of home didn't much interest me. She found no connection with stories of the people I had met or things I had seen. We sat in silence for a long time, holding each other, hoping, I'm sure, that the night and the next morning would change our time together for the better. After watching the sun set, we drove again over the valley toward the motel.

"What do you see in all this?" she said. She quietly smoked a cigarette and looked out the driver's window at the long line of cottonwoods that followed the river banks. "What do you hope to gain?"

In that moment I had no way to communicate what I felt about the places and people I'd seen and met. June saw empty, boring, crushing space outside that window. She understood the plains in terms of unrelenting and extreme weather. She had read stories of people driven crazy by wind, flattened by history. She knew people in rural towns lost their friends, relatives, and children to cities. To her the city was more exciting and held greater opportunities, products, and material satisfactions.

Certainly all that was true. But I had met people who were interesting in the way that no person or group, closely examined, are ordinary. They had possessed startling beauty in their strengths, weaknesses, and contradictions. Their enduring qualities ranged from good to ill, gentle to savage, loving to hateful. They cared about God and country even as they abused each other and sacrificed community and connection to land and place for personal gain. They believed they had a right to give the land cash value and political worth. They indulged in a God-mandated and patriotic obligation to calculate that worth against human and nature as sharply as actuaries. Most refused to see or understand how the land had changed and become a part of them, and they a part of it. Almost universally they were unquestioning devotees of the sacred American ideal of hard work, love of country, and order, however much that ethos led them to participate in their own exploitation. Their generosity and kindness, suspicion and defensiveness, and complexity and complicity made them wondrous, unpredictable, and impossible to stereotype. How could I explain to June why some people hurl themselves into the prairie sea to explore its secrets? How could I tell her why some jump from the sea at their first opportunity, and why some already drowning there refuse to swim ashore?

How could I tell or show the comfort I was finding in my own insignificance when I walked beneath the plains sky?

Back at the hotel we grasped at illusions. We wanted intimacy and love. But these things would not appear over a weekend if it wasn't there already. We watched a movie, talked, and made love, as if sex could bridge the distance growing between us.

As she fell asleep I stared at the shadows that streetlights cast on the ceiling and tried to put things into perspective. Before I'd left Kansas City, I was afraid to lose a budding romantic involvement with June. I didn't want my daughter to suffer from my selfish and vague search for something meaningful in the day-to-day and within myself.

None of that mattered now. The joys of the road were worth every step, every uncertainty, all the blistered feet, and the fear and fatigue. I was becoming separated from June's world and was just realizing how comforting it would be for me to become content with being a part of a relationship rather than responsible for it. The fear that had haunted me for so many miles was dissipating, giving way to an ethereal pleasure in the solitude of walking lonely stretches of highway and county road. At the same time I looked forward to meeting the next person, who, like Frances and Peg and the Jims, would unselfishly reveal my world by taking me into his or hers. With June, my daughter, or anyone else I met, my feeling that the affairs of others demanded my constant physical presence was arrogance on my part. Whether I was missed or not wasn't my business. The garden would keep growing without me.

In the morning, I packed my things and took off west down U.S. 30. June drove back home.

The landscape became a solid and beautiful backdrop for my fleeting passions. I walked fast, investing my confused thoughts in physical labor. Soon I was thinking of June driving on the interstate and considered myself lucky to be on a two-lane highway under the intimidating sky above the Platte River Valley. I would talk with June again. We would try to have a relationship—this was certain. But how all that might work out I didn't know, and I was no longer sure it was any of my business. I missed her a great deal—and didn't want to see her for a long time.

Just two or three days before, it had been cold. Now the pavement sizzled. Shimmering lakes of heat appeared on the road and in the farm fields. Trains rushed by, their bulk and speed drawing me to them, much the same way that a cliff's edge drew me into the void. Several miles from Lexington, at a highway pullout, three scrawny cedars shook in the hot wind. A large stone affixed with a bronze plaque memorialized seventeen white settlers that a band of Pawnees had killed. I parked myself on the stone and felt it shoot molten tentacles up my spine and into the back of my neck. I took off my shoes and socks and set them on the rock to let the sweat dry some before I took off again.

A stiff gust bent the cedars. Without boundaries of trees, great masses of buildings, and telephone wires, the landscape seemed a canvas tacked down only with the trill of meadowlarks and the screech of hawks. I took in the warmth of the rock and stared out over the hazy distance. The breeze felt good on my toes.

Later that day, I set up camp in the Cozad Municipal Park. The swimming pool there sat next to a baseball diamond with grandstands, high school emblems, and advertisements for local businesses painted on the whitewashed wooden fence surrounding it. I called my daughter on a pay phone. She was just home from daycare and talked about a kid who liked to bite other children.

"Did that kid bite you?" I said.

"Yeah."

"Are you hurt?" I watched the kids splashing in the pool. Water never looked so good.

"No." I could tell that she was watching television.

"What happened?" I said. "I mean what did you do when he bit you?"

"I bited *him*."

I told her that it was wrong to bite people, but couldn't help but laugh. It was this kind of candidness that refreshed me after long days of being alone. Our conversations every few days were never long. Invariably she would be distracted by a toy or television. But our short talks did me right. That day, long after I'd hung up the phone and rolled my bed out under the trees at the park camp-ground, I was smiling.

Evening sun threw long shadows from the oak and cottonwoods. The color and sharpness of the shadows were surreal—dusk, awash in postcard yellow and red. I lay on my sleeping bag in the grass and tumbled the lucky stones I kept in my pocket. I looked at them individually in the light of my candle, taking note of their color and mentally melding each with the person who had given it to me. I read and wrote a long time before the sun set. Union Pacific freight trains—strings of red and white lights from one side of the stars to the other—woke me every twenty minutes with their roars and whistles.

The next day began mostly clear, with a few thick clouds, and it was cool but not unpleasant. I bathed, as I did daily, head to toe with a quart or so of water, using a washcloth and half a bath towel. Then I boiled coffee, ate a granola bar and a piece of fruit, and then wrote and walked around, talking to myself, avoiding the chaos that radi-ated around my bed. As usual, nearly everything was out of the pack. My sleeping bag was spread over a thin mattress that filled with air of its own accord with the twist of a small valve. To find the clean pair of socks, shorts, and shirt, all the clothes came out. On the ground lay the gasoline-fueled pack stove, my cup, a small metal pan, spoon, knife, and fork. Among the mess were also three paperbacks: *Leaves of Grass* by Walt Whitman, *Collected Poems of Carl Sandberg*, and a novel I would read and replace.

When I'd finished scribbling for the second time in the small, hardcover notebook that served as my journal, I began my ritual. I picked up small things on the outer perimeter of my muddle and moved in circles closer and closer to the pack. First into the pack were the stove and eating utensils, then my sleeping bag and mat-tress. I packed clothes and other items as I puttered along. Then, as if suddenly, my things were gone, disappeared into the pack, never failing to leave me surprised and pleased with myself.

The road, U.S. 30, wound out of town next to the railroad tracks. Every now and then trains rushed by with spooky draws of wind. Nearly twenty-five miles of pavement flowed without effort. West of Gothenberg the sky clouded over and a sudden wash of cold wind flowed over the fields. Rain came soon after, a small spatter at first, then buckets. The sky turned black. Random flashes bathed the road in eerie, blue-green light. Spits of hail bounced and skittered on the pavement. The cold returned and I was soon wet and shivering. Just as I finished pulling on my raingear, a kid in a small black car pulled up.

"Need a ride, mister?" he said.

"No, thanks, I'm just going up another mile or so to Brady."

"It's gonna really hail soon. That what we had earlier was just a warm up. I don't mind taking you into North Platte. That's where I'm going." His straight hair whipped in odd streaks of color around his eyes. He was smiling.

I climbed in the car, just as the rain and hail got heavier and the day even darker. The driver, Ronnie, was an optimistic, pleasant guy, with all the innocence and hopefulness of his nineteen years. His dream in life was to become a rock star.

"I got a baby on the way," he said after we had talked about his ambitions a while. The car didn't have heat, and I was shivering. The cold didn't seem to affect him, although he wore only a T-shirt, shorts, and windbreaker.

"I want to be a dad and can't wait," he said. "I live in North Platte but I'm ready to go. There ain't much for a guy like me. My girlfriend's a lifeguard at the pool, and I work fast food. But I play guitar at night with my band. That's really what I want to do. North Platte just ain't the place to do it."

Ronnie drove with one hand draped over the steering wheel. His blond hair was tinted purple and pink in the front. He bobbed his head slightly to the beat of the music on the radio. He was a good-natured kid and didn't have a bad word for anyone. Even when he talked about the lack of a music scene in central Nebraska, or at least one he considered good and lively, it was without bitterness.

"Yeah, if I'm going to do what I want to, I'll have to move to a bigger city," he said, turning to look at me. "You don't have rock stars in North Platte."

"What about being a dad and a husband?" It was a question I wanted to answer for myself. If his response was good, I was going to steal it.

"I know I got to make some money and provide," he said. "But hell, look at you. You're sitting around one day, saying to yourself, 'I got this thing I got to do.' You didn't let being a dad stand in the way, did you? No. You thought about what it might be like if you did this thing, right? How life might be better."

"Actually, I was thinking more about what might happen if I didn't do this thing."

"Same difference," he said.

He seemed to have a better sense of where he was going than I ever did at his age. At age nineteen I had spent most of my days drinking my wages and living in a perpetual hangover. I believed I had everything I would ever have. Years later I sobered up and found I had drunk up just about everything I ever had. I had been fired from my job and couldn't get on with other people. I had alienated my friends, most of whom hated watching me destroy myself or refused to put up with my bad behavior any longer. Since I had come to my senses, I attempted to remake myself to fit what I thought others wanted of me—as if I could ever know what others wanted of me, or if they wanted anything at all. I went to school, but a master's degree in history didn't get me work as a historian. The work I found paid better than anything I had before but didn't provide me any more soundness of mind or happiness than I'd had when I was drunk. Ultimately I wound up where my story began: standing in the middle of a concrete floor feeling doomed to paint the same floor over and over for the rest of my life. Sober, but still lost.

Ronnie didn't seem to have a problem either with being a father or pursuing his dream. His confidence came out of an utter lack of arrogance. I liked that. We drove a while in the drenching rain. Lightning lit up the dark sky from time to time, and thunder rocked Ronnie's little car. He offered me a cigarette, which I took and lit. I hadn't smoked in years, except the odd cigar, and I wasn't about to start. But the smoke tasted good and seemed to take some of the shiver out of my bones.

"No, man," he said after a while, as if his mind had not given up his previous thought. He shook his head. "You can't let your kids stand in the way. They'll hate you for it. It's better to try something and apologize later than not to try and apologize all the time—to yourself, to your kids, to your wife."

I had to smile at the way he felt he had to counsel me. He spoke as a father would to a son, or an older person to a younger. At the same time, I knew he needed to say these things to himself. He was determined, and his advice to me was his reaffirmation of the rightness of his decision to move on with his life as he saw fit.

"Listen," he continued. "I've been going with my fiancé"—FIE-ants, he said—"for a long time. Sometimes she doesn't get it, the music thing. She's got a baby on the way and she hasn't seen one dime from me playing music. She's working at the municipal pool. Hey, it's not a bad job, keeping people safe while they're having fun. But jobs like that's all there is around here, unless you want to work for the railroad, and those jobs're drying up. And I don't want to work for the railroad.

"Everything and everybody in North Platte is the same. All us kids start smoking in ninth grade, start drinking after that, and polish it all off with bong hits and other drugs until we get old or busted by the cops. We work for the Union Pacific or at convenience stores.

"Now I ain't going to knock it. Lots of people do just fine. But it's not for me, not for my wife, and I can tell you it ain't for my kid."

The rain had let up but the sky was still black when Ronnie let me off at the municipal pool. His girlfriend, who stood near the pool entrance at a distance, wore a bikini top of deep blue with white shorts and comfortable tennis shoes. She was obviously at the very beginning of her pregnancy. Ronnie beamed when he saw her.

"Yeah, man," he said, looking at her between his hands on top of the steering wheel. "There's something out there for us."

He was smiling, his purple lock hanging down his forehead. Ronnie reminded me of why I'd had to leave the battleship gray my life had been. I remembered a few lines from Whitman I had read just the night before:

Why are there men and women that while they are nigh me the sun-
light expands my blood?
Why when they leave me do my pennants of joy sink flat and lank . . .
What is it I interchange so suddenly with strangers?
What with some driver as I ride on the seat by his side?

The girl came up to the car. She was pretty, with blond hair and the long, well-defined arms and legs of a swimmer. She was about the same age as Ronnie. He hugged her and she leaned against him as they kissed. She climbed into the car and turned to smile and wave at me. It was as if the sun had come out.

8

NORTH PLATTE

"Mostly, you go to the river and get drunk"

I CAME TO know the contours of North Platte's Cody Park in the middle of the night. Acidic light and peafowl made sleep impossible. Peacocks caged somewhere in the park yowled as if tortured. Sodium lamps flooded the picnic shelter with orange light. Instead of sticking it out on the shelter floor, I made aimless circuits of the park, poking my head in where it didn't belong. I was going over a chain-link fence meant to keep people off a couple of antique locomotives when the peacocks' howling ended abruptly. I jumped and hit the ground running, hoping this was my chance to get some sleep. The sleeping bag had not settled in around me when the park's geese started hacking and honking at each other. This time I'd stay put. It's best for all of us, I thought. I like animals, large and small, but right then I wanted to strangle them dead.

I had just fallen asleep when groups of young men began grooming the park. Weed whackers whined, lawn mowers growled, and electric hedge trimmers buzzed. It was the first of June and I'd been gone from home for a month. Helena lay another month or month and a half away. If I didn't get any decent sleep before July 15 I was going to go crazy. I kept my eyes shut, hoping the workers would go away if I ignored them. Soon a crew of them banged into my picnic shelter, paint rollers rattling in big plastic buckets. Eyes half open, I asked them to take a break—"fuckin' break," more specifically—and offered them tea since I was going to have to make some for myself. The three men in their twenties sat on the bench above my head and introduced themselves as Dan, Rich, and Tom. From underneath that table my view was all butt cleavage and hairy calves.

I served tea in my limited ware: one drank from my cup, one from the pot, the other from a paper cup retrieved from the trash and washed at the spigot. They had never had hot black tea with sugar before. After a series of squints and sniffs, they seemed to like it. After explaining what I was doing, I asked them about their work. They were equally plaintive about making a living pushing paint rollers or machines powered with Briggs & Stratton engines. The youngest of the bunch, Tom, didn't seem to mind the work as much as the others. He stood after a while and walked around the shelter with the paper cup, halfheartedly slinging paint here and there.

Dan was a large guy with the broad shoulders and wide neck of a high school wrestler. Great sadness haunted his eyes. Working for the city of North Platte was not his idea of a good time, he said. It didn't sound like it.

"I make five bucks an hour," he said. "I got a kid at home and I walk around worried about money all the fuckin' time. Plus marriage just ain't what it's supposed to be, you know, like happy and joyful and all that like you think it's supposed to be when you get into it. It's kind of frustrating all the time. Money. Where you're living. What you're supposed to be doing with your future. The stuff that never gets done but gets bitched about all the time. All that. The one joy I got is my daughter. She's six months old."

He stopped and looked up from the cup, then set his hammy hands on the picnic table and stared at his fingers. Rich, a tall man with a yellowish, peach-fuzz goatee, sat next to Dan. He looked into his tea and shook his head while Dan talked.

"There's just nothing here for me," Dan continued. "I got nothing, never did. I don't know why I thought being married would fix all that. I don't know what we're going to do. I'm pawning my stuff just to live day to day. When it's gone I think I'm cooked."

"Have you thought of doing something else?" I said. I thought of Ronnie being drawn like a moth to brighter lights.

"Sure, I thought about it," he said. "I think about it all the time. But the money, you know. I don't even have the money for community college."

"What about scholarships or grants?" I said.

"Ha!" he guffawed again. "Who's going to give *me* money?"

"What about finding something that pays better?" I said. Just coming awake now, I realized my questions were insulting—questions a person who always had opportunities, even if he never used them, would ask.

"You got to be shittin' me," Rich said with a guffaw. "You ain't getting nothing without an education. Big towns, they're just as bad as here, maybe worse, if you got no education. No. I'll save my money when I can and maybe get over to the community college someday. Learn to be an EMT. I think I'd like that. They have a good EMT program. With all us drinking and driving around here," he laughed, "there's got to be something in it."

Tom was a young, blond kid who reminded me of Ronnie and was about the same age. He was an impertinent, rebellious type. But unlike Ronnie he struck me as a person who would have to wear himself out before he tried anything else (a type I knew plenty well). He agreed with Rich and Dan that there wasn't much going on for people their ages in North Platte.

"You go work," he said from across the shelter, where he was dripping paint onto the floor in patterns. "Then, mostly, you go to the river and get drunk."

"Why go to the river?"

He dipped his brush and slapped paint on a roof support. "To get drunk."

"It's just life in North Platte," Rich said. "Drink, work for the railroad or for some factory that's going to Mexico anyway. Or you can work for the city, like we do. You grow old, have a few kids, and die."

Their fathers had made living wages with the railroad or in factories that had moved out of the cities in the 1940s and 1950s. In the mid-1990s, corporations were driving down wages in those factories before moving those operations to Mexico. For men the age of my new acquaintances, convenience stores, fast food, or city work was what they had. But these guys didn't want to work at gas stations, and they certainly didn't like working for the city. They would have to go elsewhere. And if they did, chances of returning to North Platte were slim. The lights where they were going were too bright, the activity too great, for them to return to the slender life they perceived they had in North Platte.

The boys didn't start back to their work until I was ready to go. The day had grown hazy and humid and I was exhausted already. I decided to take up a bench downtown and drink coffee a while before heading into the heat of the day. Three- and four-story buildings lined the streets, with storefronts and small shops at street level. People just coming out of the office buildings for lunch began filling up the cafes and stores along the business strip. After an hour or so I was about to pull on the pack and leave when a tall, slim, but powerfully built man in a white T-shirt and new jeans plopped onto the bench.

"Say, you visiting?" he said, indicating the pack leaning against the bench next to me. He slung his elbows over the back of the bench and crossed his booted feet on the sidewalk.

"Sort of. I'm walking through."

"Going anywhere in perticular?"

"Helena, Montana. Then to Kansas City on the Missouri River in a canoe."

"Sumbitch." He leaned over and held out his hand. "Name's Joe Lockard."

Joe had wiry, calloused hands, and gentle, but troubled, dark eyes. He looked like a tall James Dean, only older. His clean T-shirt glowed against his dark blue jeans, which were pressed; the creases ran up his legs from shiny cowboy boots. He seemed to be in his late thirties but he had a youthful exuberance in his angular, weathered face. He kept a pack of cigarettes rolled in his sleeve. His muscular arms were smooth and tattooed with a tiger and a heart with an arrow through it, inscribed "Jenny." He was deeply tanned.

We had talked for a few minutes about my trip when I asked him what he did for a living. He looked away down the streets, now clearing of the lunch crowd.

"I've worked construction here for almost twenty years," he said in a voice tinged with regret. "It's a good living. The scenery changes all the time."

"Yeah, but it sounds like there's more," I said.

"I wish I'd gone to school," he said. "I suppose there's still time for that." He unrolled the cigarette pack from his sleeve and knocked out a fresh smoke.

He'd been married and divorced three times. He had a son and two teenage girls from his third marriage. His kids didn't live in North Platte, but he never said where exactly. "I talk to the kids all the time," he said. "I wish they were around. But their mom and me don't get on too well."

He said that between the kids and wives, he'd never had the time to get to school. He lived by himself in a trailer on the outskirts of town. The trailer and his pickup were his only real possessions.

"You oughta think about staying a day or two," Joe said, changing the subject. "I know some folks, including me, who'd love to show a guy like you around. Plus, if you're up for it, me and some friends are going up to Grand Island for the weekend. You should go with us. If you need a place to stay, you can call me." He scribbled his phone number in a small black notebook that he pulled from his back pocket, and then tore out the leaf.

I spent the day seeing what North Platte had to offer, and called Joe the next day. He again invited me to his trailer. The day was warm, clear, and bright. I crossed downtown and the railroad tracks into the area of town called Flat Rock—a place that suited its name. Many of the houses spread over this plain had the earmarks of rentals—peeling paint, multiple doorbells, and weeds and prairie grass to the windows. The yards around ubiquitous trailers stood deep in loose trash, junk cars, and scrap metal. Out of the disorder and decay, people on porches waved, said hello, and asked where I was going. Several offered plastic cups of cold water. One woman insisted I sit on her stoop while she mixed up a pitcher of lemonade. "I got mix right out on the counter," she said. After a few minutes she brought out a couple of quart mason jars of sticky-sweet lemonade topped with ice. We drank from those sweaty glasses on her front steps, looking out over an empty gravel parking lot across the street.

I walked into the North Platte City Cemetery, where neat rows of stones spread across trimmed bluegrass. The order of the stones, shaded by spruces and cottonwoods, contrasted with jumble of salvage yards, tired and dark taverns, and trailers beyond the cemetery's wrought-iron fence. I lay back in grass among stones, closed my eyes, and felt the sun on my face. Traffic whined outside the fence. Railroad locomotives and freight cars boomed in the switchyard. For me the sounds of mechanized, manufactured, prepackaged, and transported life were not the jangled sounds of confusion and nervous pressure. They were the sounds of human beings being human: living, moving, and doing whatever it was they did to remain living. They were as much a part of my world as the trills of mead-owlarks on fences and the rattle of cottonwood leaves above me in the wind.

After an hour of listening, thinking, and writing down these impressions, I left the cemetery. Flat Rock had the comfortable look of being lived in. Almost anything went—good and bad, attractive and ugly—in these poor neighborhoods. People showed their ability to improvise and create what they could not afford. There was something good in that.

I was well along from the cemetery when Joe pulled up alongside in his pickup. He had been out running errands and was on his way home. As we drove he explained that he had business with his kids' mom regarding tuition and child support. His three marriages had produced three divorce agreements. Two weren't burdensome but still had property responsibilities. He devoted more attention to his third wife because of the children.

"I don't mind, really," he said. "My first two wives and I have a couple of houses I pay for still, and I'm about done paying child support to the third. It's been good to keep up with that. I got behind once and didn't like myself for it. I ignored it and the guilt for a while. But after I got on my feet I made up with the court and my wife over the money. It's worth it for nothing other than seeing the kids without hassling all the time." As a payer of child support, I understood the obligation and dreaded a day I might not be able to pay. Being cut off from my daughter would be more than I could bear.

Joe said that his daughters seemed to be happy. One was going to community college while working in an accounting firm. The young-est was eighteen and had aspirations to finish modeling school after high school and strike out on her own before college.

"Plus my wife's never asked for an increase in support," he con-tinued. "With that steady and the house payments what they were twenty-five years ago, well, things get a little easier over time. My wages keep going up. Pretty soon it will just be tuition, which the kids'll help with. Things are looking up.

"My son's done a turn in jail. But it turned out all right. It was vocational school for him. He learned how to tattoo up there in that jail. He's making a living now at a parlor downtown. It keeps him out of trouble."

We drove toward the edge of Flat Rock and pulled into Joe's trailer park. He had just recently moved there. The trailers were little different from one another except in size and age, but they showed the individual personalities of the owners or renters. Some of the tiny yards were shabby, some were trim and neat; a few had blue kiddie pools set in the short spaces between parking slots and front doors. Many had small storage sheds just beyond their stoops. There was nowhere to put anything in excess of life's necessities, no basements or attics, no yawning space in which to spread things around. The surplus was all visible. It was as if a lack of space turned peoples' priorities and needs into readable texts that revealed the individuals who wrote them. In one yard might be a boat and fishing equipment, in another detritus from a recent renovation. In between were mirrors and toilets, children's toys and kayaks, stacks of used lumber. This made life in the trailer court seem more communal, and for me much more comfortable and interesting than the wider spaces of suburban or upscale urban neighborhoods where it was easier to hide what was so exposed here.

Joe waved to people as we passed. He noticed my eye lingering on untidy yards. "The neighborhood's generally pretty good to start with," he said. "But there's not much you can do when the neighbors start trash collecting."

"I kind of like seeing what people have," I said. "You know, like what they want or use. It tells about them. People who make fun of trailer parks are rude and small-minded."

"People make fun of trailer parks?" he said with a sly smile. "Yer shittin' me. Whatever for?"

"Yeah, yeah," I said. "But I like them."

"I suppose it's all right," he said, "until you have to live in one." He looked at me again, head cocked, with a mischievous look. He laughed, which made me laugh. "Once the trash starts stackin' up outside your window, you know, it don't look to ever move. It becomes permanent, and you can't move it around 'cause it's someone else's furniture. It stays where it lands."

Joe's trailer was new and shiny among the fiberglass and aluminum boxes that were shades of beige, gas-station red, and swimming-pool blue. An aging Mercury was parked in Joe's yard among a few piles of lumber and rebar. We sat in the truck a minute and Joe pointed toward his trailer. He paid five thousand dollars for it, he said, and a hundred dollars a month for the small yard and water. When we stepped inside, I found the trailer as nice a home as one could wish, with plenty of windows, two bedrooms, and a surprising amount of room. It was comfortable and clean.

"This is about as good as it gets for a guy like me," he said. "And that's not too bad."

"Don't apologize for it, Joe. I've known people who have trailers and they are pretty happy with them. About the only thing they ever complain about is the neighbors, but everyone does that."

"It's my little rancho," he said. "All mine, except the land. But one of these days I might move this thing out on the prairie. I'll be master of all I survey. Then—world domination."

Joe had only a couch, waterbed, and a few dishes in boxes. A brand-new oak cabinet stood against one wall, empty behind the glass doors but for a boom box. The place had yet to serve a hot meal. The range was spotless, hardly a fingerprint on its smooth, porcelain surfaces. Joe and his friends ate out most of the time, he said, when they were hungry, when it just was the time of day to eat, or when someone had something to say. At the Formica counters and tables of local chain restaurants, the food was simple, usually grilled or fried, with a bottle of ketchup and shaker of salt nearby.

"But if you want," he said. "I'll cook you up some grape pop and peanut butter and crackers. Top the feast off with Oreos."

We sat in the living room, Joe on the couch and me on the floor on my air mattress, eating Oreos and drinking grape pop from cans. We listened to an AM country-music station that sounded tinny and distant, the announcers' voices cracked and tinged with static. Joe stood at one point and lifted a creamy white stone from a glass shelf in his cabinet. "Take this," he said. "I used it when I was in trouble. You'll want it when you find yourself in the soup." As evening fell we left the lights out and watched the moonlight splash through the open front door and creep across the floor. We talked and laughed late into the night. When conversation died, Joe turned the radio off. The sounds of the wind and the crickets lulled us to sleep.

I woke a while later, shut the screen door against the mosquitoes, and stood looking at the trailers. The crickets had stopped and nothing moved. The few lights around the park only made the moonlight brighter and shadows starker. Joe didn't have much and didn't want or need much. He lived in a humble house. He drove a used truck. He had an almost unfathomable faith in the present. I knew his life was more complicated, but from the outside it looked simple, easy to get a hold of.

Before he'd fallen asleep, he had spoken of the people we were to meet the next day, describing them as if they were family. Conversation revealed that he depended on these relationships and did his part to make them steady and reliable. Being the son of deeply unhappy people and dependent on my friends and my daughter, I understood that. To Joe money didn't seem to matter much except as a way of surviving—it was certainly nothing to worry about. When it was time to work, and he wanted to, he picked up his tools and he worked, generally with people he knew. When it was time to travel or see something different, he and his friends left town. I wanted some of Joe's life in mine. I stared out for a long time over the trailer park, the quietest place I had ever known.

9

GRAND ISLAND AND KIMBALL

"You're a damn fool if you spend all your time worrying about what you ain't got"

JOE AND HIS friends had planned to meet more acquaintances in Grand Island, which was back across the state near Hastings. I decided that I was going with them. Joe made crisscrossing Nebraska seem like the most normal thing in the world.

"After all," he said, "what's the big hurry to get to Montana? There ain't nothing up there but mountains and whatnot."

He was right. Montana would be there in a month, two months, or a year. Leaving Kansas City, I had a notion that five months wasn't such a long time. Now a month into the trip, time had become abstract, subject to change. Anything that was supposed to happen more than a day hence might as well have been ten thousand years in the future. What mattered, what made sense, was the change that occurred between waking and sleeping. The feeling that I had to be somewhere, anywhere within a certain period of time, ceased to make sense. I was no longer living for scheduled moments.

Joe's friends had intended to camp in Grand Island in a small pop-up trailer they wanted Joe to pull behind his truck. But nothing went according to plan, which didn't seem to bother anyone, Joe least of all. We met in the center of town, at a house that a woman named Denise rented. Men and women from their late twenties into their fifties showed up on motorcycles, in rusty cars belching smoke, and in old pickup trucks. They all wore shorts and running shoes without socks, and everyone drank cans of pop and shared bags of potato and corn chips. Most of them were smokers and tobacco spitters. We stood there until the last of the group arrived, two hours after we were supposed to have met. It was decided in the meantime that camping was out and a motel was in.

It was late afternoon before we finally hit the road, and Joe had decided to drive the Grand Marquis I had seen in his yard, instead of his pickup. The day had been clear and warm. The Platte River Valley spread wide and flat under a wispy-clouded sky that seemed bigger, deeper than I'd noticed before. Joe was quiet and contemplative for most of the four-hour drive. He smoked and drove, and hummed to himself. Once in a while, he spoke about living in Nebraska, his new trailer, some of the people we would meet. But never more than two or three sentences, never more than a random thought or memory brought on by a road sign or a passing car. He cracked single-line jokes spontaneously and with a roguish smile: "Know what Jack and Jill did when they went up the hill? Nothing, you dirty bastard. They was just kids." "Know about Kentucky Freud Chicken? It's motherfuckin' good." "Ever hear of a buttfor?"

The fat Grand Marquis soared quietly across central Nebraska. Joe didn't like the air conditioning. The hot, dry air was pleasant and good; the light of day sharp and bright. From time to time we could see the two-lane highway I had walked along just days before on the other side of the river. From I-80, the landscape was like a two-dimensional picture on a postcard. The prospect was one long vista of distant hills and valley edges, tufts of trees on hillsides spotted with cattle, and cloud shadows flowing over all of it. There was less sky and grass, fewer windmills, farmsteads, and people's faces in their car windows. When we left the interstate and pulled into the motel parking lot, it took several minutes to lose the feeling of such swift and sustained movement.

We checked in—the place smelled of antiseptic and air freshener—and went immediately to the motel restaurant to meet Joe's friends. The faces of these people, now some twenty in number, beamed across plates of chicken-fried steak and mashed potatoes, beside glasses of iced tea. Cigarette smoke filled the room like fog. Later we shot pool. Talk went back and forth through the evening. Few of these people had secure jobs. But unemployment or barely making do seemed less of big deal to them than it ever did to me. I mentioned this to Joe later in the room. He lay on his bed, back against the headboard, television remote control in a hand perched on his knee.

"Well, you know, you don't have much but what you have today," Joe said, turning to me, his face growing serious. "Most these folks have had it rough one time or another. Lots crawled out of shitty lives to live pretty good ones. Plus it's North Platte. All of us are over thirty or forty. It's not like we're going anywhere." He leaned his head back and turned on the television. He smiled, his eyes illuminated. "You know, if you live in a place without much, and then you get a little something, you're a damn fool if you spend all your time worrying about what you ain't got.

"I used to think of myself as a big shot, too good for people like my pals here. But I was scared to death to admit I was one of them, just a normal guy in North Platte with a normal-guy job and a normal-guy life. I wanted more TV-show stuff, cars and clothes and whatnot. I made out like I was important. North Platte was a crappy place, I thought. But I never tried to go anywhere else. I complained and moaned about the place. Once I even bought a convertible and stuck some golf clubs in the back seat, though I never played golf.

Imagine, I was driving around, trying to look important and getting angrier and angrier until I found myself all by myself. Alone isn't bad, you know. But I was lonely, and that's different."

I knew what he was talking about, particularly after my most recent romantic engagement. I understood posturing and isolation. The television flashed blue light in the room. Joe was looking up at the curtained window, as if he were trying to work something out. I wanted to know how to avoid worrying about what I didn't have.

"The more lonely I got, the further I drove people away," he continued after a while. "Most people go to the coffee shop regular and strike up conversations. And there was a time I did, too. But after a while, I wasn't capable of it. I was too big a man. Too important, you know. Then the loneliness was just too much and I realized what an arrogant bastard I was.

"I started to get out, you know, to start a new life as Joe instead of some guy who wanted to belong to the country club. I found all these other people, my old friends and a bunch of new ones, happy to just be living day to day. It was like crawling from underneath a rock. I bought used golf clubs to replace the new ones I had to pawn, and actually played golf for the first time in my life—with the characters downstairs. I started having fun. I still wish I had the convertible, though. That was a sweet, sweet ride."

I laughed and Joe smiled.

"Nice car?" I said.

"Fiat 124 Sport Spider. Blood red. Wood-panel console."

I knew the car. A friend of mine once had one.

"Sweet, sweet ride," he said again.

The next evening we met at a Chinese restaurant for dinner. A young couple, James and Mickey, sat across the table from me. James was a good-looking, buff man, with receding blond hair. He and Mickey were dressed in U.S. flag–decorated T-shirts, shorts, and hats. Mickey constantly kept a lit cigarette in her mouth. In the midst of conversation, I didn't see her light a cigarette for over an hour. But there was one always smoking in her mouth or hand. It seemed she was puffing the longest-lasting cigarette ever made.

"You know, Joe tells me you're going west once you get back to North Platte," James said. "We live in Kimball, south of where you're going, I think. Let us give you a ride. We'll put you up a night and get you where you need to go."

I had sedated myself with an oversized plate of fried rice and dropped out of the chatter for a while, just listening. Outside, neon and incandescent lights blinked down the strip of stores and strip malls. Strings of red and white lights on Interstate 80 shot into the distance. Over a month had passed since I'd left Kansas City. Some moments it seemed that only a day had gone by, others it seemed a lifetime. All the time, all the miles walked and ridden, had led here, to a stop off an exit on the interstate that looked like everywhere else—except for Joe, for James and Mickey, and the rest of this ragtag group. James smiled. Mickey lit another smoke.

"Sure," I said. "That'd be great."

Later Joe and I lay in the hot tub and dunked in the swimming pool in the motel's sprawling natatorium. The place was noisy, with a volleyball game going on in the pool. Kids tore past parents ensconced in chaises beside potted plants. Night bloomed inky over the skylights. I took up beside the hot tub in one of the chaises and read a book. Joe paged through a host of increasingly soggy magazines. When we noodled out of the pool area, we stood out in the warm night and stared for a long time at the great vault of stars spread over the town.

"You know," Joe said just before we went in, "there was a time when I never saw the stars. Since I've been outta my shell, though, I always sneak a look. And it's amazing, you know. When you're out in the country, you think for all the world you never seen stars before in your whole life. But I've been to big places like your town, where you can't really see the stars at all. You realize just how many you can see in a place like North Platte or Hastings or Grand Island. It makes you happy you live in Nebraska."

Later Joe fell asleep and I wasn't ready to put myself to bed. Just after ten thirty I left the room to wander around the hotel grounds, out near the highway. Air conditioners hummed and people pulled to the front entrance from the highway. I was going to miss Joe. Our time together had been fine, comfortable. I had been across the state of Nebraska twice, standing again not far from where I had met Jim Wach a few weeks before. It would be nice to get to know James and Mickey. But in the meantime, I watched cars whiz past on the interstate in the distance and thought about how many people I had come to know since leaving Kansas City, and just how many more I would meet.

I called my daughter from the hotel lobby, hoping she would still be up. Sydney answered the phone.

"Whatcha doing, Dad?"

"Thinking of you."

"What were you thinkin'?"

"Just how much I miss you and what a great kid you are."

She was watching television and I could tell in her voice that it was past her bedtime. Our conversation was short, but it was good to talk with her. I said good night and wandered back out to the road in front of the motel. I wanted so much to have her with me and yet was grateful I was on my own. After a while the contradiction was too much to think about. I lay in bed awake, listening to Joe sleep in the bed across the room, until somehow, mercifully, I began to dream.

Late the next morning James and Mickey waited in the parking lot in a rusting Ford LTD. Bits of stringy, faded vinyl chips clung to the corroded metal roof. The day was already hot and unforgiving. As we drove, shards of sunlight reflected off the North Platte through breaks in the cottonwoods. Mickey slept and James drove, one hand on the bottom of the wheel, one crooked on the door. He recounted sights and memories of his past trips as we passed small towns. "We stopped here once—they have great steak. You like steak, doncha?" "Boy, here they got a nice park, a little pond and everything." "I had a blowout on this stretch one time in the winter, at night. It took me that night and all the next day to get a ride into town with that busted tire. Froze my ass." We shot through North Platte, which looked like any other town from the interstate. At Big Springs, I-80 crossed the Platte River and climbed out of the valley over a long, treeless ridge. After that, hills rose in waves until chalk bluffs popped up out of the grassland near Sidney. Cloud shadows gave the green hills definition and depth until distance melted them into sky in dark blue and gray mists. Dark specks on the sides of the ridges looked at first like tufts of sagebrush or stunted cedar, but were, in fact, cattle grazing some five to ten miles distant.

Near Dix, a lonely group of houses in the middle of the hills, James pulled off at his favorite "sit-down" restaurant. Trade was slow. Women in aprons hummed country tunes while they wrapped flatware in paper napkins and filled ketchup bottles and salt and pepper shakers. James and Mickey sipped iced tea in sweating amber glasses. Their hands were strong and calloused, forearms muscular. Mickey had brown hair that seemed to have a mind of its own but fell around her shoulders most of the time. They again both wore T-shirts emblazoned with the stars and stripes. James's, with sleeves torn off, also had an air-brushed wolf and some patriotic sayings. He was wearing red, white, and blue nylon shorts.

I asked about the flag motif.

"I just love this country," James said. "I don't know why anyone wouldn't. It's the greatest country in the world."

"There's not another country on the face of God's earth like it," Mickey joined in.

"I just get so angry, you know, when I hear those loudmouth liberals criticize it," said James. His face was intense. He balled his fists on the table. "Anyone that doesn't love this country, I say, just get the hell out."

"But isn't it a good thing we can be critical of the nation, of the government?" I said. "I mean, isn't that part of the American deal?"

"Government's another issue altogether," James said. He waved his hand across the top of the table. "I don't know that there's more than a thimble of intelligence in all of Washington. There's too much of it, government, if you ask me."

"So you don't think people should be critical of the nation, the culture?" I said.

"I don't know," said Mickey. "All that MTV crap and porno, all the perverts. I think you can be critical of that. But those people who hate America, like we can't do anything right—"

"The package is pretty big," I said. "America is really a bunch of places, a mess of different feelings, a lot of different things to different people. It's pretty tough not to be critical of some of it."

"But aren't *you* proud to be an American?" Mickey said.

"You're free," James said. "Freer than anywhere else."

"Being an American is in my blood and bones," I said. "I could never rid myself of it. Because it is so much a part of me, I think I can be no more proud of being American than I can be proud of my feet. I can't be who I am without having had my feet my entire life. I couldn't be who I am now without innate American-ness. Freedom is a state of mind, an inner thing that has to be teased out, I'm finding out. I'm not sure you get it given to you or that anyone else can protect it for you. They are things you have by birth, as a human being. A person can be so chained to an abstract idea of freedom that other people use that devotion to manipulate and destroy *real* freedom— the freedom, for instance, to criticize power or money, the economic system, anything. I suppose I'm saying that people can become so chained to the ideas of freedom that they haven't really ever explored for themselves whether they are ready to sacrifice their freedom to be and act and think as they wish."

"That sort of makes sense, I guess," said James. "But don't you feel pride when you see that flag waving? You know? When you stand up at a game and put your hand over your heart and sing the anthem?"

"Well . . . ah . . . I never sing the anthem."

"What?" said Mickey. She dropped the hand with the cigarette to the table. "You've got to be kidding me."

"I don't say the Pledge of Allegiance, either," I said. I knew I was treading thin ice in the conversation. I hoped my views on being an American wouldn't spoil it. But James and Mickey were sincere and I couldn't help but tell them the truth.

"I just don't feel comfortable marching in that line," I said. "Or any line, for that matter. I'd rather spend the time noticing the people around me, who they are, what they feel. I suppose that makes me feel more a part of something than singing or saluting a flag with everyone else."

"Supposing tanks were coming down your street," James said. A waitress stopped wrapping forks two tables away and turned an ear to listen. "Suppose they were attacking your home and family. What would you do then?"

I had to think a moment. I liked these people. I wanted, above all else, for James and Mickey to like me. It was a time for diplomacy. America, whatever that was, was important to these people. I'm sure, at some level, it was important to me, too.

"I'd get my family the hell out of there," I said with a smile. "It would be time to run away. There's not much I can do about tanks."

"Well, I mean, if some foreign army was attacking us, you know?"

"First," I said, "I have to tell you right up front that I'm not going to kill anyone. Period. It's just not an option for me.

"Second, anyone who attacks this country has his or her hands full. Whatever Americans are, they are too many people like you and me. The attackers may take over but they won't win. Plus there's just too much country. Just think about it."

James was silent, mulling over the idea. The waitress went back to wrapping forks, her ear cocked to our conversation.

"I suppose you don't pray with anyone either," Mickey said finally. She wasn't being snide, just inquisitive.

"No, I don't." I didn't tell them I didn't pray in the conventional sense.

"I understand that," James said. "Prayers ought to be a man's own business."

"Amen," I said.

"Well," said Mickey, shaking her head and puffing her cigarette, "we certainly don't meet many like you. People around here are generally God-fearing, America-loving people."

"Mickey, now, I think Patrick here loves his country," James said. "Doncha?"

"Certainly," I said. "It's my home."

"Can't argue with that," Mickey said.

"Fear God?" James asked, shaking his head.

"I fear just about everything," I said and smiled. "So, I suppose God fits into that."

We laughed.

These difficult negotiations navigated, we had a wonderful meal—steak, hamburgers, fries, big green salads, gallons of iced tea. When we climbed back in the car again, James shook my hand. "Thanks, I mean, I think it's great that you say what you think. I respect that. Sometimes people just say things to get along, you know, to keep the water smooth."

I almost felt like a liar except that smooth water was what we all wanted, and I had not told a willful falsehood.

We drove the two-lane through stony ravines, sagebrush-covered plateaus above. We slid through lines of cottonwoods into the rocky bowl in the plains where Kimball lay. We drove past the town park—

picnic tables and cottonwoods in the shadow of a hundred-foot Air Force Titan missile at the entrance, legacy of the over two hundred ICBM silos that once dotted the western Nebraska hills near the town.

James's family's house was a two-story that needed paint, its brushy yard a trim. Car parts, kids' toys, doghouses, and old clothes littered the yard and the house's long, wood-plank porch. The porch and front steps sagged across the front of the house as if tacked at both ends and loose in the middle. A dozen or more mutts mobbed us before we made it to the front door. The house was spare and bright with natural light. It smelled of cigarettes, laundry soap, and dogs. Teenaged kids and adults, some ten people, sat on worn couches and in armchairs in the living room. Children played on the floor amid sleeping dogs. The television was on, but no one watched or listened. Conversation went a thousand directions.

James's sister, May Jean, was the center of attention. She had just arrived home from driving a forklift at the Cabela's warehouse in Sidney. She was a stout woman with muscular hands. Kids stormed her. Dogs ganged up at her feet after they quit paying attention to us. James took me aside to the kitchen.

"You got anything against lesbians?" he said in a quiet but serious and determined voice. "I gotta know."

"Nothing," I said.

"Reason I ask is May Jean's a lesbian. I just don't want any bad feelings."

"It's none of my business," I said.

"Thanks. That's good to know. I's just concerned."

"Why?"

"I like you is all." He looked out the window as he popped the top of a Coke can and took a long drink. He didn't seem to have many people outside of family he could talk frankly about this. "You know, she came home one day and told us she liked girls."

"How'd it go?" I said.

"Well, first we all thought the world was gonna end," he laughed. "Then we thought it was a phase, you know, something she'd grow out of. Now it's just something we accept. We ain't gonna change her. She's May Jean. She's our sister. I don't know how you feel about it, but I use to think people chose to be that way. You know, chose to be different. But she's always been that way. We had long talks about it, me and her. And when the rest of us, the family, I mean, sat down and talked about it, it made us think. She never lied to us, so we had to believe her. To start, the whole thing's an education for us, but we got used to it. It sort of changed the way we look at people." He drank off the rest of his cola and rinsed out the can in the sink.

"We love her and we love her girlfriends," he said, looking out the window above the sink. He reached up and rubbed away a drop of water on the glass. "Now she's got someone steady for about three years. She's really great and we hope it works out."

We stood at the kitchen door and watched May Jean in the living room. The children and her brothers and sisters tended to her with great affection. The children, in ragged T-shirts and with dirty knees below cutoff shorts, gathered around her, taking turns sitting in her lap.

We talked and listened to other random and loud conversations. After a about an hour and a half, everyone rose from the couches at once, as if by signal. It was time to go see James's father, who was in the hospital in Sidney. The conglomerated family saw the rest of us—James and Mickey, brothers Joe and Tim, and me—out the door. All packed into the LTD, we were soon on U.S. 30, a two-lane highway, straight and narrow through landscape that made one feel small, insignificant.

The towns of Dix, Potter, and Sidney were situated in green spots in the otherwise treeless and rocky landscape. We arrived at the small, one-story hospital to find that James's father, Don, had been released and was standing in front. He was a short man with a long, flowing, salt-and-pepper beard. He had on jeans with black suspenders, and a worn red T-shirt that rode over his paunch. His strong shoulders drooped with fatigue. He had a small bundle of clothes under his arm that he refused to let anyone else carry.

All of us shoved into the car again and soon added our headlights to those strung across the hills on the interstate. Back at the house, I pretended to watch the television amid the ruckus of now fourteen screaming adults, bunches of squealing kids, and a pack of barking dogs. I paid attention out the corner of my eye to the doting that went on around the old man, now laid back in a shaggy recliner. He scooped dogs and children into and out of his lap.

Somehow this family worked, even if everyone had to shout. Tim, a young and pimply teen, never put down his boom box between lighting cigarettes, fiddling with buttons, levers, and dials. James's sister Laura was a big woman and breathed heavily all the time when her cracked voice wasn't in gear. Her son Joe was a playful and mischievous kid who kept throwing things for the dogs to fetch. Joe Sr. stood near the kitchen, accommodating his cigarette and soda by pulling back his big, full moustache with whatever hand wasn't busy at the time. A young girl, Jody, constantly hiked up her sweatpants and pulled at her heavy Cabela's jacket that was far too warm for the sweltering house. Allen was the adopted son, a quiet and shaky boy. He had put a movie in the VCR, which everyone watched between shouting. Duane stood near the windows, puffing cigarettes and downing colas. He was a skinny, wiry man who worked in the lab at the chemical waste facility. ("The only 'real job' in Kimball," James had said.) Don, the patriarch, kept watch over his brood, affectionately petting children and dogs.

And other people came and went. The men wore trucker hats with various patriotic or biblical sayings and inscriptions. Everyone smoked except Don, James, the kids, and me. Everybody yelled. The phone rang when someone wasn't talking on it. The television and boom-box volumes went up and down. The dogs were friendly and the people open. Moments of frenzied conversation were lost in rounds of barking and howling.

When James, Mickey, and I left to go to their trailer, walking into the prairie night was akin to leaving a baseball stadium after a game-winning home run. The quiet was enormous and cathartic. We drove along brushy dirt roads to an old Airstream trailer in a park on the outskirts of town. It was midnight. James and I arranged my bed on a couch under a wall-sized U.S. flag, surrounded with Indian dream catchers and pictures of the crowd we had just left. Mickey hugged me and smiled before she disappeared behind the curtain on the other end of the trailer.

I listened to branches of a Russian olive tree brush the outside of the trailer. James, Mickey, and Joe seemed not to worry much about the future, perhaps because the past had been as devoid of security as the present. I thought about the fear I had felt so strongly just a few weeks ago, the way that it had haunted me nearly every day I set out on the road. It was slowly, inevitably becoming a memory, and I looked forward to the time I could live completely in the moment, without a thought to what might come. In the end it was as Joe had said: one is foolish to worry over what one doesn't have. It is important to see the wonder at hand. I had a place to stay. The people I had met had been friendly and good. I loved my daughter, and I had a relationship to build with June—or not. The country and the people were settling into me, and I enjoyed the feeling. When I closed my eyes I slept without dreaming.

10

GERING, SCOTTSBLUFF;
TORRINGTON, WYOMING

"I want to meet people, not shoot them"

WICKER BLINDS LAID ribbons of dawn light across the wall hangings, the flag, and the photos. Mickey and James's trailer was a neatly arranged but crowded den. Paperback westerns and spy novels, comic books, and popular magazines stood in neat rows under the windows on either side of the trailer. A tiny television rode the edge of the kitchen counter atop an old stereo. Only the Russian olive branches swishing over the metal skin of the trailer broke the silence.

I read and wrote until James and Mickey woke near noon. They came out of their bedroom in the clothes they'd had on the day before. We sat around the tiny, foldout dining table, drinking coffee.

"We want to buy a house," James said. "But for that you have to have steady work. We're pretty happy here already, although the trailer gets a little small sometimes."

"Especially when you're arguing," Mickey said with a laugh. "Really, it's a good place and the neighbors are good. We don't have anything to worry about here."

"Buying a house means we'd be stuck, working, you know," James said. "We wouldn't be able to travel when we wanted to."

"Sounds like the trailer does you well," I said. "How much do you get to travel?"

"Not much yet, not really," he said. "Just around the state, mostly. But that's good enough. We don't really have the money to get out and do anything really adventurous, something that'd really open us up. Like going down to the Grand Canyon or someplace like that."

I asked what they did for money.

"Mostly we don't," Mickey said. "I got a little job at a store a couple days a week. James works when he can. But besides the trailer and the few things we got to have, we don't need much."

Frankly, it looked like not working and not doing much else was exhausting. I saw in them the symptoms of boredom and restlessness that I had felt. They had dark rings under their eyes. They were nervous. Lack of exercise and intellectual stimulation made them fidgety. Driving long distances back and forth across the plains to accomplish necessities left them ragged and on edge. They reminded me of people in jail, locked into a life that couldn't satisfy body or soul. Both could have used something to get them out of the trailer—steady work, steady travel, anything.

"So, since we don't have the money to leave the state," James said after a pause, "I figured we get in a little travel with you today, if you don't mind."

"Sure," I said. "If it's still not a bother."

"Bother, heck, it's eighty miles," he said. "I figure that's, what, a hundred and sixty miles of Nebraska we take in today? Miles we wouldn't have seen if you hadn't been here. Whadya say? There's really nothing between here and Scottsbluff, no real towns or anything. And it's not like there's a lot of traffic. If you were out there, someone would stop and take you on, but it would be a while. But we aren't doing anything today, a least not till later."

We loaded into the LTD and left the trailer and the Russian olive trees in a flurry of dust and exhaust. We drove past the last of the trees at the city limits and up a vast grassy slope that led out of the valley. The two-lane shot up and down successive waves of hills like a boat on the ocean. The grass grew sparsely in places and revealed the ridges to be sand dunes that bled soon into a succession of sandy bluffs and worn mesas. Cloud shadows blotched the landscape, giving it greater depth. Distant, broken farmhouses or clusters of cattle were the only signs of human presence. An occasional oil well or windmill broke the horizon.

We stopped along a commercial strip in Gering, across the North Platte River from Scottsbluff. James and Mickey now had to hurry home to get their car to May Jean, who worked the second shift at the Cabela's warehouse. After a round of handshaking and hugging, they were off again, the LTD smoking into the distance.

In a grocery-store parking lot, a rusted car with Ohio plates pulled up and stopped just before me. The driver was a scraggly-haired man with a deep tan. He was remarkably skinny. Tattoos colored his arms. A woman slouched in the seat next to him. The back seat was loaded with kids.

"Where you headed?" he said with a growl.

I turned to walk away, but he pulled the car up next to me. "I'm just walking, downtown maybe," I said.

"Passing through, are ya?"

"Yup." Once, outside of Lexington, Nebraska, a man in an old, rusted car had slowed to look me over. A feeling of malevolence had washed over me. I felt it now again but was confused. Just what would this guy do with all those kids in the car? I hurried toward the store.

"Where to?" He idled the car up next to me and stared at my

pack. He spun in his seat to slap an unruly child's face and turned back again. "Whereya goin'?"

I walked faster but he again pulled aside. "I hope to make it to Montana," I said. I turned between parked cars to get away.

"You're a crazy sumbitch. What the hell ya wanna go ta Montana for?" He pulled around the end of a line of cars and drove up next to me again. He hung a browned arm over the door. "We need to buy a tent," he said. "You know where we can get one?" I looked over my shoulder at the store, which still seemed impossibly far away.

"Whatcha got in the pack?" he said.

I took a deep breath and slowed down. I began to figure he was harassing me for his own entertainment and that I was playing into it.

"My stuff," I said.

"Got a gun in there?" he said.

"I want to meet people, not shoot them."

"That's idiotic," he said. I wanted to laugh, remembering what my workmate Zaid had said to me months before I left Kansas City. But I was silent. "I bet you got some pretty expensive stuff in there." He took a long pull from a cigarette with over an inch of ash.

"Yeah, sure do," I said. I remembered that I could get my daughter to quit whining and crying over silly stuff if I asked her to yell louder. I thought I'd give it a try.

"It's all for sale," I said. "Every bit of it."

"For sale?" He looked puzzled.

"Everything has a price," I said. "You need a tent, I'll sell you one. Whaddya want to pay?"

He was quiet and stopped the car, giving me a look of derision. I walked into the store and looked through the glass after him. He continued to stare in his side mirror at me. After what seemed a long time, he eased out of the lot and into the street. I waited to see if he'd come back, studying the street and taking in the bluffs to the west. I bought a bottle of cola from a machine and sipped it at the window.

"Man, that's quite a get up," a man said behind me.

I turned. "Eric Kautz," he said, hand out. "It looks like you're going someplace."

"Yeah," I said. "Patrick Dobson. I'm on my way to Montana."

"Really? What for?"

"To go back home to Kansas City on the Missouri River."

"You don't hear that very often. In Gering, anyway."

Eric was tall and slender, but muscular. His face was open and friendly. He smiled and seemed to have a soft innocence in his eyes. Although he had a bag with a few groceries under his arm, he didn't seem to be in a hurry. "What do you say I take you for a little drive around?"

He stood there with the bag under his arm as if asking to tour a stranger around were the most natural thing in the world. Behind him, checkers pulled groceries across laser check-out counters, customers chatted with one another. Although the man in the car had unhinged me, I had decided that the world wasn't a harmful place. It was a place where people bought food and caught up on personal stories while they waited in line.

We put my pack in the back seat of Eric's Suburban and took off through town. Red sky silhouetted Scotts Bluff and other blue and black mesas that rose west of town. A cool breeze freshened the evening. Soon we were on the floodplain of the North Platte. The distances grew and the highway blinked with headlights like a long string of Christmas lights. We pulled off the side of the road into the parking lot of Kautz Nurseries/Gering Garden Center, a plant and flower retail operation with greenhouses out back.

"This is what I want to show you," he said.

Eric and his brother grew organic tomatoes in a greenhouse shaped like two Quonset huts pressed together at the sides. The clear plastic structure housed a quarter of an acre of cultured ground and was equipped with cooling and irrigation systems. Despite the warm evening, it was cool and humid inside. We walked around the quarter acre, Eric pointing out the operation's high-tech features. A series of magnetized lines on the water-fed cooling system kept salts in the water rather than depositing them on the large, cardboard evaporators. Solar panels provided electricity for fans and pumps, and, in winter, heat. Sensors hooked to monitors kept track of soil pH and nutrients. Gauges tracked soil moisture. A computer controlled the irrigation system, a series of hoses that dripped a predetermined amount of water to each plant. He used catfish for fertilizer.

"It's a fantastic waste of energy to feed corn to fish, and then grind the fish up to feed tomatoes," he said. "But it grows tomatoes like the dickens. And as long as the fish are organic, I keep my organic certification. This whole thing together," he raised his hands and waved them toward the roof of the greenhouse, "creates a nature that's perfect for growing tomatoes."

It was an interesting thought: creating nature.

He dropped his hands and leaned into a wooden table lined with test tubes and gauges. "Although I grew up in the nursery business, I'm not much on farming," he said. "I'm also not much on organics. But we have a big customer who needs organic goods and is willing to pay. Organics is the only thing that separates us from other people growing hothouse tomatoes. As it is, it makes money or I wouldn't be in it."

And, like any other business, he had to keep his costs down to insure his profit. Eric was able to produce fifteen tons of tomatoes per crop three or four times a year and sell them for "a buck sixty-nine a pound" to a chain of natural foods stores headquartered in Denver. The chain then sold the tomatoes for something over twice that price.

"It sounds like a lot of money for tomatoes," he said. "But the store wants fruit in certain dimensions with a consistent look. As long as those tomatoes," he pointed out over the lush mat of green that covered the entire floor of the greenhouse, "fit into dimples in special boxes and look good, our customer will buy. Regardless of the conditions we create here, vines still produce some less-than-perfect tomatoes. We sell any that don't fit in those dimples or have blemishes, for sauce. And since there aren't many organic tomato sauces around, I get regular market prices for imperfect goods, which are far below the cost of production."

The last of sunset glowed red-orange through the greenhouse. Long fluorescent lights buzzed and popped on automatically. Fans hummed and a sort of steady wind blew over the orange prairie dirt, wetted and dark about the roots of tight rows of plants. Eric was listless and breathed a deep sigh.

"I like the money and I'm 'excited' about opportunities in the organic market," he said, lifting his hands and making quotation marks with his fingers. "But doing this all the time takes it out of a guy. We can't keep up with our demand. Everything we grow, we sell for the price we ask, so the money's not the problem. But it is. It's the hook and it's the chain. It's hard to get out of growing tomatoes all the time because it is so lucrative."

Eric explained that besides working full time in the greenhouse, he still helped run his family's flower operation. He struggled to find time to spend with his wife, Julie, and their newly adopted baby girl. Once a week he played softball with a local men's league. But he had other interests and was thinking about going back to school. The dark rings under his intense eyes told some of his story for him. He was tall and strong, angular. But his skin was sallow; his shoulders drooped.

"I wonder how long the money will keep me in it," he said. "I don't want to grow tomatoes for the rest of my life. Chances are that this particular product will fall from favor or we'll have stiff competition soon. But look at all this. We built it. It was a good idea. It's a beautiful thing. It just doesn't move me. This is a big tomato factory.

Funny, huh? We take raw materials and turn them into tomatoes. It's work; the same work every day, every crop. You know what I mean?"

"Boy, do I," I said. "I left Kansas City for the same reason, really. The job paid well and I liked doing it, at first. But I suppose I have a shelf life. I expired but stuck around and rotted a little."

"What are you looking for out here?" he asked. "I mean doing this isn't like finding work that will make you happy. Is it just being able to say you did it?"

"No," I said. "It's not that. It's never been that."

Eric walked over to a small refrigerator on one of the tables and drew out a couple of cans of cola for us. He looked at me and shrugged his shoulders, prompting me to answer.

"I love the plains and have since I was a kid," I said. "When we went on family vacations, it was the only time I really felt calm and secure with my family. Later I went there looking for that feeling of security. Sort of nostalgia to see those places again. But the prairie seemed to be a place that made everything at home new again. Gave me energy to keep going. So when I took off, I wanted that energy. But I also wanted to see the world at home in a different way. I have a little girl, and I want to be able to show her the possibilities. What's happened, I suppose, is that I've met a lot of people and seen a lot of land, and I like it all. I'm finding out how other people make their way. I've learned a lot."

"You don't really know what you want, do you?" Eric said, smiling. "I can hear it. It's familiar because that's where I am."

I took a long drink of cola. The bubbles stung my throat and felt good. "Really I think I wanted some miracle that would make life perfect," I said. "But I'm beginning to see there's nothing that can do that for me. I'll have to make good what each day brings. I don't know that I'm comfortable with that yet. I suppose I'm still hoping for a miracle. But it's beginning not to matter. I just want to be in the space, smell the grass, meet the people."

"What about your kid?" He took a drink and looked over the can at me.

"I miss her but I don't want to go home. Sydney's only a kid and we're stuck with one another. We have plenty of time."

Eric's question had made me think about what was happening on this trip. Certainly the anxiety I felt at striking out was disappearing. But I hadn't, in all my journaling and walking and riding, thought about what I really wanted in the end—except to escape a claustrophobic and restless feeling that had haunted me for years. Just by leaving home I had crawled from underneath that. But over the course of the last month and some I'd found that much of my discomfort arose within me and not out of any job or kid or routine. I was becoming calmer and more comfortable with living out of a backpack, and with not knowing what the next day would bring or where I might wind up. The trip itself had taken on a life of its own. It lay outside of my control. I was beginning to like just seeing where it would take me.

We drove to a local burger joint to fetch his wife some dinner, an errand he was supposed to have run an hour earlier. We returned to the greenhouse after we dropped off the food. The plastic bubble was a safe, protected place where he could think. It was nature he'd created for himself, even if it had its drawbacks. We talked another good long while about travel and women and work. He delivered me late in the night to an RV campground, where I spread my bed on the dew-wet grass.

Dawn came in shades of yellow, orange, and dark blue, pushed up against the night, and pulled me from restless sleep. The camp was a large, treeless expanse of grass-covered parking spaces, each with an electrical hookup and water spigot. A shower house stood at one end of the campground against a hill that rose suddenly into a sandstone-topped bluff. There was just one vehicle, a pickup truck with a camper, in the entire camp.

When I called my daughter she was watching cartoons. She

seemed happy enough that I called. But a three-year-old in conversation didn't quite fulfill what I needed. I wanted to be able to tell her about tomatoes and knowing the presence of evil intuitively, and about strangers who opened their doors. Instead, we talked about what she ate for breakfast and what she learned in day care. Hearing her voice was balm in itself. When she asked when I was coming home, I told her I'd be home when my trip was finished. In fact I had begun to feel I would be on the trip a long time after I arrived home.

As I was walking back to my pack, the people with the pickup, Dee and William, invited me to breakfast, a spread of coffee, eggs, toast, and juice. We sat at a picnic table under a canopy they had erected off the side of their camper. Steam rose from the ceramic coffee mugs Dee had delivered to the table. William had once been a large, powerful man who was now gray and contemplative. Dee was shorter, also with white hair. William had taught at Wichita University before it became Wichita State. Dee and he used to backpack a great deal in the 1950s and '60s. Now in their seventies, they lived in Ohio and spent summers traveling the country in their pickup.

"It's sort of a habit we got into back when I was teaching school," he said. He brushed back his white hair with the ham of his hand. I couldn't see his eyes through his thick glasses.

"We're out this time to follow the Oregon Trail and take in as many of the trail sites as we can," he said. "We had a bit of trouble in your town at the start. Trail marks are pretty much built over or bulldozed there. But once we got into Kansas, deep, anyway, we could see plenty of sites—you know, wagon swales, trail cemeteries, and the like. We've also stopped at a lot of museums. It's been quite rewarding."

I liked their company and compulsively asked for a ride. Suddenly I felt rotten and regretful. Our conversation broke down and diminished to halting phrases and comments. At an opportune pause, I hefted my goods and started to walk, bidding them a good day. I cursed myself. I was embarrassed. People could offer rides, and I might take them. But I would never ask again. I shook off my embarrassment by just putting the whole thing out of my mind, ignoring the incident, my role in it, and all the stinging negative feelings around it. I made my way across the green to the gatehouse to pay.

"You have an RV?" the man said from behind a newspaper. A cup of coffee steamed next to him. "You have a tent? And if you don't have a tent, do you have a car?"

I didn't.

"I saw you out there sleepin'. And I saw you go over to the shower. But you don't have a car, didn't use any electricity, and water don't cost nothin'. I can't see why you gotta pay."

The road rose past the last watered lawns and then shacks with chicken coops. The wind blasted. I bent into it and plodded on, thinking of my daughter and feeling a long way from home. Suddenly I wanted to be there, but didn't. I wanted to be here, feeling the rough, hot wind on my lips, my eyes half closed against the dust and sand. At the same time, I wanted to be home. Great swells of sobs began to well up in my chest and flow through my throat and neck. I looked around to make sure that no one was around to see, and then really let it go. I felt lost, and it had nothing to do with where I was. This road winding through sagebrush and red sand into the base of the mesas beyond town was beautiful. The blue sky fluffed with white clouds, stunning. No, I wasn't lost in space or time. I was really lost between two lives.

I tramped up the long hill from town toward Scotts Bluff and the other mesa-like bluffs in the distance. After a while, I was all cried out, and started laughing at my selfishness. Of course coming loosed from one kind of living would produce a sense of being directionless. What did I expect? Leave home and become the CEO of MegaCo? Win the Nobel Prize? The Medal of Honor? I began to chant in time with my steps, "Big head, long haul, big head, long haul." I got louder and louder until I was screaming as loudly as I could. The chant changed: "Big Ed's Long Johns." "Pig head got it wrong." "Instead, smoke a bong." A car full of family drove past, gawking, which made me really lose it, and I just started yelling whatever came to mind, listening from time to time for echoes that survived the stiff wind.

When the gatehouse at Scotts Bluff National Monument came into view, I shut up. My head rang. I heard rock wrens twittering in the bushes. The wind howled between the mesas and rustled in the sagebrush.

I was laughing when I tried to pay the ranger at the gate. She asked what was so funny.

"Sometimes being an idiot is funny." I said.

"Speaking of that, you walk here?" she said.

"Yeah," I said, giggling. "You just call me an idiot?"

"Just joshin' ya," she said. "Anyway, hikers don't pay."

"You're kidding."

"No. Look at the rate sheet under the window here," she leaned out the window and looked down. "It only says stuff about people with cars."

The monument, a large flat mesa, rose eight hundred feet above. The footpath to the summit of the bluff slinked in tight curves down the rock-studded grass- and sagebrush-covered slopes that fell from the straight walls of the upper elevations of the monument. Meadowlarks and wrens hopped from one tangle of sagebrush to another. The North Platte wound in ribbons of blue and green below. Highways and dirt roads snaked hither and thither, and the towns of Gering and Scottsbluff sprawled out in an emerald fan of right-angle streets across the floodplain and into the valley, red and brown outside the green squares. Traffic in the towns below flowed in anemic streams. From the bluff I could see Chimney Rock some twenty miles to the east, standing like an upturned ice-cream cone in the haze between mesas to the south of it. To the north, long ridges, part of the same formation as Scotts Bluff, sprawled in soldier-like lines. A haze of dust and humidity cloaked valleys between the ridges like fog.

A park employee had offered—and I had taken—a ride to the Wyoming line. The sign there read "Wyoming—Like No Place on Earth" and pictured a bucking horse and rider jumping in the plains before blue mountains and clear sky. I felt a sudden sense of anticipation and excitement. I wanted to feel that I was coming home, that I was going to be in familiar territory, and I hung onto that. I had lived in Laramie for two years when attending grad school, and had backpacked and fished much of southern Wyoming during that time. I'd never seen the country ahead but for one family vacation to Yellowstone when I was young. The only memory I had of that trip was the azure of a steaming hot spring in the park.

In Torrington I wandered off the main drag and up past a trailer park and into residential blocks. The city was a sedate, quiet place off the highway. The five thousand residents lived in wood-frame houses with yards studded with cottonwood, ash, cedar, and pine. Dogs barked behind fences and people were sitting on porches here and there. I walked past a couple of pretty parks before heading back to the highway through the middle of town, where I entered a pet shop. I dropped my pack at the door and walked among the cats and dogs, parakeets and fish. It amazed me to see so many animals crowded in one place after having been in the wide open. The woman running the shop asked me if I was the guy walking through town. She was in her late thirties, with wavy hair pulled into a braid in the back.

"I suppose that's me," I said. I had to laugh at how quickly word got around—and I hadn't told anyone. "How did you know?"

"Candy over at the doughnut shop called," she said, rolling her eyes. "She's probably calling everyone we know, right now. Is there anything I can get you? I don't mean pets. I can't imagine you're taking pets. But anything else? Are you staying in town tonight?"

She brought a glass of cold, fresh lemonade. I didn't exaggerate a bit when I told her it was delicious. It was banner lemonade day.

"I made it myself at home, you know," she said. "Being at the store all day, I get a little tired of going out for Diet Coke or drinking that god-awful iced tea from next door."

I leaned back to take a look at the little mom-and-pop place next door so I'd know where not to get iced tea.

"It's just colored water, you know," she said. "But the people are nice, and sometimes when you're cooped up with dogs and cats and birds, and all the things that can go wrong with 'em—when people bring 'em back in, you know—it's nice to have someone to chat with. So when things get a little dull around here, I hitch up my go-cup and head over for a little talk. Can you hold on a minute?"

She found an inexpensive place in the middle of town called the Blue Lantern—a short walk from the pet shop.

"I made a reservation for you," she said. "They'll be looking for you."

"Thanks," I said.

"Listen, hon, you have a nice stay in Torrington," the clerk said. "And get where you're goin' safe. Oh, but I know you will."

The woman who ran the Blue Lantern Motel had rough, calloused hands and strong arms. She was in her mid thirties, and seemed to be in transition, as if recently divorced. She wore jeans and a white tank-top. She had a broad smile, soft, sad blue eyes, and bleach-blond hair. She showed me to a room, a dark affair with a bed, reading lamp, and nightstand. It was a bare-bones operation, the kind that might be used for less-than-legitimate commerce. But it was quiet, clean, and cheap. I sat out on the little porch in front of the room and read. The woman tended to her work in the heat, as if she owned the place. It was nice to see how her effort at keeping the place together created an atmosphere, made a more comfortable place.

Toward sunset I walked to the Burger King next door to use the phone. My daughter was on her way to bed, but she seemed glad to hear from me. Her little-kid voice rocketed a charge of warmth through my chest.

I bought a burger and sat down to my journal. But it and the new book I'd bought in town could not keep my attention. I looked out at the street and gazed at the cars, feeling the ground tremble as semis rolled by. I kept thinking of my daughter as the place filled with farm workers, police officers, and women with children. They caught my eye and smiled. It felt good to be with them, watching them talk and drink cold pop and eat baskets of fries and burgers. I watched traffic slow to a trickle. After dark the blond woman at the Blue Lantern came out front of the motel with a hose. Water arced into mulch at the base of young trees still supported with wire and stakes. She stared into the star-studded darkness beyond the street-lights. I thought one day I would be happy to be with Sydney, eating a hamburger in an ordinary place just like this.

11

FORT LARAMIE NATIONAL HISTORIC
SITE AND GUERNSEY STATE PARK

"Life ain't easy, but it ain't always tough"

WEST OF TORRINGTON the frenzied line of semi-trucks and muf-
fler-less pickups that had sped down the main drag had grown even
more frenzied. The shoulder shrank to a rocky path and then fell
sharply into the ditch. Thorny brush and sagebrush choked the
right of way. Soon I was dodging oncoming traffic, running from one
bare foothold to the next. My nerves frayed. Drivers passed me, only
inches from the white line. Even spookier, the backpack blocked the
sound of passing cars going my direction. The motion and reliability
of traffic coming toward me had already made cars in this lane seem
alien. But when they sped by on my side of the road going the same
direction as me, passing another vehicle, it was a terrifying and heart-
stopping surprise.

For over sixteen miles I alternately evaded oncoming traffic and
panicked after a passing car sped up from behind. It had made me
paranoid to the point that when I had a break, I was too jittery to

enjoy it. *Screw all*, I said, *I've been walking into traffic for six hundred fifty miles, doing what I've been told for over thirty years. I've had enough.* I passed over to walk along the right side of the road, and it was good. I wasn't able to see the traffic coming up in the lane next to me, but it was a damn sight better than the living nightmare of surprise appearances of cars and trucks hurtling ninety or more miles an hour past me in a lane where traffic was supposed to be going the *other* way. Walking on the right, at least I could see oncoming cars passing in my lane.

It wasn't long before a large delivery truck pulled up behind me. I didn't hear it until the driver honked. It was like getting a stick in the butt. "Get in," the driver said when I turned around. I looked through the windshield at a broad-shouldered man with sparkling turquoise eyes, shadowy beard, and smirky smile. The collar of his button-up cotton shirt fluttered in the hot breeze. His arms bulged out of rolled sleeves. I considered what kind of a day he was having and walked over and opened the passenger door.

"Fort Laramie?" I said.

"As a matter of fact, I got a delivery there."

I climbed up into the cab and settled my pack in the wide space on the bench seat. I introduced myself to another Jim.

It turns out that Jim wanted company. He started talking as soon I had opened the door. He said that he loaded retail goods and grocery items on his truck at a warehouse in the evening. He then went to work the next morning, unloading his goods bit by bit at truck stops, groceries, and convenience stores from Cheyenne to Guernsey, a round trip of ten to twelve hours, depending on traffic and the size of his loads. He made nine dollars an hour and worked fifty to sixty hours a week with no overtime pay.

"Nine bucks. For such a big truck?" I said.

"It's normal around here," he said, leaning forward over the wide steering wheel. "And it's not like you can do much bitching about it. They turn us over quicker than killing chickens at a factory farm.

You don't have much choice—either you do the job or you don't. And if you don't, the next man will. He needs the job as bad or worse than you. When I used to drive truck coast to coast, I had my own rig. I had a nice apartment on the beach in California. It was sweet. But the road wore on me, you know, and I sold my truck about three years ago. I was thinkin' I'd settle into a nice regional job, make enough to pay the rent or buy a house and save a little. Worst decision I ever made. You sell, and you think you're getting a good price for your truck, but then you find out you've jumped in the shit. The local route turns out to be slave work, and new trucks are so high you can't ever get back where you were on the pay you get. Without capital or my own truck, I'm a short hauler on another man's clock."

Jim said, however, that he was glad to have gotten away from the hassle and the paperwork of running his own business. "Frankly, after the repairs, taxes, licenses, and all that, I was getting sick of lying all the time. Like a lot of over-the-roaders, I was keeping one log for the companies I drove for—so I'd get paid—and another for the state. Plus I wasn't working all the time, even if I was flush. I spent a lot of time on the beach between hauls. Lotsa girls and sun. But that gets old after a while, if you can believe that. I wanted something steadier. The bunch I was running with at the time told me I'd never get a job driving hourly. But I showed them. I have one. But the joke's on me, I work all the time." He laughed. "And I'm damn near broke."

Jim leaned forward, hands and elbows on the wheel. He turned to me and his smile grew broad. "Here's the shitter," he said. "I got the best damn job around. I get paid better than most people you see in these towns you been in. People who work in stores and shops and whatnot, if they don't own something, they get western Nebraska, eastern Wyoming wages. It's the Third goddamn World."

"I'm sorry it's so tough," I said absently. I was thinking about that "lotsa girls."

"Like the sign says, 'Like no place on earth.'"

Despite his cynicism, Jim was an agreeable guy—smart, happy, and glad to have someone to talk to. He chattered in a way that was pleasant, his voice resonant with the whine of tires on the highway and the engine revving between gears. We drove out of the rolling hills into the Laramie River Valley, at the center of which the river ran like a shiny blue ribbon through lush, treeless green. The weather changed quickly from sunny to windy, chilly, and dark with rain.

Jim let me off at a little store outside of Ft. Laramie, a tiny town down the road from Fort Laramie National Historic Site. A military road, now long abandoned, once crossed a solid, gothic, iron bridge next to the highway. Just across the bridge and around a grove of cottonwoods stood the barracks and buildings of Fort Laramie. Outwardly little about the fort was spectacular but its presence in the vast prairie made both human and nature impressive. The wide compound of scattered buildings sat in a grassy valley between tree-less hills. The river flowed, swollen to its banks, through the middle of the fort property. Humans were small, their tenure here surely temporary and more beautiful and precious because of it. On the other hand, human objects increased the stunning aspects of the land, almost as if they magnified the size and scope of the land.

There were few visitors. Most had come and gone earlier that day before the weather had turned cold and windy. A park volunteer, Justin, toured me through post stores, stables, and administration buildings. He explained what had occurred here, told me the dates of the structures' construction and who the post commanders had been. The beds in the barracks were made as if the men had just gone off for roll call. But through the paint, newly hung walls, and repaired ceilings, history felt ghost-like, ethereal. Like any book or story, the reconstruction itself was a construction of time, culture, and place. More than history, it told about the priorities of a nation during the Great Depression (the fort was restored in 1937), a nation that was looking for reasons to believe in itself. The breath of time had blown the odor of men out of the barracks and left open rooms smelling of old wood and dust. The only sound was that of the rain spraying across the wooden roof and on the clapboard.

The fort was reducing my significance in history and the future, and it felt good. This became apparent at the post brig, a rough wooden structure with a dungeon. We stood outside the barred windows of the drafty structure that stood over a deep pit. Rowdy, drunk soldiers and Indians once milled about here, pestering inmates— or threatening to kill them. I imagined young wives bringing food to their husbands in the damp, stark jail, and Indian women at the windows, whispering soft words through the thick iron bars into darkness. I wanted to know them or believe I knew them because of our mutual ordinariness. Then I had to laugh at myself. The thing I hate most is when someone patronizes me by reducing me to alleged individual characteristics and knowable quotients. Trying to connect with these chimeras meant failure to recognize the variety in human existence. With this writ large, I felt again immensity in the sweep of time—and my gnat-like place in it.

By closing time the wind had grown still colder, the rain now laced with sleet. In the visitor center restroom I changed out of my wet clothes into long pants and an insulated shirt and jacket. Park employees cinched their collars up against the cold and dove out the door and into the wind like paratroopers. As I stepped to the door, a tall woman with long, coal-black hair walked out of a back room.

"You really mean to camp out?" she said.

"It's not so bad. I'll be warm and dry."

"That's silly," she said. "You'll sleep on my couch if you take my offer."

I peered outside. Sleet was falling with bits of hail.

"You have to know when to give up," she said. She smiled, dark eyes sparkling. "We'll have some dinner tonight and you can stay over tomorrow if it's rainy. I'll take you up the road tomorrow after work where you can get some shelter. Sometimes these things come up and they don't go away for a while. Summer here can hardly be summer at all."

Ilona was the business manager of the historical society that ran the book and gift shop at Fort Laramie. Her two teenage daughters had been among the living-history actors who worked the park's grounds. The four of us packed into the cab of Ilona's pickup and drove across the river and down a tree-lined dirt road to their house. She had a number of acres along the river that she leased for pasture and hay. She and her daughters lived in the house and kept the dooryard for vegetable and flower gardens and fruit trees. The land drew upward from the house and opened beyond a thin line of cottonwoods along the river. Uncut, unplowed prairie stood outside of some grazing pastures and alfalfa fields in the river bottom. Hardwood groves graced the tops of long rises. In the rain and growing darkness, the place seemed to be taking a long, quiet breath. The house was a hundred years old and was comfortable, subdued, and warm.

Ilona had strong Native American features. She said that she was descended from Lakota people, with family ties to reservations in Montana and South Dakota. With a strong personality and a dry sense of humor, she had a way of joking that was offhandedly personal but not confrontational. Her children were independent-minded and well-read. We sat in a warm living room, surrounded by family pictures, and talked about books. All three of my hosts rendered opinions on political subjects without hesitation, and our discussion during dinner was contentious and deep. After dinner the girls went to bed and Ilona and I talked for a long time over tea in the living room. Her work at the fort was important to her, as were her kids. She struck me as a complicated person.

"The Park Service gets cut every year," she said. "Even if they don't get cut, inflation eats them. And when they get a raise, it's not nearly enough to do everything they want or need to. Historical societies like ours help that a little. And we have a strong one. A lot of important things happened here, and it's important for people to see."

"How do you square that with being native?" I said. Fort Laramie had been, after all, a government post. The U.S. government violated the Fort Laramie Treaty almost as soon as it was signed here in 1851. Then, in 1854, a band of Lakota had killed nineteen settlers and soldiers. Tensions had been high. Settlers coming across the Oregon Trail weren't comfortable with the native presence at the fort. On the other hand, natives depended on the fort for food in lean times and trade at all times. When the army retaliated for the killing of the settlers and soldiers, soldiers killed one hundred Sioux. The incident marked the moment when the U.S. conflict with Native Americans broke again into open warfare. The Indian Wars lasted for thirty-six years, pushing Plains Indians onto reservations, reducing native land holdings, and nearly extinguishing the bison.

"Yes, but Indians have always been at war," Ilona said. "Winners in wars almost always lose in the end." She tucked in her chin and raised her eyebrows.

"But don't you think things could have been different?"

"No, not here. The Fort Laramie treaties [there was another signed in 1868] held promise, but a treaty is a fixed thing, something you're supposed to trust not to change. The U.S. government couldn't keep its own people under control, much less the Americans. The States couldn't and wouldn't enforce treaty terms if those terms ran up against their interests. More people came in, and Americans demanded more from the government and the government then demanded new treaties and forewent old ones. That the treaties signed here were violated was nothing new, and a lot expected it. On both sides. But in my own way, I try to make sure history doesn't cover up those things. Imagine if the winners wrote history without people like me. We'd never know what happened to the losers and the way they lived and how they live today. Not long ago Indians weren't considered human, and if they were, they were lesser humans worthy of extermination. They were either savages or animals. More recent history made them out to be victims. It's more complicated than that."

She shifted on the couch, finished the last of her tea. "If no one stands up to say that there's more, every time a tourist came here, they would think they're another Columbus discovering America. Discovering it. This valley is not a place that's easy to find, and it was *discovered* a long time before whites came."

Ilona had grown up in white society, she said, and she was in her twenties when she began to feel something missing in her life. "My parents taught me things that didn't seem to work well for me, American things," she said. "Many of them were good and I could see that. But there was something else, and I suppose it was given me by my classmates, the people around me. It was almost like it wouldn't have mattered if I was Indian unless someone made it a big deal—and people around me seemed to make it that. It mattered to them. I had to find out for myself how to make American ways work in Indian ways. I went back to relatives, found other Indians, and made those ways and ideas work for me. It's the Indian way, really, to take old ways and new ways and put them together. Not just in life but inside. It's not kind out here or anywhere for an Indian, and certainly not for an ignorant Indian."

I made my bed on the living-room floor. An upright piano stood against one wall, with Ilona's high school pictures next to it—a montage of headshots of a young woman with a Mona Lisa smile. Other pictures were of the girls and their father, an Indian man who Ilona had left years before. All around were paintings of and by Native Americans. There was also Native-American sculpture. I fell asleep thinking of bareback-riding Indians meeting white emigrants who were far from home and had their lives and possessions packed into wagons. I no longer knew what happened next. Though I still saw the Great Plains from the outside, I was connected with all the Jims, Joes, and Ilonas. They spoke in ways I understood, and had ambi-

tions similar to mine. We lived lives under similar conditions and had
our individual problems and challenges. We were also connected in
a common history whether we knew of it, understood it, or saw it
though lenses that distorted it or not.

The next evening, as Ilona and I drove down U.S. 26, the rain
that had been falling all day turned to sleet and hail. The green light
of the gauges shone brightly in the van. I looked out into the black-
ness beyond the rain on the window and thought of settlers and
Indians, of soldiers riding forth with determination, the great waves
of whites that would come after. Unstoppable and sometimes sadistic
economic and social forces made this place, and it made us.

Ilona dropped me at Guernsey State Park. The campground was
perched on a bluff overlooking a reservoir in the deep canyon the
North Platte had carved in dark sandstone and granite. Pine and
cedar grew in the steep creases in the rock. I poked around in the
dark and found the campground picnic shelter. Built of thick stone
walls about waist high, the shelter had large pillars that supported
large, rough-hewn timbers below a shingled roof. Concrete benches
lined three of the walls. On the fourth, fan-like windowless openings
rose above either side of the mantle of a large fireplace. The floor was
made of flat sandstone. To me it was like a small house where I could
kick back to read by firelight.

The shelter felt connected to larger things. I sat on one of the
heavy wooden picnic tables there and breathed in the sharp smell of
wet stone and pine resin. There was no wind and no sound except
for that of the rain on the ground around the shelter. I kept staring
at the fireplace. When the rain diminished to drizzle I walked up
the rocky slope from the campground and snapped dead twigs and
branches from the pines. A good armful soaked with stove fuel sent
a cloud of oily smoke up the chimney. After a while the fire burned
brightly and radiated warmth that went deep. Cup of tea in hand, I
walked out into the mist to the edge of the bluff. The lake stretched
quiet, black, and smooth in the yawning canyon. Lights from park

bathrooms and maintenance buildings punctuated the landscape. A gentle breeze came over the point and blew the few mosquitoes away.

It was June 9, Sydney's fourth birthday. I hoped that she had received the card and stuffed animal I'd mailed her a few days before. I liked thinking that she was lying in bed with that teddy bear in her arms. It was a nice thought. In a way I was sad that I hadn't been in Kansas City to make her a cake. But when I'd talked with her from Ilona's house, she seemed well taken care of. I had wished her happy birthday. She had told me that she was glad I was her dad.

I made my bed on the floor of the shelter. In the night the rain fell softly. I played the sound of Syd's voice over and over again in my head and felt a comfortable optimism about our lives together. The place was beset with a comfortable, quiet calm that came from within and without. Though I was sleepy I noticed that everything around me had a freshness I had not been aware of before, anywhere.

12

CASPER

"Probably wouldn'ta killed you, but it woulda hurt"

DAYLIGHT LEAKED THROUGH the crags above and down through the creases in the canyon's rock walls. The rain had stopped, the sky had brightened to light gray. Sharp with pine and sagebrush, the air was cold and still but for occasional wisps of breeze that pushed up through the canyon.

I had slept more deeply and awoken more refreshed and relaxed than any time since Kansas City. Something about the trip had changed overnight. A new feeling suffused my insides. It had nothing and everything to do with the wondrous, silent surroundings and a night of solid sleep. For the first time since leaving Kansas City, the uncertainty and dread that had so plagued my mornings was gone completely. Buoyancy filled the space that fear formerly occupied. I didn't put one thought beyond packing my things. Then the pack felt good on my back, the road solid and fine beneath my feet. Blood filled my legs and drove the chill from my limbs. The air smelled of pine resin and ozone, and it was good. The rain-washed scenery was sharp and pretty. It didn't matter whence the change had come. I was on my way again, free to walk a world that would be new with every step, turn in the road, and crest of a hill. I found myself suddenly in a world where I belonged.

At the park a two-room museum was the same kind of serenely quiet place that I remembered from family vacations to Yellowstone, Grand Canyon, and Crater Lake. It was an ancient place, like an old church, and like an old church it inspired wonder—not of God or history or nature, but of the people who had conceived and built it. I thought of the knotty hands that had hewn the stone for the floors and walls, made the huge timber rafters and the antiquated window casings with brass fittings. Light from deco fixtures in the corners of the room illuminated dusty dioramas and hand-painted wooden plaques. Rays of sunlight fell through smoke from a big cedar log in the fireplace. I walked slowly among the exhibits—dioramas with stooped, small Indians and tall, straight-backed white settlers. I remembered again the black-and-white pictures of unknown ancestors in the steamer trunks in my grandmother's basement and connected myself to a past barely recognizable to someone who had grown up in a cheaply manufactured and standardized suburb.

The lake meandered between high, sheer cliffs and pine-topped hills of red and brown sandstone. The Laramie Mountains rose up solid blue-gray in the distance beyond them. Puffy clouds eased the sun and added depth to the sky and land. I walked the length of the lake along a road cut into steep, rocky inclines that tumbled into the water below. The dam, an earth and concrete structure, spanned the mouth of a narrow, deep canyon. Eddies below the power plant slowly eased out into the river.

At the highway I walked up a long incline to a stone marker where the road crossed the Oregon Trail. The trail remnant was obvious. Thick brush grew in lines parallel to the road in some places. In others, two deep tracks ran through skeleton-white stone. Cows roamed in small herds across scrubby, rolling plains. Power and telephone lines crisscrossed eroded cliffs and badlands. Few cars passed. Grasshoppers buzzing overhead and light breezes swishing in the grass broke the silence. Atop a hill about twenty miles from the state park, I sat against my pack, kicked my boots off, and waggled my stocking feet in the warm sun. A feeling of contentment settled in, and I laid my head into the grass and closed my eyes. Wrens twittered and fought in a bush behind me.

When I took up my pack again, the road fluttered on and on and on. It didn't matter how far I had to walk or where the road would take me. I took a break five or six miles on. A wide valley opened below me, with the Laramie Mountains standing in a blue wall on the opposite side. Brown-green prairie stretched out over winding arroyos and the North Platte River. I took off my boots again, and my socks as well. Lying back with my head on my pack, I watched a brutally dark storm descend from the mountains and advance in lightning flashes and lithe gray veils. Yellow and brown fringed the clouds where storm met sky. As it neared, it became more awesomely beautiful—and powerful. Gray veils of rain turned into opaque curtains. The breeze kicked into stiff gusts, and I rose to put on my socks and boots. When the rain came to within what I guessed was a mile, I pulled on my rain gear. I was thrilled, excited even, by the feel of the electricity and the smell of the rain. Then, suddenly, something told me to get out of it. I turned and stuck out my thumb.

Almost immediately a pickup appeared over the hill and pulled over in front of me. When I opened the passenger door, the man inside shouted, "Get in! Hurry—it's almost here!"

I threw my pack in the back of the truck and jumped into the cab. The curtain closed over us, cloaking our world in late-evening twilight. Hail the size of large gumballs smacked the windshield.

"Probably wouldn'ta killed you," the man yelled over the deafening ruckus. "But it woulda hurt."

"Thanks," I said. "I was going to walk in it, but—"

"But you got smart," he shouted. He stuck out his hand. "Wayne," he said.

The rain and hail beat on the windshield, obscuring sight a foot past the glass. We couldn't talk without shouting, so we sat back in our seats. I was glad to be in the truck. The treeless range beyond the fence was bare of buildings, barns, or even overhanging rock. Ditches and washes, dry just minutes before, now foamed with a slosh of soupy red and brown runoff.

When the storm let up, Wayne bumped the truck off the shoulder slowly. He was a short, wiry man, about thirty-five years old, with a determined but open face.

"If you can get me to the interstate, I can take it from there." The road we were on ended at Interstate 25.

"Well, we'll get you there," he said. "But I can't guarantee you anything but hard-luck stories after that. It's one of the few places you can hitch on the interstate in Wyoming because there just isn't any other road. But it's mostly long haulers who won't stop for anyone."

"I don't like to hitch, really. I just want to walk. I'm going toward Casper and thought I'd stay tonight at Glendo State Park."

"I tell you what. It's no fun walkin' interstate with everyone driving by at a hundred. I have to go into Wheatland, I live there. Then I'm off to Casper. I'll take you if you can wait a few minutes while I gather some things at home. It'll be my pleasure."

"Thanks, I appreciate it."

"Well, you hate to leave a man out in it," he said, pulling on his sunglasses as the sky brightened. "But, you know, you make it easy for a guy to pick you up."

"How so?"

"You've shaved. You're hair's clean. You got good equipment. And you're clean dressed. It's a little easier to trust a guy like that. Except for the storm, you didn't look like you needed help from anyone."

I didn't know what to say. I had made it a habit to take sink showers in whatever restroom I could find every day before I hit the road, tying my small washcloth and towel to the outside of the pack to dry in the sun. Such a cleanup was, in part, for presentation but also for comfort. It just felt better to hit the road with a clean face and a shave.

Wayne dropped me at a private campground outside of Casper, suggesting it might be a good place for me to camp the night. As I walked up to the camp store and office, I spied a hot tub amid the RV's and pickups with campers and fifth-wheel trailers. A deep sigh welled up from within me as I thought of drifting in those bubbles. In the camp store, a small building lined with big windows, a portly man with oily skin stood behind a counter. He wore a dirty ball cap and tattered T-shirt. He had bad teeth.

"You mean you got no VEE-hickle?" the man said. He raised the bill of his cap high on his head, revealing strings of oily hair.

"No."

"No camper?"

"I don't have a VEE-hickle."

"Then you gotta tent?"

"I don't have a tent."

"No tent?"

"No. Just a canvas I set up when it rains."

"No shit."

When I asked the price for an empty tent space, the paunchy man motioned through the window to a square in the grass outside under a sort of carport awning. It looked like a perfect snake den except for the inches-deep water in long, uncut grass. He held out his hand.

"Twelve bucks."

"I can't sleep in the water.

"That's what I got."

"You'd take my money for that?"

"Look, buddy, if someone gotta have a place to stay, I take their money. I own the place. If they don't like it, theys other places for them to stay."

"Really? Where's that?"

"I can't tell you."

"Why not?"

"'Cause I gotta make a living here."

"But if I don't like it here, I'm leaving anyway."

He looked at me, face blank, hand still extended.

"I tell you what," I said, "if you have an empty park bench, that'll do."

"You can't sleep on a bench," he said.

"Why not?"

"It's unseemly. It'll upset the customers."

"But I'd be a customer, and it upsets me to have to sleep in the water."

"Look, I got one tepee left." He motioned to the line of comic-book concrete tepees out front. "I can let you have it if the reservation don't show up."

Good choice of words, I thought. An Indian attack might be what the place needed. I left him with his hand in the air.

Casper looked like a town that needed a bath and a shave. Rows of weekly rental motels and shabby bars stood beyond broken sidewalks and weedy yards. The eaves of the tiny houses sagged. Paint seemed a scarce commodity. Convenience stores and a couple of gas stations were the only businesses besides the motels. Here and there was evidence of pride in ownership, but I had a feeling most of the property along the strip was owned by people who didn't live there. There were no pedestrians.

A mile or two later, I strode into a small, plain café and ordered some coffee at a counter lined with stools. There were a few customers scattered among dinette tables set with glass sugar dispensers and ketchup and mustard bottles. The only other person at the counter was a tall, gaunt, horse-faced man. He turned and looked at me, brushing wiry gray hair out of his eyes. He had shining, ice-blue eyes and a friendly, open look. His teeth were a nightmare. I sat down and looked over a well-thumbed *Casper Star-Tribune* from two days previous.

"Say, that's a nice get-up you got," he said after a few minutes, pointing to my pack. "Where ya headed?"

I told him. He moved his plate and coffee and took the seat next to mine. He was so thin that his jeans and denim jacket sagged on him. Wiping his hand on his jacket, he stuck it at me after he sat down.

"Johnny Whisenant."

His strong and calloused hand matched his leathered face. He said that he was a former carny. The carnival he had worked for had come through Casper about a year before. He'd had enough of it and couldn't do the work any longer.

"I tried ta stick one place or 'nother before. You know, get a real job," he said, running a hand through his hair. "But I been workin' the carnival business since I's sixteen. That's when I joined my first circus in Texas, where I growed up. But circuses weren't worth shit. Travelin' carnivals, well, I really liked 'em. I got behind them counters in a midway and it was jus' like magic. I'd run ring-toss or duck-shootin' scams on folks, take lots of their money, and watch 'em git mad and line up to give me more. I loved it."

He turned his stool to me and hung his hands between his legs. His voice loosened and became a little deeper. "But it's bad, bad bidness," he said. "Famblies, ya know, reg'lar moms an' dads an' kids. After a while, yer conscience gets ya. I given it up a million times. Once I give it up and even had a wife. And a house. Real purty nice set-up in Montana. But ever' time a carnival come ta town I jus' couldn't stay away."

He looked up and became animated again. "The life's rough," he said. "Goin' and goin' alla time. Late nights, lotsa drinkin'. Anna drugs—whee-haw!" He rolled his eyes toward the fluorescent fixtures above. "Hard work. But then there's them lights an' music. The smell of car'mel corn annat funny smella cotton candy. Alla noise 'n 'citement. It's great."

Johnny had sobered up in Casper, rented himself a little apartment, and worked as a laborer for construction and oil-drilling projects. It wasn't much of a living, he said. "But it still is nice ta git away from da midway. I been doin' it fer ten years straight 'fore I quit this time. I still feel like I'm takin' a rest."

Outside the sky had cleared, and the threat of rain lifted. I asked Johnny if he knew where the police station was so I could ask about camping in a park later.

"I don't know ya wanna do that," he said. "There's lotsa rough characters 'round town. Not dat you'd be in danger or nuttin'. Just you don't wanna be out there."

Johnny's eyes widened. "My place is purty nice, and you kin have da couch. I gotta little thing goin' later. But yore welcome ta come 'long. I'll introduce ya around ta some friends a mine."

We talked a while longer. He had a way about him that I liked. Years of hard travel had toughened him, but he was childlike, still excited about this new life. When we were finished with coffee and paid up, we walked out to his pickup, an old, green Chevy that was hardly holding together. He pulled on a manual choke under the dash and worked through a series of maneuvers to get it started. When the truck coughed to life, a plume of white smoke rose behind.

Johnny lived in a dirty, stucco, U-shaped building that stood in the shade of huge cottonwoods. The apartments faced a bare-dirt courtyard filled with a jumble of plastic children's toys. Front doors stood open behind screens. The sounds of televisions, radios, and screaming and laughing children flooded the courtyard. A man with thick horn-rimmed glasses and a bare, muscular upper body opened one of the screen doors as we walked by. White tape was wrapped around the temples of his glasses.

"Say, Johnny, what up?" he said, squinting through his thick glasses. The glasses magnified his eyes and made them look crossed.

"This here's Billy," Johnny said to me. "He's from Lou'ziana. An' this here's Patrick, he's walkin' da Oregon Trail." Johnny had misunderstood me when I told him I had been on the Oregon Trail but not specifically following it in the way many tourists do. But at this point, it was too complicated to make the distinction.

"Bayou Cajun," Billy said, holding out his hand. I couldn't tell which way he was looking. "Just a old swamp Coon-Ass. Oregon Trail, is it? Must be quite a a'venture."

"It's all right," I said.

"Take a million dollahs ta git me ta walk that far." His Cajun accent was heavy, and his laugh was high and squeaky. "But, I suppose if'n I had it in me, I'd do it. Hell, I been lotta places ya never wanta hear about. Some're kinda exciting. But never hadta walk. Hadta run, sometimes. But never walk."

Johnny's apartment was a dark place of cheap paneling and worn shag carpet. Cane blinds hung at odd angles over the windows. Posters of rock bands were nailed to the wall. An electrical cord fell from a plastic clock with gold-colored spikes radiating from the center. He had an armchair and a small television. An old clock radio (with hands) stood in the middle of a small table. The place had the fust of dust, cigarette smoke, and fried food. But Johnny was a friendly, outgoing man. His would be a good place for the night.

We dropped my things and almost immediately headed out again to the old truck. Casper didn't change much as we drove out to a truck-stop restaurant on the edge of town. Sprawling trailer courts and tract housing from the mid-1970s oil boom decayed in weedy lots and behind rusty chain-link fences. Two of the three major refineries in Casper had closed in the 1980s, and the third had cut many of its employees. Many of the former refinery workers had abandoned the town. Those who remained eked out an existence in gas stations, restaurants, and convenience stores.

At the truck stop, we pulled up seats with several people who seemed happy to have Johnny with them. He introduced me to a few men and women in jeans and button-up, short-sleeve shirts, ball caps, and cowboy boots.

"We're a sort of supper club," said Dan, the man seated next to me. He had a round face made more so by his circular glasses and rotund figure. "Johnny's a good man. But you don't change your life overnight. To go from making a living on the midway to settling down and doing whatever work's around. That's tough. 'Specially here. He'll come through all right. We just have to keep him from carnivals."

I listened to the talk around the table: weather, town politics, people catching up with each other. Johnny and I headed home in the light of dusk. He opened a couple of cans of cola, and we sat on the couch listening to the people and televisions in the apartments around us. He was silent, but smiling.

"Tell me about your wife," I said.

"She's purty, real purty. But we don't talk much," he said, his head settled into the back of the chair, eyes staring at the ceiling. "I have a daughter, too. Smart kid. Whole lot smarter 'an me. I don't see her much, but I talk ta her on the telephone sometimes. Sometimes I write a little on a postcard. But I don't write too well. She sends me back letters. Man, how she can write. I can't read so good, so Dan readsa long ones ta me. They sound purty good."

I used Johnny's phone to call my daughter. She was upset that her mom wouldn't give her any ice cream.

"Honey, it's late and you shouldn't eat ice cream before bed," I said.

"But, daddy, I *nee-e-ed* ice cream," she said between jerking sobs.

"Listen, be good to your momma and she'll give you some ice cream tomorrow."

"Daddy, she doesn't *have* any ice cream," she sobbed. I couldn't help but laugh.

When I had broken through the crying and settled her down, her mom got on the phone and complained that Sydney had been impossible all that day. Then she hung up the phone abruptly. I tried to feel rotten but couldn't.

The dark walls seemed to absorb light from the single lamp that stood on an end table. Johnny smoked one cigarette after another, and the smoke hung in the room in layers.

"Sometimes at night, I dream 'bout dem lights onna midway," Johnny said after a while. "You know how dem lights hang in strings and flash aroun' da games and along dem trailers. I miss 'em. Ever a carnival comes ta town, I stay away. I know I get 'round dem lights, start smellin' popcorn an' cotton candy—dey smell like money to me—an' I'll be gone again. I don't want dat. I got a kinda good thing goin' right here. I don' wanna fuck it up."

He lit another cigarette, said good night, and stepped into his bedroom. Dry breeze came through the window, sagebrush and motor oil, and stirred the layers of smoke. The shouts and screams from the courtyard had abated to the babel of different television programs. The radio came on in Johnny's bedroom. The scratchy sounds of AM radio country music, then a talk show, something about the KGB and the JFK assassination. The people calling into the program sounded like astronauts. I laid out my sleeping bag and pulled a couple of couch pillows up around my ears to block out the sound.

I dreamed. Floating above the sagebrush I saw lines of wagons, a great cloud of dust rising, orange in the sunset. Indians on foot and horseback trailed up over the rises and down into the river valleys. The wagons and Indians turned into bison, flowing in great streams into the river and disappearing under the iridescent sheen of crude oil bubbling out of the ground below refineries. Suddenly there was a great clap. Bison scattered across the plains and I sat up in bed, startled.

"Whatcha got on yer plate ta-day?" Johnny said. He was standing in his briefs jittering and fidgeting around like an excited kid. The radio played in the bedroom as loud as before. The sun slanted though the cane blinds. Hands on clock with the spiky rays indicated that it was eleven.

"Gee, Johnny, I don't know," I said, trying to open my eyes in the light. "I thought I might head on today toward Waltman and Natrona, you know. Or see Casper a little. I hadn't really thought much about it."

"So, here's what I's thinkin'," he said. He sat on the edge of the armchair, bent forward at the waist, his elbows on his knees. "We go get some coffee and some breffast. Then, you said las' night ya might haf some things ta get done in town, an' I figgered we'd get 'em done. Then, tomorra, if your stayin', I's thinking we'd drive over ta Register Clift back in Guernsey, see somma dem Oregon Trail ruts and things you's talkin' about. I never seen 'em, an' ya missed 'em on de way in. Whadya say?"

I didn't have time to say much except we'd see what happened. But to him the deal had been sealed. Before I even had my shirt on, Johnny whisked me out the door. We ran into the Cajun in the sidewalk. He was shirtless still, standing in the same pants as the day before, holding a can of cola. He stared out into the dusty courtyard. He seemed to be waiting for something to happen.

"Whatcha got onna cooker t'day, boys?" he said, turning to us.

"I have some things to do," I said. "Johnny's going to drive me around."

"An' tomorra, we're going out ta Register Clift," Johnny said. "We'd be up for some dinner tonight if yore aroun'."

"I'm good," Billy said.

We went to a dirty café for coffee and eggs. Johnny seemed at home. He knew the waitresses and the cooks.

"I useta work with a coupla dem cooks when da carnival's in." He lifted his eyebrows and smiled at a busty waitress as she walked by. With a pen in one hand and an order pad in the other, she hiked her breasts up and winked at Johnny in a television-cliché sort of way. Johnny laughed and turned to me. "She's dreamy, ain't she? Anway, dem guys in the kitchen wasn't widda show but was set-up-and-tear-down help. Never envy a guy widdat job. Just plain work. I useta do it sometimes for extry money when I first started as a carny. But it'll make ya old too quick."

Dan came in and took a chair next to Johnny. He asked if I was going to stay around a few days. I said at least the next two—Johnny seemed to be having a good time hauling me around. Usually, Johnny said, he sought work, sat in the courtyard with Billy (who also didn't seem to work much), and dined out with his friends several times a week. I was a break in his routine.

"Well, he's the best," Dan said. He slapped Johnny on the shoulder. "Plus," he said to me on the side, "I have an idea you're gonna show him a world he's never seen." I figured it was going to work the other way.

We drove up to a county park on the side of the Bessemer Mountains above Casper, then hiked to a rocky outcrop. The city spread around the North Platte. Tangles of pipes and blank concrete pads littered the brownish fields where the refineries used to be. Johnny was intrigued. He had never traveled past the edge of town or seen Casper from this angle since he had arrived a year before. He looked silently over the valley. The innate tension in his face loosened. He said that the last time he'd climbed rocks was when he was a kid. After a while we drove over the top into alpine meadows filled with wildflowers and sagebrush. The sky was overcast, and it was cold. Johnny was surprised to find large fields of snow there. We built a small snowman and slung wet, icy snowballs at each other.

We smacked and rubbed our hands, now red and numb, and climbed back in the truck. Descending the mountain took us into clouds and back out again. Winding our way through the city, Johnny was careful to point out things he knew—the public library, the park and swimming pool, city hall, the police station. "I don' know what de inside'a dat one looks like," he said. "An' I ain' plannin' ta find out." We went by to pick up Billy, who'd finally put on a shirt. Before we left, Billy had us in to look at his kitchen. His apartment was the same as Johnny's but shabbier. The walls were covered with velvet paintings: Elvis, camels crossing the desert, flowers, belly dancers.

"I get 'em from dem sellers on the road," Billy said when he saw I was looking at the paintings. "I like 'em."

"They're awfully nice," Johnny said. "I like the colors. But dey ain' really my style."

Chattering between themselves, they walked into the kitchen, finishing each other's sentences. Billy's entire apartment centered on the television in the living room. An assortment of racing and girlie magazines, empty paper cups, straws, full ashtrays, and empty pop bottles radiated from one empty dip in the deep-blue, plush-velvet couch. In the kitchen Billy was showing off his cooking utensils and spice rack to Johnny.

"This here's the cayenne I use," Billy said, holding up a bottle when I came in. "It's good stuff. Ever use it?"

"Not this brand, no," I said.

"It's good stuff. Leave your draws smokin'," he said—that was how he said "drawers"—"but it ain't jus' cayenne I use for Cajun cookin'. I use alla dem spices. I get 'em down at da Safeway. Ever made gumbo?"

"No, I haven't," I said. "But I like gumbo."

"If I can find some okry, I'll make up some for tomorra when y'all git back from Register Clift."

Johnny and I drove to a restaurant much like the others I had seen with him. The food was American fare—hamburgers, fries, tenderloins, and iceberg-lettuce salads. This restaurant, however, was a little seedier than the others—the kind of a place you feel a need to wash off yourself after you leave. But dinner was a pleasant tumult of conversation. Dan was there, and Billy, and several other people who had been at dinner the previous night, along with new faces. As night fell outside the steel-barred, Plexiglas windows, bevies of young children raced around couples and single men and women. They were a rough-looking bunch—ragged jeans, cowboy boots, leather vests, faded T-shirts with airbrushed images of wolves and Indians. They watched a lot of television, but no one, it seemed, had satellite or cable. They all drove old cars, and none had kids in private school. Some wished for a return of the oil business, others never wanted to do the body-breaking work again. Johnny just wanted something steady. Billy never wanted to work again.

"If I get a job, what'll I do all day?" he said.

I looked down at my glass and wished it wasn't clear. The water was milky, the surface iridescent with oil.

The next morning Johnny gassed up the old truck and we hit the interstate. The wind was warming pleasantly and smelled of sagebrush and dust. It promised heat that would dry sweat grainy on our skin and burn the tips of our noses and ears. But it meant we were outside and that was the most agreeable of promises a person could feel in the height of summer on the high plains.

Johnny drove with a ceramic coffee mug in one hand, the other draped over the wheel and holding a cigarette. Not far out of Casper we saw a man walking on the shoulder—at first a tiny speck in the brown, sagebrush hills. It getting hot; the sky was cloudless. The man looked out of place, not only because he *was* but also because we had seen no one else on the road, in town or out. The man had no pack or suitcase. He walked with a sort of waddle, plopping along as if he was hurt.

"We should pick him up," Johnny said.

Unsteady and breathing heavily, the man climbed into the truck.

His clothes were new and he wore rubber boots. He had clean, chiseled features, and a mass of unkempt blond hair. He looked like a surfer who'd lost his way. He seemed shorted out.

The man introduced himself as Jonathan. "I am on my way to the East," he announced. He had a look of great sincerity in his eyes. "See, I'm the next King of Israel. In the Bible, it says Jonathan would be the next great king after David. The apocalyptic things occurring around the world now, and the ascension of the devil to the most powerful political position in the world—I'm the Jonathan the Bible speaks of. I am him. Everything in my life has led me here. My time is at hand."

"Was ya stayin' at da mission in Casper?" Johnny said, looking over from the wheel.

Jonathan's ocean-blue eyes were clear but unfocused. I offered him some water, which he drank deeply.

"Take it easy a little," Johnny said. "Too much'll make ya feel bad."

Jonathan shook his head slightly. He looked sick. He fished a bag of tobacco and papers out of his pocket. But his shaking hands whisked tobacco over his lap. Johnny gave Jonathan a smoke from his pack. I lit it for him and rolled him a couple for the road ahead.

"Listen, it's damn hot ta-day," Johnny said. "Ya sure ya wanna walk?"

"These shoes hurt," Jonathan said meekly, looking down at the floor.

His rubber boots were open and flopping around. They were the exact wrong kind for walking on hot pavement. They were too big and he didn't have socks. Swimming around in there, his feet were hot and raw, probably blistered. We drove in uneasy silence until we came to the exit for Ayres Natural Bridge State Park. We dropped Jonathan at the exit, at his insistence, but told him we'd be along in an hour if he didn't get a ride. He waddled off down the interstate toward Douglas.

"Cops'll git him," Johnny said. He put the truck in gear and took off down the dirt road to the park. "They'll take care of him if he don' git a ride."

The dusty road through the sagebrush led to a closed gate, where a sign warned of high water on LaPrele Creek. But it didn't say that the park was closed. I convinced Johnny that we needed to walk in, to which he responded with enthusiasm. The road dropped into a canyon along the river, flowing in a long loop through the gulch and into a flat, grassy area. Picnic tables and barbecue grills were scattered among cottonwoods. It was a calm and peaceful place except for numerous signs forbidding rock throwing in the park. I stooped, picked up a rock, and threw it into the water. I skipped another across the width of the stream. Johnny looked around cautiously, as if expecting someone to scold us. Then he picked up a rock and bounced it off some boulders into the river. Laughing, we began to throw rocks, singly and by the handful, tossing them with abandon into the canyon walls, into the river. After a while we walked over to an abandoned stone-and-brick building that looked like it had been a small power plant, and crawled through the empty window. Our voices echoed as if in a cave. We climbed through the building, hanging precariously on pieces of pipe stuck in the walls. When we came back out, the air was fresh and chill after the still atmosphere inside. A wide, yellow-and-orange sandstone arch skewed over the swollen river. Hundreds of bank swallows flew into and dropped out of honeycombs of nests plastered under the bridge. They flashed here and there, skittering over the clear water.

We walked back up through the sagebrush and rock to the truck, and then came across Jonathan again, flopping along not far from where we'd dropped him. This time he revealed no biblical truths but said he had stayed in the mission, gotten new clothes and boots, and had a good meal to eat.

"But it was time for me to go," he said. "It's important for me to travel light."

"Ta Israel, ya mean?" Johnny said.

"What?" Jonathan said with a quizzical look.

He stared at the expanse of sagebrush around us, the highway disappearing in the distance, as if he had just come to.

"I can't understand so much land in one place," he said. He stared out over the plain. "It goes on forever. It's scary. I lived in Hawaii my whole life. Surfed a lot. I thought it was time to see how things went on the mainland. But I never thought I'd end up where there was so much empty space." It made me wonder what he thought of the ocean.

He said he had bought a ticket to Boise with a stopover in Seattle. After a long stint on the waterfront on Puget Sound, he'd missed his plane and hitchhiked to Boise. From there, he'd taken off on foot. He didn't give a sense of how long all this had taken, but to hear him it had been a while. Johnny and I suspected that there was something he was not telling.

Johnny dropped Jonathan off at a truck stop in Douglas, where Jonathan insisted he could find a ride with a truck driver. Then we drove over to a restaurant and motel called The Pump, an old log building with wide glass windows across the front. It was comfortable and dark, but the employees were smart-alecky and slow. They clearly didn't feel like working for a couple of single-digit payers. We got our coffee in heavy milk-glass mugs and took a table by the window. There we looked out over the quarter-mile drag strip in Douglas, the stands fat with spectators. Below, smoke plumed up from time to time, and rumbles shook the glass. I told Johnny how strange it was to be in places I had seen from the interstate days before—and thought I'd never see again.

On the way out of town Johnny pulled off at the truck stop to see about Jonathan, who now leaned against a corner of the canopy that connected the building with a set of gas pumps. Someone had given him milk and blueberry pie, which he had lathered into his face. When he saw us, he smiled, blueberries in and on his teeth, seemingly happy that we had returned. We loaded him back into the truck and pulled back on the highway, and drove on, passing the whistle-stop towns of Orin, McKinley, and Glendo. As we approached U.S. 26, which we would take east to Guernsey, Jonathan began to tell us more.

"I spent a lotta time on the beach," he said. "Shot a lotta dope, heroin mostly. But I'd use just about anything if connections weren't hittin'." He paused and rubbed his forehead. His hands were shaking terribly again and his eyes had become bloodshot. "I was ready to quit. But I was always ready to quit. I wanna quit now. But I can't."

"Let us take you back to Casper, kid," I said. "We can hook you up with people who can help you."

"But I don't wanna stop."

"I thoughtcha said ya did," Johnny said.

"I do wanna quit, the bad stuff, but I don't wanna quit the drugs."

I looked at Johnny. We both knew that Jonathan wanted the pain to end but not the euphoria, the escape. Johnny had known it with the carnival. I had known it with a hundred other things.

"But it's driving you insane," I said. "I mean, look at where you are. Walking in the hot sun. Bad shoes. Screwed up feet. No water."

He stared vacantly out the windshield. "I know," he said. "I don't know."

When we turned off the interstate, Jonathan insisted on getting out. It was time, he said, to continue his journey. We'd be back in a few hours, I told him. If he wanted to head back to Casper, we'd find him the right help. When he climbed out of the truck, he looked up and grasped my wrists tightly, his pale blue eyes wide with fear—where to go from here, what to do. It was a familiar feeling. The land was large; he was alone. He tried to smile and wave after he stepped out on the shoulder, but, back on his aching feet, he hesitated. As we pulled away he was looking after us, one hand raised.

We drove toward Guernsey. "We're never gonna see him again," Johnny said.

"I know."

We drove past the rise where Wayne had picked me up just a few days before, and then coasted down a long slope into the valley and into Guernsey, a lively, if worn, town where the Wyoming National Guard had training grounds and reserve units. We followed the signs to where we could stand in the tracks that thousands of Oregon immigrants' wagons had worn into the sandstone. Some of the ruts were troughs nearly three feet deep.

Johnny walked off up the wagon ruts, toe to heel, talking to himself. "How it musta been. How it musta been." As I watched him I thought about how travelers on the Oregon Trail had only had two things to show them the way—these tracks and the sun. After the first few adventurers and immigrants, the path was set. The maps some carried were indistinct and uncertain, and could never tell their owners how the journey and landscape would make vast personal changes in them along the way. But if my trip had shown me anything, it was that once on a road, or a worn path, one is never lost. One may be disoriented or unsure of the direction he or she is headed. But a trail, a path, a road leads somewhere.

We walked over to Register Cliff, a large sandstone boulder behind chain-link fence meant to keep modern graffiti writers at bay. People had previously hacked their names into the stone to be remembered—letters scrawled by the hands of working people, hands that had driven oxen, baked bread, handled babies and scythes and hammers, hands that were gone now but whose owners' descendants lived all over the country and the world.

A bent and rusted wrought-iron fence marked a small cemetery in the shadow of the rock. Unmarked stones ringed the graves where small children, fathers and mothers, and old people lie. When the river dipped into the sand at the height of summer, these people drank water from wagon tracks and hoof prints and it wreaked havoc on stomachs and colons. Cholera and dysentery wasted them. Influenza and the common cold choked them. There were thousands of graves like these across the prairie, from here to Kansas City, most disappeared, plowed under, just plain forgotten. Johnny wandered along the face of the cliff, reading names and dates aloud. He wondered at archaic and biblically inspired names—Cletus, Jeddah, Malachi, Otis. He was awestruck that the letters had been scrawled by human hands. When we returned to the truck, we had nothing to say.

When we pulled up on the interstate, Jonathan was gone, which disappointed us both. The sun on Johnny's face was yellow, and all around shadows had turned the prairie dark in shades of green and brown. After forty miles or so, we heard loud bangs against the bed of the pickup, and stopped. The wind smelled of sagebrush and grass and dirt. We considered vacant spots on back tires where pieces of rubber had come off the tread. Both spares were flat. We comforted ourselves by saying they'd be all right. They'd get us to Casper. If we broke down, someone would come along and we would get a ride. That's just the way it was.

But before we left, we leaned against the truck a while longer, feeling the heat of the metal, and listened to the wind in the sagebrush. Johnny smoked. The sun dipped into the horizon and turned the sky orange and purple.

13

"People seldom seen by the rest of the world"

So RELIEVED THAT the tires had made the rest of the trip to Casper without blowing out, we hopped back into the truck with Billy and went out to dinner at a café with Johnny's friends—another riot of random conversations started and ended quickly over greasy glasses of pop, bad food, and semi-dirty flatware.

After we ate I spread my map out on an empty table next to our group. I told Billy I was walking out the next morning along U.S. 26 toward Natrona and traced the route for him with my finger. Billy hummed in approval, nodding his head from time to time and saying, "Ummm, ummm . . . Yessss . . . Yessss." Kim Merchant, a short, cheeky man with a mischievous smile, whitening beard, and trimmed gray hair, rose from the tables of pals and sidled up.

Kim looked up with bright eyes and a determined grin. He leaned forward, his hands on the table. "Why don't you come out to my place near Emigrant Gap tonight?" he said. "I'll put you up, and we'll hitch the horses tomorrow and take a ride down the Oregon Trail, the real one. I'll take the horses back after we get in a good ride and come back and get you back down to the highway at Independence Rock to stay the night."

It almost felt as if I was being handed from one Wyomingite to another. I liked the hospitality but wondered what I had done to deserve it. I told people my story, what I wanted to do, and they responded. I thought it might be due to my openness and willingness to trust people at their word and for who they were. But being fatalistic from a lifetime of disappointments I always expected the kindness people had shown me to end. It didn't today, and that was enough. As we finished up dinner I told Johnny that I was going to head off with Kim.

"I had a great coupla days," Johnny said. "You'll come by agin, I hope. I should be here, if I stay away from carnivals." His blue eyes shone through the long locks of stiff gray hair. He reached into his pocket and pulled out a small piece of pyrite. "It'll bring you luck when you need it," he said. He smiled with those teeth that were so hard to look at.

Kim and I drove a smooth two-lane that flew over and between long, treeless hills. Grassland rolled up the side of the Bessemer Mountains, where dark stubble of scrub cedar washed up the foothills into dark-green, almost black, blankets of pines. Bluish-gray clouds swept over the top of the mountains, trailing rain in soft fringes. The sun fell toward the horizon. Lengthening shadows began to swallow up the landscape.

As we drove Kim said that he taught mentally challenged children in a small town near Casper. On school breaks in the winter and summer he took tourists on long horse treks to a wilderness camp that he ran in the Big Horn Mountains. He hosted hunters and guided them on elk and deer hunts. Due to cold that prevented the snow from melting up near the camp, and the general wet weather, his season was starting late.

"When school's out, I got nothing but time to do what I like to do," he said. "I paint a house here and there, and I keep some horses up at my place. They're a hell of a hobby."

He also kept a spate of period clothes for reenactments of Oregon Trail rides in Casper and across the West.

"Every summer we get together with the Indians and do a trail ride," he said. "We use utensils and outfits the settlers would have used. Then we enact historic battles with period arms and wagons and things—real cowboys-and-Indians. It gets real knock-down, drag-out. Sometimes the white guys win. Sometimes the Indians win. We all win and lose when we're not supposed to. Nobody knows the difference. It plays well for the crowd, 'specially the foreigners, and it's a helluva lot of fun."

"White guys and Indians?"

"Yeah, real live Indians," he said with a smirk. "We got real Indians out here, you know. Some live up on the [Wind River] reservation, and some are from around town. A lot of them are good friends. It gives a sort of feel to history to act out these things. The settlers, trappers, soldiers, and cowboys are white guys; the Indians are Indians. We all take it pretty seriously with the clothes and boots and guns and things. Still we make it a good time."

We drove through Emigrant Gap, a breach in a ridge of low hills, and departed the North Platte Valley. We stopped where a dirt road split from the pavement, and then climbed from the pickup to watch dusk fall. A copse of pines marked a small seep on the ridge about a half a mile away. Tires whined on the highway in the distance. A slight breeze whisked over the landscape, rich with the scent of sagebrush and dried grass.

Kim lived on a road fashioned from what was once the Oregon Trail. A trim yard and swaying Russian olive trees abuzz with honeybees surrounded his neat ranch house. Rows of flowers ringed the house and yard, next to which stood a tepee and the skeleton of a sweat lodge. Behind the house stood a horse barn and an assortment of horse-drawn wagons, with a camper and pickup between. Green cattle fencing marked off a dusty corral with gates that led out into wide, barbed-wire squares of prairie meadow where his horses stood, faces in the wind.

A few cats and an aging black retriever lounged on the covered deck that ran across the back of the house. We sat on the deck, leaning back in soft chairs and staring across prairie that reached into the dark red remnants of sunset. A breeze swished now and then in the fronds of the Russian olives and rattled in a grove of cottonwood and ash at the edge of the yard. We stayed up long after night revealed blue-silk wisps of stars.

To prepare for the ride, Kim and I split my things up and secured them in leather saddlebags astride a lean and strong mare. He set me astride another. She was red with short legs and hefty haunches. I was scared witless of horses, having been bitten, thrown, and stomped in my short interactions with them. Fortunately Nugget was a stupid man's horse—she didn't have to be spurred, goaded, or steered. She followed the packhorse tethered to Kim's mount without any other direction.

The sand and claypan road followed the old trail along easy rises and dips in the prairie. Where the trail deviated from the road, brushy greenery ran up the ruts where the fragile ground had been broken so many years before. White runnels ran through sandstone where there was no green.

Tourists and history students know more famous landmarks along the trail, such as Independence Rock, Split Rock, and Devil's Gate. But the accounts of Francis Parkman in *The Oregon Trail* and those of numerous settlers documented other, more out-of-the-way sights. Kim and I began to come across them, our horses swaying slowly and the prairie quiet but for wind. At Avenue of Rocks, white, yellow, and red sandstone outcrops lined either side of the road as it dropped into a small valley, rife with jagged washes and ravines. We stopped and climbed up on bone-white rocks to take in the vast treeless land, picking up pieces of emerald-green quartz along the way. We rode through the sagebrush with few words between us. The area grew more arid as we left the rain shadow of the ridges behind us. Sheepherder wagons stood alone on the plain like white and silver skiffs in a sagebrush sea. Here and there, single power lines on wooden poles crossed or followed the road a while before dodging off to oil rigs or lone farmsteads far from sight. The silence was at once calming and overwhelming. The wind soon died away, and we could hear the occasional scuffle of a jackrabbit.

Kim looked back and forth across the plain under his wide-brimmed cowboy hat—so big for such a little guy. But he was a strong, wiry man who possessed no fear. The night before, he had projected the confidence of a well-adjusted man. His wife, Leah, smiled in the photos that hung on the walls. She was a pretty woman with a warm smile—a teacher who taught at a small grade school on a dirt road two miles from their house. Leah, Kim told me, tended the sprays of flowers and the large vegetable garden. As he talked, his powerful voice echoed in the vaulted ceiling above the living room. His eyes were afire, clear and deep and bright. As the day caught up to him, he was like a child who fights sleep until the last possible second, and then passes out before the pillow cradles his head.

Now he turned from time to time and asked how Nugget was doing. As far as I knew, she was doing fine. "Not bad, as horses go." She walked in an easy lope most of the time, but on occasion took off in a trot for reasons only she understood. At these times my knuckles turned white on the saddle horn. I imagined dying of head trauma or from being dragged, one foot in a stirrup, across sand, boulder, and sagebrush. Usually such panics were short-lived. When Kim heard Nugget take off, he shouted a few words, and she slowed again to a walk.

"You know what horses like?" he said after one of Nugget's bursts.

"No. What?"

"They like it when you don't grit your teeth all the time."

After ten miles, Kim dropped me off to walk on my own and turned to take the horses back. Sagebrush, buffalo grass, and blue grama covered the plains and the hills, a few scrubby cottonwoods grew in the washes. A radio antenna, a telephone pole, and a sheepherder's wagon shimmering in the distance caught my eye and kept it. All day only two cars passed. White plumes of dust had risen and engines whined in the creases of the hills a full five minutes before the cars raced by, and then many minutes after. Late in the afternoon I slouched under a lone juniper perched on a small rise next to the road. A slight hot breeze rose from the south, and I fell into a dream of swirling yellow light. When I woke, a coyote stood in the shade of the tiny juniper with me. Surprised by my waking movements, it took off, dodging and jumping sagebrush, white puffs of dust rising from its footfalls.

The road meandered between the hills past Willow Springs, a wet spot in a deep valley where an old cabin creaked in the breeze. The springs had once flowed freely, and I wished it still offered sweet, cool water. The road climbed a long, steep rise up Prospect Hill. After fifteen miles of walking, it was time for me to stop and wait for Kim. The sun was setting, coloring the landscape with orange and yellow light. In the distance, the Seminoe and Rattlesnake mountain ranges rose out of pink-purple mist. Short wildflowers and red whisks of Indian paintbrush lent the wide, empty space an eerie beauty. Bobolinks and meadowlarks twittered in the sagebrush.

I was beat and thirsty, the heat and the hills having worn me into a pleasant fatigue. At the top of the hill I took a feeble, grassy lane off the main road to a log fence that surrounded a Bureau of Land Management historical marker. I dropped my pack and felt the chill of sweat evaporating from my shirt. Without the weight, I felt like I was going to float away.

The fence puzzled me. There had been no fences in the open range for miles, except this one small rectangle. Soon, however, the fence made sense. While I was reading the marker, a herd of about a hundred black-and-white Holsteins gathered around. The fence kept them back but seemed a shaky defense. Where I went, their heads followed in wide arcs. They were quiet at first but soon began lowing and mooing loudly. I wanted them to go away. I trusted bovines as much as I did horses. I shooed and yelled and shooed some more. I tried to remember what I'd seen in cowboy movies, but all that came to mind were men on horses with cowboy hats and six-guns. Shouting and waving my arms brought more cows to the herd until they were cheek-to-butt in a hundred-foot circle around the fence. Finally I sat against the plaque as still as I could, looking into their black-spotted noses. Slowly they began munching cud and one by one trod off down the hill.

The Holstein threat was long passed and my water bottle empty when Kim arrived in the evening. I was still behind the fence, however, afraid to move and bring the beefs back to stare. Kim gave me a cold cola and a bottle of water from a small cooler to put back what sun and heat had taken from me. We drove another fifteen miles over the dirt road, ever deeper into the valley. The haze in there turned dark blue-purple. Kim dropped me at the small parking area at Independence Rock National Historic Site. It was tough to have to say goodbye to this interesting, complicated man. But I was sure that for him it was something that was as natural as saying hello.

/ I walked around to the back of the rock, threw my mattress and bag out among sagebrush near a long seam in the granite, and climbed in. I watched headlights from cars approaching on the highway play over the side of the rock.

By the time I started down the highway the next day, the landscape burned orange and brown in the midday sun. It was as beautiful as it was empty. After eleven miles my bottles were again dry and I had a powerful thirst. Runoff from a large grazing area between the road and the mountains ran into a little draw at the side of the road. Water steeped in acres of cow dung and amoebic discontents, I thought, as I pumped two liters of it through my compact antiseptic filter. I hoped it would work the way it was supposed to and filter out the little monsters. I was careful to keep drops—likely tasty with cow chips and hoof rot—from the outside of the bottle and away from the opening. After all the precautions, the water, despite my doubts about the efficacy of the filter, was sweet and cool.

I sat back in the tall grass and took off my shoes to let the ache drain from my feet. Birds and crickets made small creaks in the silence. Tires of the occasional car or truck whined. After a while I rose and was far more energetic and ready to walk than before. I was also now confident the cow-urine-hoof water I'd pulled from the ditch wasn't going to kill me. I pulled on my socks and boots, dry and warm from the sun.

The shoulder widened but the concrete and tar and gravel were much more reflective than the gravel shoulder I had been walking on. The heat soon filtered through the bottom of my shoes. Growing hot, achy, and tired, I looked forward to making it to Muddy Gap, a kink in the road where another highway intersected it. There I planned to refill my water bottles and find a night of solitude in the sagebrush and saw grass.

When I arrived in Lander the next evening, neon and large lighted signs gave me the feeling of being on the Vegas strip after the dark nights at Kim's and Independence Rock. The Downtown Motel was a quaint 1940s-style motor court for discriminating Packard and DeSoto drivers that had suffered the shifting of the age. The woman at the desk was about fifty. She had trimmed and styled bleach-blond hair, and wore a white blouse and blue jeans. She had a pleasant smile.

"You in for a while or just tonight?" she said. I signed the registration card.

"Just tonight."

"I notice you don't have a car." She raised an eyebrow above her black horned-rim glasses.

"No, I kinda walked here, kinda rode here."

"Well, honey, a car doesn't matter much, everything's walking distance. What do you want to see?"

"I just want to take it easy. I had long day."

"Lotsa walking?"

"Plenty. Tomorrow I need to go to the post office and do some laundry. I might want to go to a bookstore."

"There's a couple of bookstores. One's Christian."

"I'll be needing the other."

She walked over to the door and pointed down the street to the bookstore. Evening had set and the street had grown quiet. Streetlights and neon glittered under a dark cobalt sky. Stars shone white and hardly twinkled. She led me to the room, which was small and clean. A table lamp burned on a writing desk. The bed filled the room.

"You just holler if you need anything," she said. "I'm in the house next door after the sign's off. Just knock. It doesn't matter if it's three in the a.m."

I talked with my daughter and then walked a while and puffed a cheap cigar. It was 9:00 p.m. and most of the town was closed; pickups of all ages and styles were parked in knots before taverns. I thought about the events of the last few days. I'd had plenty of time with people, interspersed with long moments of contemplation. As I walked, my thoughts turned elsewhere—to the cloak of stars now seeming to float above the town, to what it might be like in the smoky bars along the street, to the sound of the lone motorcycle that kept racing up and down unseen side streets. The night was still and getting cool. Walking around in it was comfortable and easy on the eyes and the soul. I realized again I wasn't wondering what the next day would bring. I had a room in a small motel. The air was so clear. The wind smelled of sagebrush. That's what seemed to matter. When I arrived back at the motel, I opened the window and fell asleep listening to what few sounds the town was still making.

I wandered around town much of the next day, just poking around. In the late afternoon I set my pack down in a park on the Popo Agie River. The stream was brusque and swollen and smelled of rosemary and fish. The grass was warm in the sun. I lay down and began to doze, only to be awakened a short while later by a little mutt sniffing at my pack.

"Got some food in there," said a little man at the end of a leash. "Nitro can tell. I'm Willard Hugo."

I stood to shake his soft but strong hand. He was wearing a black bowler with matching pants and jacket. He also wore a tie. When I told him where I was from, he smiled and laughed with delight. He said he'd grown up in Kansas City and run a garage during the reign of political boss Tom Pendergast in the 1930s. His eyes sparkled.

"Back in my wanderin' days in the 1920s I hitchhiked all over the country," he said. "It was a pretty common thing for people to put out their thumbs and get a ride. Back then it didn't matter if you were looking for work or just looking around. People stopped and gave you a ride. Not everyone had a car, but there was always some-one around who would share. Then if you had a car you turned the favor."

"Today's not that way?" I said. We sat at a nearby picnic table. Nitro sat at his master's feet. "People go out of their way to give me rides."

"Well, good for you." Willard folded his arms, looking toward the river. "You hear too much about people getting killed giving rides. News is filled with freaks and perverts, it seems. But I say you never hear about people who *never* get killed giving rides, and there must be millions of them. Me, I don't think bad things happen any more than they used to, just there's more people. People's just a little more selfish now and always scared. I give a ride to anybody, especially Indians. They don't have many cars, and the cars they have, well, some of 'em don't have much life to 'em."

"Well," I said. "People have really surprised me. I get rides sometimes just into town, sometimes a long way down the road. Just yesterday I had a stranger beg me to take a ride with him—and drive his car."

"It's a hell of a thing," he said. "People, when they're real and not abstract, can be pretty good, I find."

I agreed. We listened to the Popo Agie rush by. Willard pulled off his hat and ran his stubby fingers though his thin hair.

"Yes, sir," he said. "It was good in Kansas City. I had a garage downtown, a little car-repair business. I was working in the shop one day when Tom P's boys come around looking for a stolen radio." Tom Pendergast was Kansas City's Democratic machine boss in the 1930s. Although never elected to public office, he had politicians and business and civic leaders in his pockets. He had engineered Harry Truman's start in politics.

"That was 1932, I believe," Willard said. "Well, I had a coupla guys working there, and I asked if they stole a radio. They said they didn't, and I told Tom's boys my men's word was as good as truth. They were a little mad about it. They didn't like being told what for. Wasn't used to it. A bunch of them stood at the door and shut my place down. Then they wanted everything out of the register, only they couldn't get it open. I didn't open it for them and wasn't going to, either. They got frustrated and went away, and that was the last I heard from them. Thing was, I liked Pendergast, thought he did a hell of a job for the town."

In the 1940s, Willard went to work as an ironworker. He got on with the Fluor Corporation building and salvaging oil refineries around the world. It was a good job, he said, with good pay and a decent pension.

"Plus I was able to see places I only dreamed about as a kid in Missouri," he said. He petted Nitro, who didn't seem to be going anywhere or caring much whether he was stroked or not. "Arabia, Russia, South America. They were places a Kansas City kid only gets to see in picture books. But I suppose you understand that already."

"I sure do," I said.

Willard said that after a life of exotic languages and lands, he retired in Parsons, Kansas, where he lived only a few years before his son talked him into moving to Lander to set up housekeeping.

"And you know what?" he said. "I ain't movin' again."

He slapped me on the knee and stood up. He and Nitro sauntered off up the concrete sidewalk. After a few feet he stopped and turned around.

"By the way, son," he said. "I think it's a good thing you're doing, getting out across the country. You get to meet fine people that way, people seldom seen by the rest of the world."

"Yes, I do."

Willard headed down the walk toward the river. I intended to stay the night at the park. It was one of those days in a journey when nothing more than lying around would do. The sound of the river worked on me and made me infinitely lazy. I had gone to the post office, called my daughter, and been to the bookstore. I had nowhere to go, really, no timetable that mattered, nothing to do except start my new book and nap. I lay in the grass listening to the river and the gush of my pulse in my ears.

I slept a long while in the sun. When I woke a woman in her late thirties was standing over me. She asked about my pack and sat down on the grass. Jody was her name. After a few moments, she offered to put me up on her living room floor. I had a funny feeling. But she was smiling in a friendly, benign way and seemed to have good intentions.

"My husband's working but won't mind," she said. "He'll be home late. And my kids'll get a kick out of it. I have some errands to run but I'll be back by in a few hours. I'll stop by to see if you're interested."

"I'm not one to deprive children," I lied. I didn't feel like doing anything and the promise of an easy place to stay and another hot shower was too much to pass up.

"That's a good attitude," she said.

I was just waking from another nap when Jody came by later. We walked down a quiet street under a stand of mature sycamores and cottonwoods. The light had grown dim, and the evening was still and peaceful. People sat on porches and in the yards of trailers in swings and lawn chairs. Toward the edge of town, the treed lane opened to sagebrush plain. Beyond, the valley spread to the last of the Rattlesnake Range to the north and east. Jody was tall and slim, with light brown hair that fell over her shoulders. She talked non-stop.

"My husband's a construction contractor," she said. "He's a loving man and good father, but our marriage seems to have lost something, that spark, you know."

I didn't know. I wondered if I was doing the right thing but kept right on walking toward her house.

Along the way, we met Karl, a tall, stooped man with worried eyes who had driven by in his truck. He leaned out the window on his folded arm. Though cheerful enough, he seemed deeply unhappy.

"I'm headed to Riverton tomorrow," he said. "Then I'm off in the afternoon to my brother's vacation house on some land on the Indian reservation. You don't want to walk through the reservation and try to find a place at night. The Indians, they get drunk, you know, and it won't be safe for you there. I'd be more than happy to take you. Dinwoody Lake, that's where my family's house is. You can stay the night there; no one will bother you."

The Wind River Indian Reservation was on the road north. Since I'd entered Wyoming, people—all white—had told me that the reservation was an unfriendly place. The Indians, they said, were an angry lot, poor and resentful. I'd heard this refrain from nearly everyone I talked to in Lander, except Willard Hugo and the woman at the

Downtown Motel who had said, "Indians are just folks trying to get along."

I shook Karl's hand. "Thanks. But I think I'd like to walk."

"Really, I'd love the company," Karl said. "My appointment actually will take a while. You can get around Riverton some, and I'll take you. I'll pick you up at 6 a.m., if that's not too early."

Jody's house was an expansive doublewide on a small yard fenced with chain link and scattered with toys and bicycles. The house seemed to be a neighborhood gathering place. Children ran everywhere. Jody's daughter Clarisse was a pretty girl, about thirteen years old with blond hair. She kept wildlife in cages and little fenced areas near a flower garden. She had just caught a collared lizard, and she and her friends were passing it from dirty hand to dirty hand. Darin was nine, and three of his friends played soldier, shooting each other loudly—*Bang! Bang!*—and stopping long enough to argue who was dead and who wasn't. When we approached, they dropped their plastic guns and offered to carry my pack and water bottle. It took two of them, and they got it as far as the front step before giving up and fiddling with zippers and snaps.

I sat on the step and showed them my pack—here the stove, there the bag with matches, knife, eating utensils, flashlight, compass, and a host of other small items. I showed them my waterproof canvas and survival blanket, as well as the water pump, rain gear, and first aid kit. They asked questions: "What's that for?" "How does that work?"

After a short time Jody ended the show abruptly: "All right, that's enough. Let Patrick get inside and settle in."

The kids persisted, and she raised her voice angrily. Paige, a very little girl who had been plastered against the screen in the door since we'd arrived, held her arms up to me as I walked in. She talked nearly as much as her mother and refused to go to bed. With a nasty shout from Jody, Paige disappeared into her room.

Jody's husband, Dave, came home and introduced himself, extending a strong, calloused hand. He was a tall man in tight-fitting jeans and a button-up work shirt. We sat in the living room and talked for a while, when suddenly he said it was time for him to go to bed. Jody stayed on the couch across from me, talking ceaselessly, eying me in a way that suggested intentions other than just chatter. The neighbor children had gone home, and Darin had gone to bed. Clarisse watched television. Jody told me to use the shower.

I was an idiot, I thought. Not every stranger was going to be all right. Not all the goods laid before me were worth taking just because someone set them there. I had now gotten myself into the tiny bathroom of a trailer belonging to a passive-aggressive maniac who was turning out to be a control freak. Plus Jody's husband's sudden exit from the room felt wrong. Why, I didn't know, and I tried not to think that it had to do with sex. When I came back to the living room after a shower, I had made up my mind to get the hell out. Clarisse was gone and Jody slouched deep in the couch, legs spread, one hand crooked behind her head, the other over her crotch.

"Where you going?" she asked as I went to my pack.

"It's time for me to go," I said.

"You better not," she said angrily. "You can't just come into people's houses and use their stuff and leave without spending time with them."

My teeth felt covered with sandpaper. Her husband was in the next room and the house was house full of kids. I was frozen, afraid of risking a cry of rape or a husband with a gun. Worse, I didn't want to have to make a break for it without my pack.

I sat on the couch opposite her armchair. She began to talk about her life and the people in Lander. It was a small place, she said, not very cosmopolitan. Life for a woman who wanted more than kids was less than satisfying. She had been good-looking once, she said, a high school beauty queen. She had dreamed of finding herself in a big city but found love in a small town. Now kids and responsibilities kept her from being what she'd wanted to be. (She never said what that was.) Her chatter soon became racier, and I thought that going to bed was a fine idea.

"What a fine view for a girl like me," she said when I bent to roll out my mattress. I moved to different position to finish what I was doing. "There's some fine legs you got there," she said. "A big, good-looking boy like you must have met some women along the way?"

"Well, yes and no." I was now planning how to best exit through the front door, trying to accept the loss of my equipment. I wondered if I could run fast enough to dodge into an alley before shots were fired.

"Women show guys like you a good time, I bet," she persisted.

"Not really. I have a rule about that." I said. I sat on the edge of the couch, my hands folded between my legs. Maybe, I thought, I had found a way out of the present unpleasantness.

"A rule?" she asked. "What rule?"

"Never sleep with women I meet on this trip," I said. "You never know who's got a husband or lover, and who doesn't." I was lying, sort of. I had vowed to steer clear of situations that might get me in trouble with my own heart or with husbands, lovers, and police departments. But I had already wanted to violate that oath at least once. "On foot, it's not like you have a chance to get away. Besides, a run-in like that would ruin everything."

"What's that?" she said.

"Getting used to being in my own skin and living in the moment rather than in the past or future."

"Oh, so it's some sort of mystical thing you do, 'walking around the country'?" She was being snide and demeaning, but I wasn't going to play.

"I'm interested in finding out some things," I said. "About me. About others. About the Great Plains.

"Great Plains!" she said, raising her voice. "Who the hell gives a shit about the Great Plains? It's a shithole. Look at this place. A shithole on the edge of the mountains. You'd deprive women of affection for finding out about what? That's generous."

"Listen, Karl's going to be here in five hours," I said. "I'd better get some sleep."

"This is my house. I stay up as long as I like."

For another hour she talked about herself, the things she'd done, the things she'd seen. She didn't move, but shifted every now and then, casting poses that, given the situation, were sickening rather than seductive. Despite my own discomfort I felt awful for her. I kept my eyes on the television.

"So you're really in charge," she said finally. "You have to get up so everyone has to go to bed."

"No," I said, not looking at her. "I'm scared and I'm tired. I don't want to tell you what to do, but I'm very uncomfortable here."

"Well, good night. I'll get you up in the morning."

She stood and turned off the television with the remote control. She flipped off the light and left me to fumble around in the dark. I packed my things and waited for her to go to sleep so I could slip out the front door. But I made the mistake of putting my head back and fell asleep. I woke an hour later, feeling as if someone had been standing over me. Now I was afraid to move at all. I stayed awake until dawn.

When Jody came in at 5:45, she looked as if she were hungover. Her tattered bathrobe dragged the floor behind her. Her long hair was in knots.

"I'll wait for Karl outside," I said, rubbing my eyes.

"You will not," she said. "I'm making coffee."

I picked up my pack and made for the door.

"Stay put. I'm making coffee, I said."

She slung together a cup of instant coffee from hot tap water. I looked around the house for signs of why this was so weird. The place was neat and clean, nothing out of place, pictures of a smiling family on the wall. I slugged the coffee and kept slugging after it was gone to keep from having to say anything. Shortly Karl pulled up outside.

I grabbed my things to go, but Jody stepped in the doorway and blocked my way. She stood a long time, silent, waiting. Finally she took a deep breath and stepped outside. I'd never smelled fresher air.

"You ready?" Karl said. He stood outside his truck.

"You bet."

"We had a fine time," Jody said, smiling, as we walked up to the truck. "We stayed up late, talking. Almost didn't make it out in time this morning. You doing good, Karl?"

"Yes, thanks," he said. "It's going to be a good day."

I climbed into the truck. My eyes and face felt heavy from lack of sleep. My mouth was dry. But I was glad to be out of there, vowing to myself to be more careful. Jody stood in the front yard and waved as we pulled away. I felt badly for her.

"Sleep good?" Karl said.

"Not at all."

"That's too bad. I haven't slept well for years. Enjoy your stay?"

"It was different," I said. "Jody doesn't seem to be too happy."

Karl pulled through the last stoplight in town and headed out into the open tablelands.

"She isn't," he said.

14

RIVERTON, WIND RIVER INDIAN
RESERVATION, DUBOIS

"If we wait long enough, white men'll go away"

JODY HAD SET me up. But I was angry with myself for not getting up and leaving when it became clear things had gone wrong. Afraid to make a sound, I'd been worried about jail, a severe beating, being shot—that sort of thing. But I'd also been afraid I'd blow my ride with Karl if I had to walk away from our appointed meeting place.

I was chickenshit, first for putting myself into such a miserable place, and second for staying in it. How could I be so stupid? I wondered if I was taking pleasure in having attention paid to me. But, if so, what kind of gratification, vicarious or real, was I trying to get? I had been selfish. I had wanted a shower, food, and a place to overnight. I had wanted a ride with Karl. In the end, I had paid a dear price in self-esteem and self-worth to learn that selfishness was a great way to ruin a journey.

We didn't see one car on the highway the twenty-four miles from Lander to Riverton. Karl spoke from time to time, working through various scenarios of new security and comfort, or failure to gain them. He seemed to need someone to listen to him, but I was focused mostly on my own thoughts. As I ceased rebuking myself for the incident with Jody, the relief at escaping whole and safe rose out of my chest in sighs. *Goddamn it*, I said to myself, *I was fucked.* I laughed. Maybe all the dangers were in my own head. In fact the situation I thought so dire had been the meeting of two quirky personalities, Jody's and mine. Whatever the underlying truth was, I was free from a terrible situation and never had to live through the same nonsense again.

The landscape seemed ethereal to me. I noticed the difference in perspective between driving and walking—of distance before me on the road, of space, and of time. I had never really been aware of the ways that my perceptions of time and distance blended together in a seamless whole. At any one time the day might move faster or slower. Similar distances might seem short or near at one time, and long or far away at another. But these varying perceptions all formed a continuous view of the world around me.

Shops and restaurants lining U.S. 26 at the Riverton city limits cut my reflection short. Karl dropped me at the park, a big square of ground on the edge of town. A few walkers made circuits around the park perimeter. At picnic tables and benches, men and women milled about, talking and drinking coffee. I strolled up the main street, poking my head into shops and bookstores, buying a couple of cups of coffee and making a few telephone calls over the course of the day. I wandered back to the park to take the pack off and do a little writing and reading.

Karl had warned me about drunken Indians in the park as had several people in the shops I'd visited while walking around town. Without exception they spoke of natives with the third-person impersonal pronoun: "They're angry." "They don't like whites." "They'll take everything you got if you let 'em." But the native men and women who sat around the park picnic tables and drinking fountains were sober and friendly. As I sat writing, they smiled as they walked by and asked where I was going. When I told them, they asked how my trip had been.

I noticed between breaks in reading and writing that some of the men and women in the park had been in line at—or come out of—the temporary employment agency across the street. Setting my things aside, I walked over to a man in a red western shirt lounging against a metal pole beneath a barbecue grill and asked how much work there was around Riverton.

"There's work, but more people than jobs," he said. He looked out over the park. He wore jeans and cowboy boots. Long black hair flowed from under the straw cowboy hat. He squinted when he smiled. "We come here to work when we need to. Then we wait. We wait for a ride to get here in the mornin'. We wait for work when we get here. If there's nothin' after nine, then we wait for rides back home. Lots of people don't have cars. Indians're good at waitin'. If we wait long enough, white men'll go away. They never have time. We have time."

"People tell me not to walk through the reservation," I said. I sat down on the concrete pad below the grill. "They keep telling me about mad, drunken Indians. They say it's not safe."

"Remember who's talkin'." He chortled, lifting the brim of his hat and shifting his back against the grill. He smiled. His teeth were perfect. "Indians wouldn't say stuff like that. Most Indians're friendly. Even drunk Indians aren't drunk all the time. An' they're mostly friendly when they're drinkin' anyhow." He laughed, dipping his chin into his chest and looking up again. "We don' got enough money to be mean. I think you gonna find most people's pretty nice. It's not like you want nothin'. An' I don' know what you're waitin' for, but it's not too bad here," he said, looking out over the park again. "This here's a nice park. Got drinkin' fountains and a bathroom. Sometimes the police run us out. They say too many Indians just sittin' in the park. But we don't mind havin' you."

"In my town, there are plenty of people who sit all day in the park who aren't Indians," I said.

"Goes to show ya."

The man's name was Dan, "hundred percent Indian. Shoshone, if you're askin'." He said his family lived near Ft. Washakie on land they had settled in 1863. Men in his family had fought with the Union in the Civil War. They rode with the U.S. Army in the Indian Wars, helping to chase Sioux and move them to reservations in South Dakota. He said he was a veteran, having served four years in the army.

"But it was never comfortable for me out *there*, you know," he said pointing east. "Reservation life isn't for some, but it's all right for me. I got a little house, a little land, a couple of cows. When I want to I get work most of the time.

"Whenever I was outside here," he swept his hand over the Wind River Mountains in the distance, "outside Wyomin', really, I always felt like I was someplace else."

"But you were someplace else."

"I mean a different country."

"Really?"

"Sure. I grew up on the Wind River Indian Reservation, nations of Washakie's Shoshone and Northern Arapaho. My family's from here. This here's ground I came from and always come back to. Out there's foreign land. Hell, even Sacajawea came back after all that runnin' around with Lewis and Clark. When I left, I found out how much that meant. And you know what?"

"What's that?" I said.

"When I was gone, I never missed home, not once. I knew I'd be back. Then, when I come back, I found out how much 'someplace else' there really is."

I thought about how I didn't miss home and about how much someplace else there seemed to be. I wasn't comfortable at home because there always seemed to be something unsettled in me. Over the horizon looked like a good place because it wasn't home. At the same time, Dan's comment about being someplace else dovetailed with the Wyoming state marketing motto, "Like no place on earth." To him it was like nowhere else. It was home, and home was reliable. It would always be there when he got back. When I left Kansas City, I didn't look back because I knew I'd be back. Maybe deep down inside I had the same kind of confidence in home that Dan did. I only hoped that I would find the kind of contentment my Indian friend had in his home.

We watched the traffic stop and go at the traffic light at the corner of the park. Joggers ran through the park and disappeared into town. A few more people spilled out of the day-labor agency and walked across the street to join others at the picnic tables.

"It wasn't hard to come home?" I said after a while. I remembered the difficulty I'd had being in Kansas City after living in Germany for a while. The disappointment was onerous and it took me what seemed a long, long time to get out of it. I wasn't sure, even now, if I had escaped the disillusionment that comes from comparing home to places I'd been and seen, or become used to it.

"Sure it's hard," he said, adjusting his hat again. "The world turned underneath me, you know. I saw some things. I changed. But home didn't and neither did the people. But after a while I figured that was good. That's what home is about. It's not all new and it's not all what you thought it was when you was someplace else. You don' got to be Indian to understand that."

Two men in a pickup pulled up to the corner of the park and honked.

"Like I said, we Indians got time to wait," he said, getting up from the concrete and dusting himself off. "And we got time to go. So long, amigo."

Later Karl picked me up and we drove toward the mountains. The Wind River lolled through the grassy plain. I would be climbing into the Rockies the next day. I was ready. It would be nice to walk in the rarified air. I had passed north of the southern Rockies as I made my way from Casper. This little panhandle that encompassed the Wind River Valley from Lander and Riverton toward Dubois was the last of the Plains I would see until I came out of the Rockies at Helena. As we drove, the valley narrowed between the Wind River Mountains to the south and the Owl Creek Mountains to the north. The terrain became rougher and hillier. Signs staked next to the road read, "No camping or hunting without permit of Tribal Government." The land was wilder, cropped only by deer, elk, and an occasional cow.

When we were well up the valley, Karl pulled off the highway and drove up into the sagebrush hills for a mile or two and then into a narrow valley. Dinwoody Lake spread out under long ridges on either side. A small hump of land bridged the two ridges and cupped the lake in the valley. A group of houses stood on a tongue of land at the opposite end of the lake about three miles distant. The houses were at the base of a steep grade that led to another lake a tier up in the valley. Karl's brother's place was among them.

I walked down the shore, which fell one way into the lake, the other down a dry, sagebrush-filled wash toward the road. Short juniper and stunted white pines grew in clumps near the water. Buffalo grass studded with side-oats grama and sagebrush spread out from the water's edge and around the pines. The sky had grown overcast, making the valley seem a large, closed room compared to the wide spaces we had just come from. Rings upon rings suddenly broke the lake's glassy surface, as if the trout knew it was time to feed. The wind began to rise gently.

I built a fire from dried sagebrush and pine branches. Bathed in that fragrant smoke, I set up a lean-to. With one side of the canvas staked down, two small sticks secured with rope propped up the other side. The Mylar-coated survival blanket served as ground cover. It was fine shelter, housing my bed, pack, and all the loose things that came out of the pack over the course of the evening. After dark the breeze died and the valley became completely quiet. The lake was still. Mice scrambled in the sagebrush. Lights came on in the houses and reflected off the water. In the still calm I marveled at the stars covering the sky in gauzy sheets. When my fire died to a glow, I crawled into my bag and was asleep as soon as I closed my eyes. I felt the most soothing comfort, an otherworldly calm.

Just like the plains, the mountains were beautiful to me because they were not in my everyday vision. But they were a part of me and my personal history. Their exotic nature derived from those moments I'd had as a kid when my dad bumped the station wagon up Forest Service roads to camping sites at the foot of glacial moraines and next to cold, crystal streams. Although I loved the jungle-like heat and humidity of a Missouri summer, I remembered well spending time in places where the air was so clear and dry that it made the whole world seem new and different.

Jody probably could not find comfort in clear, clean air and mountain backdrops. They were routine for her and as such couldn't relieve her emotional distress. She and Karl did not understand the treasures they had—public lands minutes from their homes, crisp, cold summer nights, air smelling of pine and sagebrush. These advantages were, for me, dreams born in the good memories of childhood. Taking the thought a step further, I realized that it was only after I'd decided to leave that I began to see my town in a new light. For the first time in decades, I saw the beauty in Kansas City's expansive parks and quiet, old neighborhoods. The journey illuminated what was good about living in there, with my daughter, and in my own skin. I also knew how waking up in a different place every day renewed my energy for life. As I thought of Jody, I realized I had to greet every day, at home or anywhere, as if it were new to me—with the understanding that problems were small in the wider scope of an entire life. This and only this would keep me from falling into restlessness and discontent.

The sun was already high in the sky when I poked my head from under my sleeping bag. Packing seemed to take forever, mostly because I found myself staring off over the lake time and again. The surface was mirror-smooth, blue but for occasional primer-gray splotches as clouds passed over. The fire I'd relit for a little comfort in the cold morning puffed out smells sharp and resinous. The ground seemed inordinately soft. When I finally got started, walking the dirt road to the highway was pleasant and easy. I had it in my mind to make it to Dubois, some thirty miles distant.

On the highway there was little traffic, and then mostly old pickups and beaten cars driven by Indians who smiled and waved as they drove by. All the talk of drunken, murderous Indians had come out of other people's fears. Indians, abstracted and attached to a few, old myths, were scary to those who had told me about being mobbed by drunken, angry, thieving natives. In the back of my mind, I had given them little credence. But the actual fact, once met, was that Jody had been more threatening than any of the natives I had met or who had seen fit to wave to a stranger on the road. I regretted taking a ride from Karl because of the people I may have missed meeting. At the same time, I was grateful that he had delivered me to such an eerily beautiful place where working these thoughts through came easily and without strain.

Once on the road, fifteen or sixteen miles fell away quickly. The late afternoon sun had dropped behind the blood-red bluffs of Red Rock Canyon. Spires of sandstone cleaved by wind and water and ice towered above the rocky, foamy Wind River. Red-tailed hawks flew the length of the canyon, and bighorn sheep defied gravity as they pirouetted on the cliff faces. Deep ravines broke the cliffs like hallways into rooms beyond. The road wound higher and higher between the Wind River Range and the Absarokas, and climbed through a cleft in the red bluffs. A narrow valley of sagebrush hills fluttered into pine slopes and snow-covered mountains. A few miles on, the valley broadened again, and pink and orange badlands rose from the north side of the valley in spiky and rough edges that seemed to change in form and color as the sun ducked in and out of the clouds. Always the Wind River meandered through the valley, sometimes close to the road, sometimes as if on the other side of a large, high-ceilinged room. It reflected the sun like broken mirrors.

Evening had fallen when I walked over a rise and could see that Dubois was a one-street kind of place. Between the town and me, dirt roads radiated from the pavement into the mountains. Farther on, the river rolled through the middle of ground leveled and strewn with gravel. A log-home builder had a house half constructed, without windows, just off the side of the road. A small truck drove up and stopped in the driveway to this barren piece of ground before pulling out on the road. I was nearly to town when the same truck pulled up, and a man with a friendly, sunburned face asked if I wanted a ride.

"Dubois is right there, isn't it?" I said, pointing to the town.

"About three-quarters of a mile."

It seemed a ridiculous distance to drive, especially since I had walked thirty miles already. But the man and the woman he was with had already begun making room for my gear among chainsaws, woodworking tools, drill bits, and drills in the bed of the truck.

"You're really going out of your way," I said.

"Well it's all right," the man said. "I've backpacked before." He handed the heavy tools of their trade to the woman, who was very slight. Both were dressed in jeans with down vests over heavy work shirts. They wore tattered and dirty ball caps. They were ruddy people with strong, adroit hands. When they had moved the last drill bit, they stood, adjusted their caps, and waited for me to make a move.

We crammed into the cab of their tiny truck. Tim and Mary said that the level, desolate ground I'd seen had once been a large saw-mill and lumberyard, and then turned to other uses. They built log homes there. Tim bought trees at Forest Service auctions, felled and trimmed them, and paid a man to haul the logs back to the "yard." There he and Mary stripped bark, cut and stacked the logs, and inventoried them. When someone wanted a house, they sat down with them to find what they wanted and then to design it. Plans finished, Tim and Mary took logs they needed from their stores, and cut, split, and notched them appropriately. They built the house first at the yard to make sure all parts fit perfectly. In the meantime they worked with an architect and excavating company to prepare a building site for the home they were assembling and crafting at the yard. Once both house and site was completed, they disassembled the house and transported it in pieces to the building site and put it all back together again. Tim had studied various ways of fitting logs together and had settled on a method that allowed him to build tight structures without chinking or mortar. Tim and Mary, I noticed, were fit for the work. Tim was strong and round-shouldered. Mary was tiny compared to the large tools but no less sturdy.

They let me out on the main street, an avenue of log buildings and clapboard facades, and said they'd be back in a few minutes. If I wasn't at the drugstore, where I needed to pick up some things, they'd find me. I didn't doubt it, since I could see both ends of town from the roofed boardwalk before a row of shops. There seemed to be enough motels and hotels to raise the population of the town three times on a good night. People streamed in and out of the Rustic Bar, a big log building across the street. A man drove a stagecoach up to the boardwalk, where I was leaned against a wooden post.

"You here for the party?" he said.

"Well, I am now."

"You ought to go up to the chariot races," he said, smiling. "You know Ben Hur kind of stuff."

"Big wheel spikes?"

"Nope."

"Charlton Heston?"

"No. It's not that ghastly," he said. "But still a damn good time."

When Tim and Mary returned, we walked across the street to

the Rustic into the middle of a huge, wood-timbered hall. Balloons and banners hung from the vast timbers holding the roof. The lights were low except for those on the stage, where a woman stood amid a jumble of band equipment and announced raffle ticket numbers. A sea of people crowded the hall. They were dressed in colorful western shirts with sterling buttons, pewter and silver bolo ties, boots, bandanas, and jeans. Some wore short vests emblazoned across the backs with names of singing and musical organizations, sports and shooting clubs, and ranches and homesteads. The biggest attraction was a potluck dinner. Spread across a multitude of tables, it was the largest I'd ever seen, and I was delighted. Potluck was my favorite cuisine. A canopy of cowboy hats fluttered around the long tables of food. Barbecued ribs stacked high started the line, followed by platters of roast beef, potatoes (mashed, French fried, baked, and twice-baked). Down the line were oceans of vegetables and salads, and a cornucopia of cakes, cupcakes, cheesecakes, brownies, ice cream, and fruit.

Our little group stood among lines of hand shakers. Everyone greeted everyone else by name. We sat at paper-covered tables where people shouted at each other across plates and bottles and cups. Mary explained over the noise that the party was the town reunion. People from all over the country that had once lived in Dubois came back for the annual event, dragging hundreds of tourists with them. It was the biggest event of the summer, and of the year, in the tiny town.

As we began to dig into the piles of food on our paper plates, music began. Dancers two-stepped and strolled across the dance floor. People made for the front door to get to the chariot races, the next round of which was to start soon. Mary offered to take me there, but I declined, seeing that she was just being nice. She and Tim still had the shocked and stunned look that comes from hard work for long hours in brisk air and full sun. Only these two people who'd peeled and hauled logs all day matched my own gluttony. We ate and ate, drank gallons of iced tea. Tim and Mary introduced me to tens of people until our collective fatigue, compounded by mounds of good eats, ushered us, sleepy and numb, out the door.

Tim and Mary's place, Spring Ranch, was on a piece of land saddled between the foothills and the Wind River. Rough planks and logs sat at the foot of one of the hills. Pine trees, willows, and tall grass grew between the houses. Tim and Mary's two-room cabin was in the back, highest up on the hill. Their living space was spare: pine-plank table, three wooden chairs, a roll-top desk, a wood-burning stove, and a large, antique gas range. A window in the living room/kitchen gave a view of the ranch buildings and pink badlands across the valley.

We talked late into the night. Mary and Tim's log home business was a struggle, but with the inexpensive rent on the cabin, and building opportunities in Jackson about fifty miles away, they made ends meet. I walked outside to puff on a cigar and stood on a small bridge just past the door. A brisk stream running from the spring for which the ranch was named flowed there. It smelled of rosemary and reminded me of mountain freshets I had pulled young trout from. The light from the cabin flickered off its surface.

When I woke the next morning, Mary was cooking piles of bacon, eggs, and potatoes, and then laid them out on plates on the big plank table. The wind was up. Willows lashed the window. But the day was fine and brisk. Sharon, the owner of Spring Ranch and curator of the local museum, joined us. She was a self-assured woman of strong opinions who didn't hesitate to offer them. She dominated the conversation.

In the afternoon, Tim, Mary, Sharon, and I drove up to an alpine lake in the mountains that spread across a rocky, pine-stippled valley. The mountains climbed in sharp, steep slopes out of the water, up red and brown feldspar-laden boulders and cliffs, emblazoned with hundreds of petroglyphs. The sun dipped below the mountain and the valley began to grow dark. We walked, reading pictures and marks chipped into the surfaces of the rocks and bluffs—turtle-shaped humans with rays emanating from eyes and fingers, mythical and realistic animals with human-shaped heads, and spaceship-like ciphers and helmeted figures. Rivers of wavy lines and curious dots streamed across the rocks. Lichens obfuscated some of the pictures. Others looked to have been made only yesterday. Sharon treated the marked stones with an odd devotion. She talked in low tones around them as if the visions of the ancients would have terrible repercussions for lowly moderns who questioned or defaced them. I thought the artists might have been restless and bored Indians waiting for the next hunt, which, to me, increased the beauty or meaning of their work. We ended the day at a pizza restaurant in Dubois, from which we all retired drowsy and lethargic from too much good food.

The next morning was crisp and clear, with fluffs of billowy clouds. I took off from Tim and Mary's early, as they had a full day of work ahead of them. Outside of town, wind whistled up the narrow reaches of the mountains. The highway rose higher and higher through the beaver pond–dotted valley, lush and green, between pine-covered hills and rocky crags. When I finally stopped toward late afternoon, I'd walked about twenty-five miles. I sat on the edge of the pavement resting before I wandered up into the forest to make camp. My eyes caught two people walking across the valley. They disappeared in the cleft of the hill below but soon appeared on the embankment. The two young men introduced themselves. The tall and lanky kid with long, blond hair was Darin. Around his neck were amulets with marijuana leaves stamped in relief. He was calm and gentle. The other, Bevan, had dark, cropped hair. He was no less skinny, but not as tall. He was more jumpy than Darin and kept his hands darting in and out of his pockets. Both wore T-shirts and baggy pants and strong leather hiking boots. They were fifteen-year-old high schoolers from Laramie, staying with Darin's father for the summer. They said they had seen me walking from their cabin at the end of the valley and came up to meet me.

We sat on the side of the road staring out into the valley below Togwotee Pass. The Wind River Mountains rose out of the valley to graceful, snow-covered peaks; the Absarokas climbed beyond the tree line, columns and stair-steps of granite. Occasionally a truck passed on the road behind us. The boys were intelligent and hopeful, full of dreams. And they were ambitious. Both said they wanted to go to college, and that they were "activists." Their conversation was filled with environmentalist, Earth First!–tinted anarchy, which endeared them to me. Darin hoped to show nature's truths to urban and ranch people by becoming a pack-trip outfitter. Bevan was undecided on his future but leaned toward environmental science. His purpose, he said, was to rebuild and restore what he believed people had spoiled.

As the shadows grew long, the valley came alive with deer and elk, and birds flitting around in the sagebrush. River and wildflower alike seemed to sway in the breeze. Cabins stood about a mile distant in the trees at the foot of the Wind River Range. The boys pointed out where they lived. The houses looked quaint and rustic in the evening light. The coolness of the evening filtered into my bones, and I told the boys I had to move on.

"We have to go home for dinner now, anyhow," Darin said. "But if you don't mind, we'll walk you to a spot about a mile up the road where you could camp. If you decide to stay there, we'll come back and spend some more time."

"Yeah," Bevan said. "There's some other kids who wouldn't mind sitting around the campfire tonight."

Alpine woods stretched in every direction from the road. Soon foothills and bluffs obscured our view of the mountains. Darin led us off the pavement and down a dirt road that ended near the river. The two walked into the woods and were gone.

Mounds of river stone hid the campsite from the road. Mats of pine needles and flood refuse made the ground soft and springy underfoot. The air was still, and a hush fell over the place after the boys left. I made a circle of stones and gathered wood for a fire. The sun's rays crawled up the trunks of trees next to the campsite. In no time, it seemed, Bevan and Darin came through the trees with their friends, Audrey and Danny, and Darin's sister Helena. We sat around the fire, gathering closer to the flames as the evening cooled.

"It's good up here in the summer," Darin said. He was burning a stick and drawing on the flat surfaces of the rocks around the fire.

"It's better than Laramie," Helena said. She fiddled with the locks of her brown hair. She was younger than Darin, but not by much.

"What's so bad about Laramie?" I asked.

"It's a small place with a small mind," Bevan said.

"Not nearly as small as Sheridan," Danny chimed in.

"Aren't all the towns in Wyoming small?" I said. "I went to grad school in Laramie, and it was a slow place. But it's like a lot of other places its size. There aren't many people in Wyoming but they seem to be interesting."

"Yeah, interesting only goes so far," Audrey said. She was a gentle, soft-spoken girl, no less determined than the others. "When you're around those people every day, they aren't so interesting."

"Fair enough," I said.

"Here, at least, you can run off into the woods whenever you like," she said.

"So there's not much for people your age if you don't like fly fishing and camping, cross country skiing, ice skating, and rock climbing?" I said.

They looked at each other. We all had sticks now, burning the ends and drawing pictures on the rocks and in the dirt, stylized birds, moose, elk, people, cars, and televisions. The firelight shone orange on the kids' faces. They all had on down parkas or vests and wore sturdy hiking boots. The clear night brought all the stars forth, and the sky beyond the trees was like glowing chiffon. The sounds of water rushing over stones and wind in the valley washed over us. The sticks made scraping sounds. I thought that maybe this was the origin of the petroglyphs I'd seen the day before. I started working on a real masterpiece.

"Maybe you've seen something of the world that people around you haven't," I said. Wise beyond my years, I was. I didn't know what these kids wanted or needed to hear. I tried to remember morsels of life lessons I had learned from movies so I could put them into conversation, sound smart, and keep conversation going. I liked listening to them.

"Fourteen and fifteen's a tough age," I said. "You're really men and women, but there's more you have to learn. At least that's the way I understand it."

"Who wants to wait?" Danny said.

"You don't have to," I said. "Your high schools have exchange programs, and if they don't you can find them. It will get you out of Wyoming and out of the country and teach you something besides. Your parents will be happy you didn't quit high school to shoot drugs."

Darin said he had already thought of an exchange program with schools in Sweden, "where they have some of the same outdoor stuff we have."

The talk rose and fell for over three hours. Sometimes it was quiet and I could hear the elk whistling across the valley. Other times the group erupted in laughter, the sound echoing under the trees and across the river. Bevan gave me a garnet he'd found in the river when he was a child. "I carried ever since," he said. "But I want you to have it." I put it in my pocket with what was becoming a mound of lucky rocks.

Long after dark we gathered our sticks and threw them in the fire, and the kids disappeared back into the woods. I climbed into my sleeping bag and watched the fire die to a flicker. Stars lay over the crook of sky in the branches above, like a silken blanket. I was sore and tired. But the ground and my bed felt good. I breathed in the smells of smoke and river and pine trees, thinking home was a place everyone had to find, even if it was right beneath one's feet.

After the flames had died, I remembered that there were bears in the woods, but I was too tired to worry about them. I closed my eyes. As sleep washed over me, I figured that if I was eaten in the night, the images on the stones might give someone something to wonder about until the next rain washed them away.

15

JACKSON

"Now you know, and that's somethin'"

THE SUN CAST bony shadows through the branches of a lodge-pole pine. I lay under that tree listening to the creek and watching my breath, trying to ignore the Midwestern work ethic gnawing my insides. Fortunately I had an excuse to stay in the warm sleeping bag. A moose had splashed around in the river all night and was still chewing on reeds at the stream bank. I wasn't about to get up and run the risk of pissing it off. Instead I lay motionless and stared at the sky through the boughs, and took long, deep breaths of crisp mountain air. About the time the sun ducked behind a bird's nest high in the crown of the tree, the moose—looking more like a moss-brown barrel hiked up on sticks than Bullwinkle—had picked its way across the stream and away into the pines.

I rinsed my hair and washed my face in the stream. The water shimmered in the sun and was so cold it made my scalp ache. After a quick look around to make sure the area was free of people and moose, I stripped and eased over the smooth, round stones into the water up to my shins. Becoming bolder, I dipped in to the neck as quickly as I could. The cold forced the breath out of me and bounced me back up like a jack-in-the-box. Then I bobbed up and down until I could sit on the rocky bottom. My breathing was shallow and quick and I waited patiently until I could relax and ease in that first deep breath. All the while I kept thinking that if the moose came back I'd be stuck. There was no way for me, warm or cold, naked or clothed, to outrun an angry moose.

When I finally hit pavement, there was a spring in my step—most probably from a good night's sleep and the alfresco dip in glacial water. Nothing mattered now except the view of the land from my next step. I had no thoughts. My head was free of vocalizations and visualizations. I'd had a similar feeling as I had walked away from the frigid Dinwoody Lake. There was only walking and breathing, pavement and landscape. It was as if I had ceased to exist except for the exhilaration that came from sharp, acute perception.

The valley wound along the Wind River, higher and higher toward Togwotee Pass. The air was so clear that it magnified the color and definition of the landscape. Rain clouds drifted over the top of the saw-toothed Absarokas. When I reached the pass about nine miles from where I camped, I was ready to doff the pack and sit for a while in the valley between jagged gray peaks. I stopped in an aspen grove and heard the sound of water splashing across a nearby meadow of wildflowers and tall grass. I found the stream bubbling from a culvert, where I sat and watched the water flow across a small concrete landing and off to a nearby brook. I dropped a pinecone into the foam and watched it skid across the concrete, disappear in the darkness below the culvert, then pop up downstream. Then a piece of wood. A small rock slid slowly across the concrete and dropped away.

"Hey! You!"

I looked over toward the road, where a red-headed man stood

beside a brown and beat-up pickup, his hands cupped around his mouth. He waved. As I came closer I could see wrinkles spread across his scrunched brow. He was dressed in jeans and boots, a pink T-shirt, and denim vest. Muscular and slender, he wasn't a vision of health so much as of hard work. He had a ruddy and dark laborer's tan and baseball-mitt hands. He looked very tired. A cloud of steam rose from the front of his truck. Two milk jugs stood on the pavement by his feet.

"Kinda got a problem," he said as I walked up. "By chance, you know where there's any water around here?"

"I was almost sitting in some a second ago."

"I'm Mike," he extended a rough hand. "I think I need water. Know anythin' about radiators?"

"A little."

I poked my head under the hood. He told me he didn't have any trouble with the truck down in the valley, but the engine had overheated on the approach to the pass. Puddles in the frame below the engine indicated he'd lost a lot of fluid through the radiator's overflow hose.

"Sounds like the thermostat's stuck," I said. "Coming up this steep grade probably overheated the engine. You have to let it cool a while. I have to get my pack over by the stream. I'll get some water."

I picked up the jugs and went to get my pack and some water from the culvert. Mike fiddled with some electrical cables, another source of trouble. He offered me a ride. Two gallons of water later, we were over the pass and down the other side.

"I just got a job in Jackson driving tourists around," he said. His thin, brown hair fluttered in the wind through the window. Around the curves he guided the truck with hands firm on the wheel, arms stiff and straight. "I don't know if I'm looking forward to it as much as I am bumming around these woods. We don't have nothing like this in Illinois. That's where I come from. I worked construction.

Finish carpenter. But I know some folks up here and they told me there was work here. I thought I'd give it a try."

He wasn't young. I guessed he was about forty. "So you just up and left?" I said.

He raised his eyebrows and rubbed his forehead with his long fingers. "Man, you get right to the point, doncha?"

"Sorry," I said. "I'm just curious."

"I kinda wear it, though, don't I?" he said. "It was my wife. She left with our daughter a couple of months ago. She won't let me see the kid—she's thirteen. Won't divorce me so I can. With a divorce, I'd have rights. But she won't, so I thought I'd come up here for a while. Only problem is the place is full of carpenters, so I thought I'd try something else a while and got this job."

"This is beautiful country to a Midwesterner," I said. "You may never go back."

"Sure I will," he said, taking a deep breath. "Mountains become like Illinois farms after a while. That kid means everything to me. You got a kid?"

"I suppose you're right," I said, wondering just how my daughter was doing. She was probably doing just fine—nary a thought of her father in her head. "I have a daughter. Greatest thing that ever happened to me."

I was also thinking about just how long it would take the mountains to become as ordinary as an Illinois farm. Maybe if I had grown up here, I might think such grandeur was run-of-the-mill. But as a Midwesterner, I once found everything outside the Midwest astonishing. Now, however, because of people I'd met, even the most common things back home were becoming extraordinary.

Mike cleared his throat. I could tell he was loosening the lump he had gotten from talking about his daughter. Any mother or father could understand the kind of emotions Mike was talking about. And they hurt.

"I'll go back anyway," he said. "I don't know how long a guy can make it up here. You haven't seen how people like us have to live in Jackson, have you?"

"I've never been to Jackson, only heard of it."

"Well, if you get in there, you'll see pretty quick. I live in a bunk-house in the center of town. A bunch of guys just like me. And none of us got a pot to piss in. The tourists don't see that kind of thing. They might think everyone in town is rich. But you got rich and then you got everyone else, and that's most everyone."

Mike dropped me at a Forest Service campground in the valley below the pass. I walked up through the stands of pines behind the campground. About a mile and half up, the dirt road broke into a clearing in the pines. A storm settled into the valley and the sky clouded quickly. I set up my lean-to and threw a rope over a tree limb about a hundred feet away from my camp to hang my pack out of the reach of bears. The rain started slowly and fell steadily after a while. A hush settled into the woods and made the forest seem like a big, calm, and quiet room. An occasional car on the highway below swooshed by. Night came on quickly, and after a few minutes of reading I fell asleep with a book on my chest. A bear shuffling by my lean-to woke me later. It sniffed and clawed trees for about an hour. Thunder rumbled through the peaks and echoed up the valley. The next morning bear tracks wound in circles in the mud under the pack swinging from the tree limb.

I packed and made my way down to the highway. Storm twilight still covered the valley, beyond which the Tetons spread out in a long, serrated line. But the sky soon cleared and the sun shimmered like diamonds on the wet sagebrush, wildflowers, and grass.

A Forest Service ranger offered me a ride into Jackson. It was out of my way by some sixty miles, as I was headed to Yellowstone. But the ranger's mom was visiting. He wanted to take her to dinner and then to a rodeo. I was invited to ride with them and meet them at the rodeo arena. I'd have time to take a look around and do laundry while they were at dinner, and they would get me back on the road to Yellowstone after the event.

We drove through the Snake River Valley toward the Tetons. Stands of yellow balsam, blue lupine, and purple larkspur broke the deep green of sagebrush. The valley widened under the Tetons and spilled through a narrow crook in the mountains into Jackson. It wasn't a quaint spot. An airport boomed in the Teton Valley beyond the fences of the National Elk Refuge. Trophy homes laced the slopes approaching the town. In town, wealth and sophistication oozed from elaborately renovated houses. Even the smallest yards had been landscaped. The heart of town looked like a carnival. Boardwalks and sidewalks were busy with tourists, who dragged packs of children. Flashing and neon signs blazed above gem and souvenir shops; rafting, ski, adventure, and expedition shops; and art galleries heavy with pictures of ducks, trout, and elk.

The ranger and his mom dropped me at the Laundromat. The place was filled with people in ragged clothes. I knew that Jackson had long been a tourist destination where most jobs were in restaurants, gas stations, and ski areas in winter and dude ranches in the summer. At first I had looked forward to the Laundromat, thinking it would be a good place to watch people and strike up a conversation. But for the whir and hum of the machines and the rhythmic snap of clothes tumbling in driers, the place was silent. The people sitting in the formed fiberglass chairs looked tired, haggard, and overworked. They were unhappy, unfriendly, and seemed to have too much on their minds.

I walked up toward the rodeo arena, past the art galleries, tourist shops, and restaurants. The tourists looked as if they had all just showered. The whole town, it seemed, smelled of dryer sheets, diesel, and pine needles. After dusk had fallen, Venus was bright among the few stars that appeared in the deepening blue. The arena's lights seemed bright as daylight. The people in the stands were tourists, their clothes and the way they sat together in families distinguishing them from the locals who worked the refreshment stands, the animal pits, and the ticket booths.

I walked before the stands, looking for the ranger and his mother, but didn't find them. I tried to focus on the rodeo but didn't find it as entertaining as I had imagined. Billed and hyped as authentic cowboy West, it seemed more like a carnival sideshow. There was plenty of action. The competitions intrigued and excited the spectators but bored the locals. Young women in Annie Oakley blouses and skirts and stiff hats roped calves and raced horses around barrels. "These girls are real cowgirls," the announcer said with what seemed like too much "gen-u-ine" Wyoming twang. "Born and bred on Wyoming's fine land. These are the best of them, folks. Real girls of the real West." At a refreshment stand, I bought a cola and a candy bar from a pair of teens who were discussing characters in a television show and listening to LL Cool J on a boom box.

During the bronco busting, the horses bucked most of their riders airborne within a few seconds. The young men landed on their butts, backs, and heads, and then spider-crawled away as clowns shielded them from agitated ponies. One kid of about seventeen, said to be the best in the bareback competition, rode his horse well out of the gate. The horse started a rhythm of kicking out with both legs and running as if thinking of what to do next. The horse took shorter and shorter gallops between kicks until it was in frenzy, kicking and kicking again. After a few seconds of this, the boy began to flail atop his mount. He fell over the side, but his hand did not come loose from the rope that passed behind the horse's front legs and over its back. The kid ran backward beside the horse. His hand remained tied tightly between the horse's shoulders and his arm became unnaturally twisted. The horse began to run, faster and faster, kicking higher and more furiously. The boy couldn't keep his feet under him.

The rodeo master and his men pulled their mounts behind the kid's horse and made chase. The clowns played Keystone Cops, dodging the angry equine. Everyone in the ring was trying to grab the horse's bridle, but it pulled its head away and eluded the men in a series of turns and bucks. Soon it ran faster and faster around perimeter of the ring, breaking randomly into a kick or a flying twist. The boy was dragged to one side, trying to keep himself from under the horse's feet. But he could not stay up, and the horse's hooves began to pound down on his legs. The boy sagged further, and within seconds looked like a rag doll flapping from the side of the horse. The mounted men's effort to corral the horse drove it closer to the fence. Hooves fell on the boy as often as the ground. The horse stopped bucking altogether and broke into a dead run, the boy's head banging against the rungs of the fence. Bong, bong, bong.

When the mounted men finally lassoed the horse, the kid was knocked out. They pulled alongside the horse and struck its nose and face with fists. Finally a man leapt from his horse onto the errant mount's back. With one hand on the back of its head and the other around its nose, he wrenched horse's head around until it fell, punching its hooves into the dust. One of the clowns produced a knife and cut the rope that held the boy to the horse. The men, now all off their mounts, dragged the boy over the horse's belly, laid him flat in the dust, and folded his hands on his chest. The kid's red hair and freckles highlighted the pallor in his cheeks. He looked like a child asleep in the cold.

The crowd, loud and cheering seconds before, became silent as a vacuum. With the horse hobbled and restrained, the men pummeled it with their fists, as if to get back at it. Spectators began to gather their things and stream off the bleachers. I grabbed my pack and joined them.

The stands were nearly empty by the time the ambulance arrived.

Spectators pushed past the gate. Clerks at the concession stands, which all faced away from the arena, stood with their hands on the counters wondering what had happened. And I never did find the ranger.

I walked out to the split-rail fence and sat on it, hitching my feet to the bottom rung. I felt horrible for the kid, who just moments before had been looking forward to a trophy and a cash prize. I hated myself for my part in putting that kid in danger. I had bought the ticket and been one of the spectators. I had been a part of it. "Goddamn it," I said aloud, balling my fists in frustration. "Goddamn it, what a shitty thing. What a goddamn shitty thing." In my mind I saw his head banging against the fence. Having myself been battered and lacerated plenty of times before, I had felt the blows to the kid's head. I knew what it was to have my arm twisted into hairy spaghetti. I hated the people who owned the arena and the show. I hated the tourists and their kids. I wanted to go home and be with my daughter. Who was I kidding? Traveling across the country? To do what? To do what?

Great sobs welled up in my chest and I sat on that fence and cried for a long, long time. Silence had fallen over the arena. A few kids walked through the stands picking up trash. Others were cleaning the dung from the competition and holding areas. After a while I hoisted myself from the fence and wandered through the streets, not knowing or caring where I might end up for the night. I couldn't stop crying. I walked out to the main commercial strip among the restaurants, gas stations, and convenience stores, trying to find some solace in the light. But the neon and mercury lamps did me no good and I pushed back into the dark residential streets. I don't know how long I wandered, but it was well past 11:00 p.m. when I came by a motel with a vacancy sign burning. Running my fingers through my hair and pulling my hands across my eyes, I walked into the office. A woman who looked to be in her late forties sat behind a wooden counter. She took off her glasses and put down the book she was reading.

"I have a room for sixty-five," she said, standing and pulling a card from behind the counter.

"Thanks," I said. "But that's a little steep. Have a good evening." I moved toward the door.

"But where will you stay?" she said, putting her hands flat on the counter. "All the motels are filled. I think I have the last room in town."

"I don't know."

"I'll give you the room for twenty. I want to turn in."

She smiled at me as I filled in the card.

"No car?" she said, looking down over my hand.

"I'm on foot."

"Well, good for you. Somethin' got you upset, honey?"

"Just saw a kid get killed or worse up at the rodeo, and I never found my ride out of town."

"Ever seen a rodeo before?" she said.

"Nope."

"Well they're all kind of like that, you know. People get it all the time. That's why I don't go. Can't stand watchin' it."

"I wish I felt that way before I went tonight," I said.

"Well, now you know, and that's somethin'. You need anything, dial zero. Rings right up next to my bed."

I wished her a good night. The lights in the office went out as I walked up stairs to the room off the second-floor balcony. It was a relief when the key clicked the lock and the door fell open to a spacious, clean, and comfortable room. I tried to find comfort in Walt Whitman. *Fuck Walt,* I said to myself after a few minutes of seeing words on a page and not being able to read them. *Fuck you. Fuck you and your hearty "I love America," "I love life," "I love people" bullshit.* I threw the book against the wall, turned off the light, and lay down on the bed. Shadows danced on the ceiling. I cried again when I thought of the bareback rider, the way he looked so much like a cold, little boy as he was lying next to that horse. My sinuses felt stuffed with sand, and my insides were heavy, as if I had a hangover. After a time my anger and emotion faded into numbness. I parted the curtain and looked out over Jackson for a long time. I tried to convince myself that life was tough. These things happen. There was no currency in worrying about them.

16

TETON VILLAGE, TETON NATIONAL PARK,
YELLOWSTONE NATIONAL PARK

"It's not all about you"

I PICKED WALT up off the floor the next morning and dusted him off. I read the opening pages of the "Preface, 1855" from *Leaves of Grass* and flipped through "Democratic Vistas" and "Specimen Days." I had been sore about the kid the night before, and in that moment Whitman seemed a mockery of the boy and what he had gone through. I had been hurt and had wanted Whitman, the rodeo master, and the owners of the rodeo to feel it. I wanted those spectators and all the purveyors and consumers of violence and animal cruelty to feel it. I wanted that boy to be whole and healthy, and I couldn't make it so. I couldn't change the past or ignore it. At the same time, because I was hurt didn't mean I could disregard, as Whitman had not, the facets of human beings that *made* them human. Ugliness was part of them, a part of me. The good and bad, harmful and helpful, glorious and tawdry made us beautiful. No one could control it. These, I thought, were the most painful of truths to face.

Reluctantly I closed the book and headed to a diner close to the motel. I dropped my pack behind the door and pulled up to the counter for coffee. It was a generic place: Formica counter, a pie rack in a glass case, a few booths along a window that ran the length of the dining room. The middle-age waiter, named Hank, was friendly. He asked if I was "the straggler who drug in late."

"I suppose so," I said. For all its faults, Jackson was a small town. At the time I had no idea how small.

"I saw your pack as I's walking up to get my morning get-up-and-go," he said. "My friend works-up-at-the-motel told me about you coming in after the rodeo. Said you was upset about the kid that got hurt. Tough thing about that boy. I heard you lost your ride."

"Yeah," I said. "I'm headed to Yellowstone."

"And you'll get there. Don't let this sort of thing hold you back."

Hank set a plate of hash browns and some fruit in front of me. As I ate, I went over the dreams I'd had. Evil presences in the dark. Giants towering over the woods. Toothy mouths, like those of bears, opening in the ground below my feet. I was trying to figure out where the images came from and what was bothering me. I thought about the anger and hatred that boiled up so suddenly, as well as the abject loneliness and fear I felt. Some part of me was still frightened at letting go and feeling guilty for having left job and kid to strike out on a new, unproven path. Would I succeed? What exactly was I looking for? I thought I knew when I struck out on the road. But here in Jackson, among the contradictions of wealth and squalor, tourist and worker, and visitor and native, as well as my own emotions, I didn't know anymore. I knew I didn't want to go home. But I didn't know how to move forward. As I finished my coffee, I settled on letting things happen as I had for awhile now. I'd see what the next step brought.

As I was getting change from Hank, a tall, blond man came in on his lunch break, took the stool next to mine, and ordered a salami-on-rye to go. A moustache canopied his toothy smile. I detected South African in his speech.

"I'm a bit of a traveler myself," he said. "But my girlfriend and I got here about a year ago and haven't left."

"They tell me work is hard to find," I said, not knowing what else to say.

"And it is," he said. "I'm a boat captain by trade. This time of year, I would normally be running tour boats in the Caribbean. Catamarans and trimarans, big boats for tourists, you know. Weekend adventures on the ocean with full gourmet meals, deep-sea fishing, island hopping, that sort of thing. But now I drill holes in elk antlers for a guy here in town. I bolt them together and wire them into chandeliers, if you can believe that. It's big business around here. Restaurants want them, hotels, motels, you name it."

Elk-antler chandeliers aside, I was still on the ocean.

"How did you wind up this far from the sea?"

"Long story."

Hank set Roland's sandwich on the counter. As he stood, Roland offered to put me up. He lived in the attic of the health clinic at Teton Village, a ski resort town. He told me where he worked and asked me to meet him later.

I walked toward the center of town. The sun was out full, the sky empty and deep blue. I breathed deep the clean, crisp air. Many of the residences along the way coupled as businesses—tropical fish, ski sales and repair, snow machine and auto repair. The streets were bare, however, until I entered the business district downtown. There people flooded the sidewalks. They were mostly the scrubbed-and-powdered tourist variety I had noticed the day before. Overweight men and women with white legs and floppy hats walked along with bevies of children with ice cream and chocolate smeared across their faces. Elderly men and women, jacketed and protected against the sun, dawdled in front of shop windows.

At an outdoor equipment store, I bought a cheap fly rod and some angling supplies and sat on a bench on the roofed boardwalk outside. Hundreds of people streamed into the stores. Many were eating ice cream cones or drinking coffee out of small cups. Kids had plastic cups with straws; some ate hot dogs or dug in bags for chips. I tied leader to floating line, daydreaming of pulling cutthroat out of a creek flowing through pine forest. A man sat down next to me and broke my thought. He was fidgety and nervous. He wore a canvas hat and a camouflage army jacket and pants. He was rumpled and didn't seem very happy. He squinted through thick prescription sunglasses and puffed obsessively on a hand-rolled cigarette. He reminded me of the Unabomber. When it was clear he wanted conversation but didn't know how to start, I introduced myself. His name was David.

"Yeah, I live in my van with my cats," he said after a minute. He pulled a pack of generic cigarettes from his jacket pocket and lit one of the flattened and crooked smokes.

"How does that work?" I said.

"Sometimes I park in town or go out into the national forest." He shifted his gaze to the ground, leaned forward, and hung his hands between his legs. "Sometimes I just drive."

"Where do you work?"

"I'm a vet with a disability check. So I got hospital and gas taken care of. I eat peanut butter most of the time but also a lot of fruit." He had a curious habit of hardening Ts and Ds, as if he were an irritated grade-school teacher. It made words pop out of his mouth.

"What's the van like?"

"It's crowded. But I have a bed for me and for the cats. I have my canoe on the top and stove stowed in the back."

"You could go anywhere, why stay in Jackson?"

He lifted his hand and swept an open palm over the wood rail next to the bench, indicating the scenery.

"It's good, but if you had to, would you go anywhere else?" I said.

"Leaving home isn't that easy."

David had the quirks of someone who spent too much time alone. He looked out at the world through squinted eyes. His face twitched. He rolled his index finger around in his nose and sucked his teeth. He believed his own stories, fawned over his cats when he was nowhere near them, and smoked one cigarette after another. He seemed troubled and bitter, almost as if he needed to be.

"I'll be headed up to the Tetons tomorrow," he said. "It'd be great if you came along for some fishing up on Jenny Lake," he said, pointing to my new fishing rig. "We'll camp and I'll take you up to Yellowstone. You have to buy the gas, though."

"How'd you know I was going to Yellowstone?" I said.

"Word gets around."

"I guess it does."

"Come on, whaddya say," he said.

"Well, we'll see. Where do I get a hold of you?"

"I'll be here tomorrow around the same time," he said and stood up and walked away, trailing curls of blue smoke.

Shops and tourists kept my attention until it was time to meet Roland. I walked down a line of houses with manicured lawns past the house he had described. He shouted from the open garage door and awakened me from my meditation. When I walked into the open garage, he was milling the ends of a set of antlers on a bench grinder. He showed me some of his work, in which he took great pride.

"It's pretty specific stuff," he said, holding up a spidery tangle of antlers solidly screwed together "Pieces like this don't work just anywhere. Nice as they might be, I think it's all quite kitschy unless hung in a dark wood room with mountains in the window."

The sky had become a deeper blue in the afternoon. I wandered around on a square of grass set with picnic benches across the street from the house until Roland bounded out of the garage ten minutes later.

We drove out of Jackson down a two-lane road that wound through dark stands of pine. It turned out that Roland knew David when I told him that David had invited me to join him in the Tetons.

"He's quite a piece," Roland said. "A little crazy. But I think he'd be good for a night of camping." Roland said he would drive up to visit David and me in the park and possibly spend the night.

The sun had sunk behind the mountains and the forest took on the halo of alpenglow. Teton Village was a collection of high-rise hotels, log homes, and condominiums at the base of a ski area. Large swaths of bare ground with spines of spindly lifts climbed the mountain. Roland and his mate Michelle had a small studio apartment on the second story of the clinic. A kitchen area stood to one side, with an open dining and leisure area next to a sliding glass door that lead to a balcony. A ladder rose from a small kitchen and living space to a loft that held a bed. They set me up for the night in the studio next door, whose resident was gone for the summer. The view from the porch took in the entire valley beneath the Tetons.

We sat at a small, neat table over a dinner of salad, homemade bread, and hard sausage. Michelle had poured cream and honey over blueberries for dessert—coincidentally my favorite. Both Michelle and Roland were from South Africa. Roland had been a boat captain in the Caribbean for a number of years when he met Michelle. She was the ship's nurse among a crew of young Afrikaners who had sailed a leaky boat across the Atlantic to Florida under an incompetent, drunken captain. In a sort of mutiny, they stayed ashore in Florida, refusing to take the boat further. The captain was fired, but before the crew could take off under a new leader the boat's owner went broke. She and the others were left standing on a south Florida beach without money or food.

"Those of us who could called home for money for the flight back to South Africa," she said. "But I didn't have that."

"Money or home?" I asked.

"Both," she said.

She met Roland on a boat dock in Miami. They fell for each other and she sailed to Trinidad with him. There he sailed tourists on big trimarans, and she worked at a hospital. After the tourist season they went on vacation in the States. They wound up in Jackson and stayed. Roland was tall and slender, his angular frame set on towering, powerful legs. His long hands were long and precise. Michelle was attractive, with tightly curled reddish-brown hair that fell over her shoulders in solid waves and framed her wide face and deep-blue eyes. She smiled nearly all the time. While he fashioned lamps from antlers, she worked at a clinic in Jackson, one of the few well-paying trades for working people in or around town. Though they were here temporarily, they seemed quite happy.

We talked until well after dark. They hadn't turned on the lights, and candles illuminated the room in flickering light. Conversation slowed, and we turned our chairs to look out the sliding glass door that led to a small, wooden balcony. The alpine meadows and bogs across from the village were silver in the moonlight. The stars were like veils.

The next morning Roland and I walked around Teton Village. I kept expecting to look up at the hotels and condos and see life, movement, activity. But most were empty. The vacant buildings and empty streets were eerie and beautiful. Roland was a seafarer and had seen entire cities close down after the last days of the tourist season passed. I couldn't stop looking over my shoulder for movement, life of some kind besides Roland and me.

He seemed to sense my displacement. "I guess that's part of the reason I liked sailing," he said. "It's a seasonal business, ferrying tourists around on catamarans and yachts. It's good fun for a while, then it ends, and it all empties out. I get to do other things. And I can always go back because tourists always come back."

We sat at a table outside a small coffee shop with bagels and coffee.

"The way I figure it," he said, sipping his coffee from the paper cup, "Other people can do regular work. It's good for them, puts some structure in life. I get that out of steering a boat. I learn new things and see a lot of people. But it's always something of a show. People expect to see a boat captain, like in the movies. The guy with the hat who's in charge and who knows everything. He stands at the helm and doesn't have anything to do but steer a ship and marry people. But it's more than that. Managing the crew, if I have one, making sure the supplies are laid in, that the boat's safe, and that all the paperwork and accounting gets completed for the boat owner. None of that matters to the customer, nor should it. They want an ocean experience, you know, all deep blue sea and Moby Dick. It's a made-up thing that has something of the reality in it. Then, poof, they're gone and it's time for me to move on, to quit trying to fit into that thing people expect. In another year or so, we'll have enough to take off. We'll probably visit folks in Cape Town. But then I think it'll be back to the Caribbean and sailing for me, at least for that season."

I met David back in Jackson around the same time we'd seen each other the day before. There was something interesting about a man who lived in a van with cats, something about such a Spartan life and what drove him to live that way. But after we climbed into his van I was sorry. It was a sanitary disaster. The place had never been swept or wiped out. Piles of clothing, litter boxes, food in plastic crates stood in stacks about the vehicle. The smell of cat pee was stifling.

He had three dollars in his pocket. I bought food and firewood, and we drove aimlessly around Grand Teton National Park, looking for a place to camp. David said he had been an army intelligence officer. I could believe he was a veteran. But a spy? It sounded as if he had read too many Tom Clancy books. He kept saying tantalizing things: "You don't know what we're up against. I know. I've seen it." "If I told you the things I know, you wouldn't believe it. But I can't tell you." "You're lucky there are men like me protecting people like you."

"I've done things," he said.

"Well, David, what kind of things?" I said.

"Things. That's all you need to know."

"That's makes me feel safe and warm."

"You joke. But national security is no laughing matter."

When he wasn't repeating that he had "done things," he complained about the road, the park, and the weather. It was glorious outside his tiny, claustrophobic world. The day was cool and bright, the sky clear. We drove through expansive meadows filled with wildflowers, the mountains rising behind. But he couldn't see it. The beauty of the landscape could not ease his pain. He soon began to complain about people following his van too closely.

"These people don't learn how to drive, and bring their bad driving to Wyoming," he said. Between lighting hand-rolled smokes, he shouted into the rearview and side mirrors: "Gotdamnit!" "Asshole!" "Jackass!" It would have been funny had it not been so pointless—or even if he'd thrown a few decent, filthy cuss words into his low-grade vulgarity. Then he slammed down on the brakes suddenly. The car behind us swerved and rode up on the shoulder. "Get off my ass, jackass!"

"Hey! Hey!" I yelled. "Why don't you give it a rest? You're gonna give yourself a heart attack or kill somebody."

I felt sorry for the poor guy. He had one cassette tape and he played it over and over—mediocre, vapid stuff. He seemed to be trying to show me he knew all the lyrics. After a while he began to complain about how people were this way or that way, how silly most people were, about how screwed up the world was. After a half an hour of this, he proclaimed, "Everyone else is an asshole."

"Listen to yourself," I said. "If everyone but you's an asshole, who's not fitting in here? At some point, you have to realize who's the asshole before you hurt yourself. For instance, you know Roland and Michelle. Two nicer people you couldn't find. Right?"

"Yeah, they're good people." He sighed. "You just called me an asshole."

"You're acting like one. Everyone has good in them. There are lots of good people; you just have to open up to them, have a little faith." Listen to me, I thought.

"You're an asshole," he said resentfully.

I focused my attention out the window while David brooded. I thought I'd walk away from David and on to Yellowstone when I got the chance. But, selfishly, I wanted to be out on a lake in his canoe. When we finally settled into the campground at Colter Bay, we had a meal of peanut butter and bread. David had securely squirreled away the food I'd bought.

We finally set his small canoe on String Lake, a narrow lake under Mt. Moran. Forest carpeted the mountainside, except where avalanches had bared paths of rocky ground through them. The sun settled behind Moran in orange and yellow. The angles and stony sides of the peaks softened in the afterglow. The air was still and the lake tranquil and mirror-flat, revealing every nip a trout took at the surface. Despite having gotten wound up over David's behavior, I felt the tension flow out of my chest and shoulders as I breathed in the mountain air.

But it didn't last long. David's canoe was tinier than I thought, with hardly enough room for one man, much less two men and cats. He had an agonizing way of gasping each time I shifted my butt. When the canoe rocked a little, he sent high-pitched squeals echoing across the lake, putting the cats in a panic. He didn't notice that we were on a lonely, lovely lake under a mountain that climbed to the backbone of the Tetons. He fussed, fidgeted, and complained. He could not sit still. The canoe turned, David jerked, and the cats danced. He paddled clumsily and without rhythm. We never made it far from the shore.

I tried to use my new fly rod but got fed up with David telling me how to cast, tie on flies, and reel in line. Besides, every cast was a new adventure in being scolded for rocking the boat. I gave up and eased into a comfortable position to study the lake and the surroundings. David and his fiddling around seemed to disappear into the background until he hooked a fish. He announced his catch with a long, loud moan. As soon as he hauled the foot-long lake trout into the boat, he paddled quickly toward a family picnicking on the shore. He sawed up the poor fish with a bowie knife for his audience. I made him let me out. He took my insect repellent with him.

Clouds of mosquitoes rose up off the lake. I slapped and fished. Despite this, the quiet and the vistas were comforting. Mixed blessings: the beauty and solitude of the Tetons, and David's curses and random chatter echoing over the lake.

After dark, we headed back to our campsite. I wanted to sit by the fire and listen to the woods and the people. We were in the midst of hundreds of people but never saw anyone. Everyone had a small plot of ground big enough for a tent and a picnic table. The rumble of conversation, the tinkle and bang of pans and forks and knives, and the closing of car doors made the woods come alive and accentuated the space we inhabited. But peace was not to be had for long. David made tending the fire a tedious and noisy business. He brought out one piece of wood at a time, allowing that to burn almost completely before announcing in a loud voice he was drawing the next. Between logs he moved his chair from place to place, cursing the smoke, wind, and wood. He alternately cooed at the cats and chased them in loud squeals around the campsite, and once in a while he disappeared up the road, yelling cats' names.

In the night, when I was dead asleep in my lean-to, one of the cats made a break for it—as well it should have. When David discovered its absence, his loud, high-pitched squeal raised me six inches off my mattress. For over an hour, David walked around our small campsite, squeaking, "Here kitty-kitty-kit-kit."

"David, won't the cat come back when it gets hungry?" I said.

"But I'm worried. She's like my baby, like a child. I can't sleep without her."

A man in a campsite down the way yelled, "Hey, buddy, shut the hell up, for chrissake." His voice trailed off into a grumble from which I could make out, "sleep," "family," and "goddamnit." David called him a bastard. "I heard that," said someone else in a campsite a little closer. "Why don't you give it a break," he said further. A woman from elsewhere in the campground raised her voice: "Hey, mister, I got kids here." I tried to get back to sleep by concentrating on what I supposed was a raccoon in the bushes. But my best efforts couldn't shut David out. When he finally found the cat, he chattered with it and the other cat for another hour. Throughout the night he fretted about, chasing cats, getting in and out of the van, slamming the doors, and making the springs squeak. Several campers next to us pleaded with David to "be quiet," which he never did. Sleep came in fits.

By the time I made it out of bed in the late morning, it was time to vacate the site or pay for another night. David insisted I stay with him while he found another camping spot. But I told David I was going with Roland and Michelle back to Teton Village.

"You mean I'll be by myself tonight?" His normally tense face turned long. I saw the whites of his eyes for the first time since we'd met.

"I'm sorry David. I need a few things before I head into Yellowstone. Roland will get me to the store and into the park."

"All right," he said. He looked dejected.

"You gonna be OK?"

"Listen, we didn't have a contract or anything." His face tensed again. He had the look of a kid picked last for the team. "If you think it's more important to go back with them, well then you just do that."

Later I climbed into the car with Roland and Michelle. David stood at the side of his van with one of his cats in his arm. Though I felt bad for him, I felt a great relief as we headed back through the forest to Roland's place.

"It was a tough couple of days," I said. "David's a little much, and I think he didn't have a great outing."

"He's a little much for everyone," Michelle said, laughing. She turned around in the front passenger seat and faced me. "You did him a big favor, you know. When we hear about this next week, you'll be the big hero. He'll have glowing stories of your adventures together far into the future."

"Really?" I said.

"You don't know what you did up there," she said. "He probably hasn't had anyone to travel with for years. And I know no one but you has been in that van since we've been here."

Roland and I took off the next morning toward Yellowstone. We got me set up in a camping spot at the Lewis Lake campground, a beehive of parking spots carved into a hillside. We walked down to the lake, a wide and lonely body of water surrounded on all sides by pines, some living and more burned away in the 1988 fires—forests of deep green and jungles of what looked like telephone poles. We cast out lines into the lake outlet, where it inconspicuously, then with increasing movement, turned into the rough and loud Lewis River. Steam rose from thermal seeps along the side of the grass-blanketed banks. The saturated earth was spongy. Snow on the hillsides wept into muddy, charred slides that stopped at the narrow stands of grass and wildflowers. The air smelled of rosemary, pine resin, and decomposing duff. Dead trees, white like bones, cluttered banks and bunched up in stacks against rocks, and in tangles on the river bottom. The day was turning yellow and shadows fell in steep angles through the stands of dead trees. Over my shoulder, the lake, deep blue, shimmered in the late-afternoon sun. I climbed over a snowbank and down a steep incline to get at a riffle in the bend of the river. There the river came fully alive, with rushing rapids and steeper banks as it ran into a canyon. On a grassy bank that reached into the river, a deer slowly walked out to chew on tufts of grass.

Later Roland and I headed back to the campground through trees black and bare of branches. Some had exploded in splinters to one side of a trunk or the other in the blaze. Others that had fallen were charred, with a black, alligator-skin crust. Still others seemed little damaged but were dead all the same.

We made dinner over a smoky fire and ate in silence. We watched the sun dip under the tops of the pines. Through the campground, pans clanged, children laughed, and fires crackled. As the evening grew darker, bluer, the sounds quieted to the sigh of parents settling into lawn chairs. Down in the valley, a wolf howled. The twilight sky soon filled with stars.

"Well, my man, it's been a good couple of days," Roland said after a while.

"I don't know how to say thanks," I said.

"You go on and keep being someone people like to meet." He sat on the table, looking through the pines at the lake shimmering in orange and purple. Smoke was rising from other campsites in blue plumes.

"Thanks."

"I mean that," he said. "Walking into people's lives does more good for them than they do for you, though it doesn't always seem that way. This trip you're on, it's not all about you, regardless of whether you know that or not."

I stoked the little fire and watched the smoke uncurl and join that of others and settle in the pines like fog. Taking a trip meant accepting whatever came. Most moments along the way had been good. Others weren't so pleasant, like with Jody back in Lander or those moments with David. Good times and bad began to meld into a series of lessons about other people, places, and, through them, me. And maybe I brought a little something to their lives by giving them opportunities to open up, practice their principles, or even be someone else for a little while. We sat on the table a long time, wordless, watching the sun sink into the lake. We both knew that when he left, we wouldn't see each other again.

Walking into other people's lives had consequences for them and for me, some not so great. I puffed on a cigar and built up the fire, if for no other reason than for the trance nicotine and fire can induce. As the twilight turned to night, the sounds around the campground abated to camper doors closing and parents telling their children it was time to get ready for bed.

Down in the valley a wolf howled. Then another. I tucked my canvas lean-to into a small piece of flat ground between some pines. The wolves' howls echoed into my dreams.

17

"Walk quietly in any direction"

I'D PLANNED A couple of long hikes into the Yellowstone back-country, and the trails both started at Old Faithful. But the road was narrow and twisting. There was no shoulder between the pavement and the steep-sided ditch. Speeding drivers didn't give an inch, even when there was no oncoming traffic. I spent most of the morning dodging RV mirrors and car bumpers. It was discouraging. I crossed and re-crossed the road, to use what shoulder there was. A few times I jumped across a ditch into the brush to avoid facing an RV. I watched cars speed by just inches from me. Seven very long miles later, I dropped my pack at a turnout with a large sign that marked the Continental Divide. I stuck my thumb out in the hope that some-one would take pity on me. After a while a car pulled up next to me while I happened to be on the right side of the road.

"It's tough walking, ain't it," the driver said through the open passenger-side window.

"Cars and more cars," I said.

"There's a store I want to go to at Old Faithful. You headed that way?"

"I'll ride," I said and put my pack in the back seat of his car. "Thanks."

"No sweat," he said as we pulled away. He was about twenty, with curly brown hair and long sideburns. "I know how it goes. Only a few of us who work concessions in the park have cars. That's why it's going to be easy for you to get around. Almost everyone who wants to get anywhere in Yellowstone just has to look like they need a ride, and they get one."

He said he was glad to be out of his North Carolina town for the summer. He washed dishes at the Grant Junction restaurant, making five dollars an hour, thirty-five hours a week. Weekly, after taxes and fifty-seven dollars for room and board, his paychecks were less than a hundred bucks.

"Hey, but it's saved money," he said. "I don't drive much, so I don't hardly spend anything. Usually I hitch rides if I want to go fishing or hiking on my days off.

"Everyone's sort of in the same boat. When you're a kid, you dream about being a ranger in a place like this. But rangers have to volunteer for years before they get on regular. For people like me, who have to get paid something, you work for the concessionaire and make out the best you can. It's a sweet deal," he said. "I don't work overtime. Hardly work full-time. I get to do what I want in the park. And I have some money to bum around with until I find a job back home."

I envied him. When I was younger, I thought work had to be drudgery, and that aspiring to work in a national park was an arrogant, impossible goal for the likes of me. As a result I bounced from one hourly job to the next, drinking my way along. I was risk averse and only apt to change something when my life reached a certain level of misery. This kid, on the other hand, was comfortable with having a job that in the big scheme of things was quite out of the ordinary—even if it was washing dishes. He knew where he was, and the great advantages of being young and being in a great national park with time on his hands. He reminded me again that regardless of the outcome of this particular journey, most risks that frightened me were hardly risks at all.

"I've done this every year since I was eighteen, and I'm twenty-three now," he continued. "It gives me time to see my town a little different, you know, rather than it just being a place where I work and sleep. I suppose running up here every summer's bad on a career. But I don't hardly know what a career is. I just know that I like living this way."

He dropped me off at Old Faithful, where I joined the crowd of several hundred waiting for the geyser to blow. The famous column rose up on schedule. After picture taking and hoo-hahing with the rest of the crowd, I took a trail into the hills along the Firehole River toward my campsite for the night. The river ran swollen and sinewy under steep banks blackened in wide swaths with geyser seep. Soon the trail wound away from the river and snaked along the backs of rocky ridges and up the sides of rounded volcanic hills. It came over a rise to a pit of steaming mud pots. A bison there raised its head to get a good look at me and went back to munching soft grass that grew in thin streaks in the mud. Dried clods of beige gumbo clung to its beard and the keel-like hair along its chest and stomach. Its coat rippled with each slight movement. It snorted, and I took the long way around.

Late the next afternoon, after filling my water bottles at a store near Old Faithful and calling my daughter, I took off up into the Firehole Valley. The day was chill and cloudy, making the dripping leaves and needles a deeper green. Ferns and wildflowers grew in thick stands next to the trail. The pines drooped under the burden of rain, fluttering now and then in the wind and showering water down in sheets. Lone Star Geyser's cone stood twenty or more feet tall in an amphitheater-like escarpment in the side of a hill. The yellow-and-red, volcanic-looking cone, which had made loud boiling noises as I arrived, now began a spectacular eruption. Steam burst from the top of the cone in a V-shaped plume. The earth growled and dinned as if it were hollow beneath my feet. Steam-fluffed water erupted and inundated the cone in cascades that both flowed down its face and splashed down from the sky. Two smaller geysers to either side of the main cone also sprayed plumes of smoky steam. Great clouds rose through the tall pines into the wet gray day.

When the geyser fell quiet, I walked in what was now strange silence down a broad trail to my campsite, which lay under widely spaced and ragged pines. Just beyond, moose wandered back and forth across a wide wetland, stopping from time to time to graze. I watched them, taking in their skinny flanks and giant heads, while they moved alone and in pairs under the gray.

I set camp, rigged my new fly rod, and walked along a trail lined on both sides with steaming thermal pools—puddles of deep azure surrounded by the colors of the rainbow. I moved up and out of the pines and down to the floor of the Firehole Valley. Pine-carpeted hills dropped into the broad, treeless valley interior. Here and there bison grazed. Plumes of steam rose from geysers and thermal pools either side of the river. Clouds dipped from the rainy sky down the flanks of the hills in white flumes. The river was swollen and ran cold. The fish were too deep, the current too swift for my small flies. But I spent a long time casting, feeling the river through my line, and watching the quiet valley until the sky drew closer and the day dimmer.

When I arrived back at the campsite, I strung my pack high off the ground on a distant tree and crawled into my sleeping bag in my lean-to set between two firs. I stared out into the silence, breathed in the now-frigid air, and fell into a deep, dreamless sleep, from which I later rose suddenly, startled, and fully awake. A bear had walked into my camp, and I knew where it was before I was even awake. I didn't see it in the dark, but I knew it was about forty feet away, scuffling around under some fallen trees. It stood and dragged its claws on a tree, producing an extraordinarily loud and machine-like sound. Then it stopped suddenly and knew I was there—I could feel its hesitation, much like the brooding silence that falls between friends when one of them has insulted or hurt the other but no one is talking. Sniffing the air, it snorted once and moved toward my lean-to. Unsure of what else to do I hunkered down and clenched myself into a tight knot. When I had to breathe, I tried to inhale in a way that I couldn't hear it. The bear suddenly stopped short of my shelter and moved the other direction, lifting logs here and there until it disappeared into the river bottoms beyond the trees.

I kept thinking about the bear returning, and then what? Anxiety returned. I tried to distract myself by thinking of the ways the national park was a garden, human-made and -tended: Yellowstone was hardly pristine. To build the garden, Americans had weeded people and animals out: Indians, poachers, mountain men, and mountain lions, and wolves. And they tended the garden, fighting fire and blazing trails. They replanted wolves and watched them grow. They built roads into the garden they made, and that access brought the outside world into the garden with stores, gas stations, cabins, and hotels. Plants, birds, and animals from foreign shores and from other places on the continent found refuge here. Tourists stole national treasures and clogged up geysers by tromping on them, breaking off pieces of them, and throwing things into them. Pristine this place was not, today or yesterday. Yellowstone was a place sequestered. Spectators were allowed to see in, through bars, gates, and laws. Did the park give people an understanding of themselves as a part of nature? Or did it perpetrate the myth that they were separate from it and in charge of it? As I fell asleep I kept thinking that the bear and I were really both just animals in a very big zoo.

As the sun rose through the fog that had settled in the river bottoms overnight, I drew water from a boiling thermal pool not far from camp and set the water jugs aside to cool. Later the water had cooled enough to pour over my head and shoulders. The quick, warm douse left behind a refreshing chill. I smelled of camp soap, sulfur, and chalk. Rain soon began to fall and the forest dimmed to near twilight, bathing the forest in muted gray and brown. Except for the pitter-patter of rain, the forest was completely still.

A ride or two later, I headed down the trail to my next campsite. Ice Lake was a rectangular dish of clear water in the top of a ridge. The campsite was perched on a short thumb of land that poked out into the water. On the opposite side, live trees, untouched by the 1988 fires, reached into the last bit of gold and purple sunset. The evening was still, the surface of the lake like a dark mirror. Soon, outside the yellow pool of the fire I'd built, it was black-dark and quiet but for the trills and knocks of woodpeckers, and even they soon ended. Quiet suffused my surroundings for a long time and I heard nothing save the beating of my heart. Suddenly something big splashed into the water on the far side of the lake. Waves of its headway soon sloshed the shore. Whatever it was huffed and snorted repeatedly as it approached my camp. It swam up close, just outside the light of my fire. It stopped and seemed to tread water, panting and grunting. I threw a bundle of sticks on the fire, and the animal swam on. Determined to be done with creatures altogether, I pulled my stocking cap down over my ears and went to bed.

The hike away from the lake was flat and sweet. The burned-over forest had the solemn uniformity of a stand of telephone poles. Sun fell without hindrance through them. Fallen trees lay in neat rows with roots aloft, heavy with dirt and rock. Woodpeckers had chiseled away large pieces of bark from many of the dead trees. New growths had taken a hold on the forest floor, and everywhere wildflowers swayed in the breeze. The place was alive with bird songs. The trail led through groves of living forest that gave way to alpine mead-ows blanketing expansive valleys between stony, brown mountains. Later I cast my flies into bends and riffles in the Gibbon River, and small trout accommodated them. Birds chittered in the grass and trees. Mice ran from beneath fallen trees, and picas sat on rocks and whistled. Overhead hawks circled and cried.

Rounding a bend into a boggy streamside meadow, I nearly walked into the back of a moose. The giant creature, whose green-brown fur bristled in the sunlight, barely looked up. I retreated as I came, slowly, evenly. Spying another moose a short way up the heavily wooded ravine, I backed away and well out of their sight. I shouted and cursed, hoping to scare them away. My voice echoed under the canopy. Then I crept slowly around the bend in the trail to find they hadn't moved. I retreated again, farther this time, and made coffee and cooked something to eat on my pack stove. The sun was setting behind the ridge, making the green darker, the foliage in the river seem more lush, and the woods dimmer. I moved forward again, this time singing and banging my pots together.

The moose had not moved. They looked up briefly and returned to grazing. I was anxious to move on, and afraid to deviate far from the trail in country I didn't know. Instead of waiting, I walked in a wide arc around them, wading through the deep bog near the riverside. I talked quietly to let them know where I was in case I got lost in their blind spots—"I'm just going to make my way through this cold-ass water," I said. "Pay no attention to the man in the reeds. Don't bother with him. Pay no attention to him." A distance away, I found my way back to the trail and started running.

At my campsite, hills descended into an oblong blue pool called Cascade Lake, nestled in the bottom of the bowl-shaped valley. Above, the pines ringed a wide meadow that spread around the lake. My camp was at the bottom of the tree line on a hump between two ravines, where streams flowed down into the meadow and toward the lake. Beads of sap hung thick below deep bear claw marks on the trees. The site was ringed with them. I hesitated, wondering if it was a good idea to sleep where bears had made themselves so famous. Ah, I tried to tell myself, the National Park Service wouldn't put us little, ignorant, inexperienced campers in danger. For a long time I wandered, fraught with indecision, before I started a fire in the fire ring. Things seemed to calm down inside after a while, and I ate while watching moose make their way down one of the ravines into the meadow and back.

Seeing the moose reminded me of cartoon moose in the books I read to Sydney. I missed her, and the longing was not soothed by the every-other-day calls I had been making to her on pay phones. She seemed to be a happy four-year-old. When I called she was doing kid things—watching television, riding her bike, drawing pictures. She wanted to talk but would be quickly pulled away by more important things. I wasn't sure what I expected by calling her, only that the frequent calls satisfied my inner need for contact with a girl who had delivered more love to my life than I had ever experienced before.

As I watched those moose walk silently in the woods and into the meadow, I hoped I wasn't just being selfish. I felt guilty, as I should have, for leaving. To some of my friends, the trip seemed to be a whim or fantasy. But at base it was necessity. I wanted to set an example for my daughter. People like us, working people, people who didn't have money or time, could do something different. Life did not have to be work and drudgery. It could accommodate happiness. And if she ever decided to live in misery, I hoped she wouldn't have to live thirty-plus years before finding a way out of it, as I had. And that she would not have to walk across the country to escape wretchedness. I hoped she would never stay in a job longer than it pleased her.

The moose started walking the tree line just beyond my camp. I took a deep breath and smelled the pine, and my mood grew lighter. The burden was on me to make things different, better, when I got back home. I didn't know how to do that, not yet. But that would come. I only knew that if I was going to leave my kid for a trip across the country, then I had the responsibility to make my way and pass that on to her to use if she wanted. I would have to take responsibility for my own happiness and fulfillment; it wasn't going to come from a house or job or city, or even another person. I made my feelings of frustration and restlessness. I could no longer use her as an excuse for anything. I knew that things would be different for her because I could feel that this was a new start for me.

By nightfall I was sleeping deeply, without dreams. When I woke, I knew exactly where the bear was, though I didn't hear it for another few minutes. I waited, daring not to take a breath. Then I heard the animal splashing in the small creek at the bottom of one of the ravines. It sounded as if it were flipping stones over in the water. After a short time, it left the creek and its footfalls became louder. The ground shook in thumps.

My heart raced. I lay dead still, hoping my daughter wouldn't be too upset when she heard her father had been eaten. My hand hurt, and I discovered I was tightly squeezing a little can of anti-doggie spray that I had kept in my pack and never used. I'd fished it out but couldn't remember doing it. What would I do with this dinky little can of pepper spray? I tried to think of how I'd defend myself if the bear swept in for a quick bite. Hit it in the nose with my fist? Maybe spray the stuff in the can right into its eye? Wouldn't that just piss it off? How would I avoid spraying myself? The bear stopped and began to scrape a tree, making the machine-like grinding of wood I recognized from a few nights before. It moved on to a tree very close to the lean-to and began the scraping again. The ground trembled as it walked by, and its nose zipped back and forth across the canvas as it snuffled and sniffed. At one point, the bear ran its nose across my butt, which made me scrunch my face so hard it hurt. The fug of sweat and shit and the sweetness of decayed meat wafted into my shelter. Smelling that, I panicked. I held my breath and clenched all my muscles even tighter. Then I remembered: the ends of the lean-to were open, ready to be pawed under for roots and bugs like any other overhang, and the fuzzy ball of my stocking cap was hanging out of the end of the lean-to like a big, red marshmallow!

237

Slowly, methodically, the bear moved on, scraping several more trees on its way down to the stream in the next ravine. It flipped stones as it moved back up the hill, loud crashes that echoed eerily in the night. I stayed wrapped tightly against myself for a long time. Slowly I convinced one muscle to relax, then another. As I fell asleep again, I promised myself to get the hell out of there at dawn.

But soon a machine gun–like pounding started, just up the hill from my shelter. I had no idea what it could be and found myself scrunched again into a tight ball. Drifting into and out of sleep, I lay there a long time listening to the sound start and stop.

I rose slowly with the dawn and cautiously peeped over the side of the lean-to in the direction of the sound. "Shit! Fuck! Goddamnit!" I shouted. A ruffed grouse sat on a log about thirty feet away, drumming its wing against the ground. I strung together long ropes of angry vulgarity. I chided myself for being such a scaredy-cat wimp. A bird, for God's sake, a harmless bird. I waved my arms and shouted. It didn't move when I ran up to it. Thrown stones didn't stop it from making the noise. When I landed a rock at its feet, it fluttered up the hill twenty feet or so and began booming again. A cannonade of rocks later, I gave up and collapsed, worn out. When I woke, the grouse was still at it.

The sun was high in the sky, bathing the lake and the boggy valley in washes of gold. The woods across the meadow were burned, which added spindly shadows to a scene of unearthly beauty.

Well after noon I slumped, exhausted and jittery, in front of a burger and baked potato at the Canyon Junction cafeteria. The place was crowded with families in various stages of bad hair and sunburn. The employees seemed to be in good spirits, upbeat and smiling, doing their best to make the tourists comfortable. I imagined how I looked and was wondering where I could take a nap. A man in a chef's hat who had cooked my burger came over and sat down at my table.

"Cains Underwood," he said as he stuck out his hand. "From Alabama. I saw your pack. Did you just walk in here?"

"Yes, I was up the woods a few days."

"Where's your car?"

"In Kansas City."

Cains was on a break from his post at the grill. He lifted his hat and ran his fingers through his thin red hair. He was about thirty-five, and his small-town origins came through in the way he talked, the way he met my tired eyes with his own sky-blues. He had big, knobby hands, and his southern drawl was comforting.

"What's it like out there?" he said.

"Man, I just got sniffed up by a bear," I said. "But besides that, I'm stunned. The park is something else."

"No. I don't mean the park, in particular. But on the road. Ya meet lotsa people?"

"Just like you," I said, wiping the mustard from my mouth with a napkin. I was thinking of a cup of coffee. "The pack's like a business card of a person with a strange or exciting occupation. People can't help but ask. Being on foot helps. It's not threatening. I can't do anything evil or dishonest and get away."

"How're folks?"

"Generally pretty good. There's a few that set my teeth on edge." I shook my head, remembering David and his cats. "But most seem to be looking for ways to be generous and helpful."

"Sorta like in Alabama," he said. "Nearly everyone from my town's like that. It's a small place, like ya see on TV. We got a main street, a courthouse, and the like. Everyone knows ya and knows what you're up to. But it ain't bad, like everyone's in your business. It's good. Neighborly."

I liked the way he talked and asked what brought him to Yellowstone.

"Well," he said, "my town's just a little place. Not many people go out and see stuff. And when they do, they don't come back. It's not like people return from adventures, or even doing like what I'm doing. I thought it'd be nice to see some things, meet some people. So I came to Yellowstone. It was just the place."

Before coming to the park, Cains had worked as a welder in a machine shop. He had to quit his job to take three months in Yellowstone. But he didn't regret it.

"Are you going back?" I asked.

"Yeah, sure," he said. He had his big hands folded on the table and he was relaxed. He seemed to be at peace with himself. "It's home, you know. Plus I can always get along there between going out and seeing places."

"What are you going to do?" I said.

"Well, I figured I get a job." He rubbed his forehead with his fingers and smiled. "But that's not even important right away. I'll have some money saved and my stuff's at my folks' house. I'm good for a while. I think I might take to doing this again next year, a different park, you know, a different part of the country. I like it here. The people's real nice, and there's lots to do. Maybe in a different park I can have the same kinda work and see some other things. I could live like that a while, maybe figure what my next move will be.

"Sounds like a cool plan."

"Yeah, but nothing like what you got. Say, whatcha going to do when you get to Montana?"

"Float home on the Missouri River in a canoe," I said. My plans for the river trip intrigued him even more than walking tales.

"Boy, that's just like a dream," he said. I didn't tell him I didn't know a thing about canoeing, or that the river was a long, dark, scary mystery to me. I could no longer imagine life at the end of the river.

Cains went back to his work and I stepped outside the restaurant to go over my map. A friendly guy sat next to me and unfolded his. I introduced myself. Mike said he was from Wilmington, Delaware, and was "just out screwing around for a while." We had talked a long time, when he stood and said he was headed for the Grand Canyon of the Yellowstone—the wide, deep gorge that was the subject of innumerable paintings, calendars, and photo essays. He asked me to accompany him, and I said I would. Everything in his car had a place—a cooler within arm's reach, a dash map rack that held maps open and readable from the driver's seat, a carrier for a water bottle in the console, smokes and lighter above the visor. He had packed sleeping bag, tent, and stove neatly next to the back doors, where they were easy to get at when he stopped for the night. I envied him. I longed to have things in my pack so neatly.

Mike was laid back and gentle. He wore sunglasses and a yellow floppy hat and sunglasses. A chemist for DuPont, he was "working on getting a chemical farmers use to flow better. It's my job to make sure the chemical is easy to use in the field. It's all pretty hush-hush and pretty interesting stuff—for a chemist. I like my job. But if I had the money, I'd leave it in a second to do something else, travel or see things. All I have now is my vacation time, about a month all together."

"There's something to be said for that," I said. "I don't think I ever worked the kind of a job that gave more than a week's vacation. I always take more, it seems. But they don't pay you for that sort of thing."

Mike laughed. "I used to think I wouldn't mind being a school teacher, you know, get some time off every year in the summer," he said. "But then I found out you work almost all that time anyway getting your classes together. Besides, at DuPont I kinda got hooked into the money. It's tough to see my salary and think about leaving it. But who knows, a few more guys like you might convince me."

We arrived at Artist Point at the canyon and stood with our mouths open among all the other visitors. When we recovered the ability to speak, we said things millions and millions had said before us, and then we turned silent again. Finally Mike cleared his throat. "It's something, isn't it? I don't know if you get used to this kind of thing."

Throngs of people made their way through the juniper and pine to the point, and each person held his or her breath a moment. Kids that had been rowdy above hushed as they made their way to the view. There was chatter in the center of the concrete and rock platform on the point, and along the steps down to it. But along the wall, where people sat and leaned with eyes cast over the canyon, there was solemn silence. No one fought for a look. Those arriving waited patiently for a spot on the wall to open. Those on the wall took their looks and moved aside for others to see.

We didn't talk as we drove to the head of the Yellowstone Falls. The humanity of words, it seemed to me, didn't measure up to what we'd just seen. We took an iron-grate staircase a hundred feet into the canyon. The throng of people on the stairs moved slowly. Everyone tipped their heads up and down, taking in the falls and watching their steps in between. The river rushed over the precipice in a solid mass, quickly turning into foggy white spray that gave everything a watery sheen. Dripping ferns hung off the brown-red cliff behind us, and lonely piñons scrabbled out a living in the crags. The wind the falls whipped up was powerful and cold, and the sound deafening. When we reached the bottom of the steps, we couldn't see where the falls crashed into the rocks below, due to the great, smoky mists.

Later Mike drove slowly. He was quiet, his forehead wrinkled. He seemed sad.

"I've been thinking about folks I meet," he said. "Like you, for instance. You seem to be pretty courageous doing what you're doing."

"I don't know that it's courage. I think it's fear of dying and having missed something. It's the product of not being whole yet."

"Still, I would like to have some of that."

"You already do," I said.

"But everything is pretty regular back home. I'm not sure I know how to change that."

"My dad worked a job he hated for over thirty-five years," I said.

"On the other hand, I'm thirty-two and never worked a job more than a couple of years. Stick with something, I say to myself, and it will turn out all right. But every day I go to a job, I'm scared to death I'll get old and die without having seen or done anything. I plod along doing stuff that doesn't matter to me until I get sick of it and run off to something else. But I don't really change things, I just change the scenery. But now I think that's because I'm scared to death of taking any real responsibility. Getting old working bullshit jobs is easy, especially if you get to say, 'I have a kid to raise.' Well, I don't want to use my kid as an excuse not to act, try something, or even to fail. I didn't take this trip out of courage, Mike. I took it out of fear. You know, like, 'If I don't do it now, I'll never do it and then wind up regretting it.' I don't want to take my frustration over lost chances out on my kid. I can't do that. If I don't get anything out of this other than having done it, she will have that."

A wall of pines shot past his window, punctuated with gaps of clear, deep-blue sky.

"I suppose that's something," he said. "But you're not talking me out of thinking that taking off across the country isn't courageous." He laughed. "So, there!"

Mike dropped me off at a junction in the road and headed west to his next destination somewhere in Montana. Soon an RV lumbered to the curb. The man at the wheel leaned out his window, "Hey, want a ride? We're going to Mammoth, where the hot springs and cliffs and things are." A woman opened a door on the other side and a set of steps dropped from beneath the carriage. Inside, everything was clean and bright. A blender sat next to the toaster. An electric can opener hung from a set of cabinets just above a small stove and oven. The dishwasher was built into the cabinets below. The refrigerator was large and built into the wall next to a microwave oven. The dining area where we sat was spacious and comfortable, and there was even a twin set of armchairs with end tables and lamps. Dainty curtains fluttered from the windows.

"Man, this is some place," I said. "Just like home."

"It *is* home for now," the man said with a wide, satisfied smile. He had turned in the driver's seat and held out his hand. "Rick," he said.

"I'm Stacy," the woman said.

Rick and Stacy were about the cutest couple I'd ever seen. Rick, at thirty, was strong and skinny, with wispy black hair and small, but deep, dark eyes. Stacy was twenty-four with a smile that dominated a round face surrounded with a poof of black hair. She was confident and happy. She wore pink, fuzzy slippers and a baggy sweatshirt that fell in folds around the waist of her jeans. They both spoke with heavy Boston accents.

Stacy armed me with a glass of iced tea. I slouched into a couch across the dining table from her.

Rick drove with relish, his back straight and his arms spread wide over the broad steering wheel. "I always admired these things," he said. "I thought they might be nice. But after the first night in it, I decided I would never travel in anything smaller. It just ain't worth it."

"I don't see how we could have made it all the way from Massachusetts without it," Stacy said.

"What's with the 'for sale' sign in the window?" I asked.

"The RV's for sale," he said. "We bought this for our honeymoon trip. We put that sign up before we left the dealership. We get a good enough price, we'll fly back."

"Newlyweds?"

"Fresh as spring," he said. "We figured we'd take a trip across the nation for a while, see some things we wanted to. I own my own business in Boston, a specialty industrial machine-parts shop. Stacy's a nurse. We've been together for the better part of three years and decided to get hitched. We bought this place to take our honeymoon trip in."

"You wouldn't believe the problems we had," Stacy said. She and

Rick both rolled their eyes in a show of frustration. "We went to a couple of places looking for the right one, because it's kind of like buying a house, you know. But we couldn't get any of the salespeople to talk to us. We were too young for anyone to take us seriously. And here we were, going to pay cash."

"Cash?" I said.

"Just driving this off the lot lost us a couple thousand bucks," Rick said over his shoulder. "If you're on installments, you're paying interest on lost money. Renting something like this would cost us a fortune. That's insane."

The RV rocked gently from side to side, took curves like a dream. Rick leaned over the steering wheel like a bus driver.

"When we're done, we won't need it," he said.

"Won't need it?"

"Nope," Rick said. "We won't make many trips like this. We'll just get another one next time we do."

I wanted to have his attitude toward money and owning things. I was afraid of money, and even more scared to make any big purchase.

Stacy asked me how I liked being on my own.

"It took time to get comfortable with seeing how things go every day," I said. "I still get overwhelmed sometimes. But I've found people mostly friendly and accommodating."

"Big deal," Rick said with a laugh. "I'm glad you're doing it. If it was me, I'd say forget it. All that walking and carrying on with tents and whatnot."

"The heat and the bugs," said Stacy. "It must be rough."

"I like it, to tell the truth, being by myself, meeting people, seeing what they work at and what's important to them."

"I'll bet you've seen a lot of great places," Stacy said. She reached under the table and pulled out a shoebox. "Want to see where we've been?" She pulled the lid off a box full of postcards. My mouth hung open.

"Why take pictures when someone else takes such good ones for us?" she said. "Postcards are much cheaper and easier. I'm always afraid I'll miss something. This way, I get the very best shots of the places we've been."

Rick and Stacy had stopped at every glittering, neon-lit attraction between Boston and Yellowstone. There were hundreds of postcards from dozens of tourist traps. She pointed to the pictures and told me short facts about each of the places they had been: "This is the world's largest electrically lighted waterfall." "The world's highest bridge." "The home of George Washington Carver, who made the most stuff from peanuts."

In a way, I was envious. Doing tourist things with hundreds of other tourists made me feel like a voyeur. The money I spent at such places represented cash I'd need someday—for emergencies, hard times, and things like cars, food, and rent. I was almost always certain I would fail and wind up destitute. Rick and Stacy loved being consumers and unabashed tourists. They had been confident and fearless in buying and planning to sell something that cost more than most houses I'd lived in. Sitting next to Stacy as she explained how wonderful this Ferris wheel was or how big that waterfall was or how many millions of cobs of corn covered this building, I realized that she and Rick never doubted that they would be all right. I wanted to fit in my world as they seemed to fit into theirs.

"How long have you been in Yellowstone?" I asked. It had taken me close to ten days to meet a bison, two bears, and a couple of herds of moose. And I was far from through. I could only guess how long their stay had been.

"We got into Cody (Wyoming) yesterday afternoon and drove into the park to see some sights," Rick said. "We stayed outside Yellowstone last night, and today we are going out of the park past Mammoth Hot Springs. So, I guess a half a day, give or take."

"That's enough to see what you wanted?"

"Sure," he said. "We stop at the sights, take a look around, and go to see more. There's so much. Hey, here's a fine lookout."

He trundled the RV into a turnout overlooking the Yellowstone River as it flowed through a jagged canyon. Rick said he wanted me to have the chance to see a few things I wouldn't have the chance to see without a car. We stepped out, and I had hardly pulled a full breath before we were driving away again. We stopped with machine-gun rapidity at several more scenic spots. Each pause ended with Stacy declaring that, "Gosh, it's beautiful, isn't it?" and "Glorious." Between, I lounged in an armchair recliner and sipped tea.

Rick and Stacy were good to be around. They were open and cheerful, curious in their own way, and generous. Their RV was, as Rick said, a *place*, in the sense of it being a space where they lived. I imagined it being a mini version of the house they would have in Boston, imbued with their personalities, bric-a-brac, and other personal touches. When we parked at Mammoth Hot Springs, they got out, looked around, took a breath, and were ready to go again. Stacy padded up to me in her slippers and asked if I would remember them when I arrived back in Kansas City. I told her I didn't see how I could forget anyone who had such a beautiful home.

I walked down from the parking area toward the Mammoth Hot Springs. Crowds ambled on the long, winding boardwalks and staircases. They looked ant-like against ice-white terraces of the springs. The day had grown hot. Tired and ragged, sweating mothers tugged screaming kids. People ran as if they were late for appointments. The volunteers at the visitor's center seemed heartless and self-absorbed.

After taking in the springs, I walked a short way with the tourists on the boardwalks and took off up Terrace Drive, a narrow, one-way road that wound between colorful geysers and seeps. The smell of grass and pine laced with sulfur floated on the air. The road was steep, and motorists stared at me as if looking at something out of place, a different sort of bear.

I arrived at the campground in the early evening. Two brothers were in the campsite next to mine, Jeff and Craig. Both were stunningly good looking. Jeff was fresh out of his New Jersey high school. His cropped, dark-brown hair accentuated dark-brown eyes and a toothy smile. He was a quiet foil to his brother Craig, a friendly, boisterous young man who had just graduated from the Air Force Academy in Colorado Springs. His angular physique and military cut of blond hair added to his boyishness. They had decided to take a trip together before having to settle into a summer job and a military career.

We made our dinners and talked. We found that we had all been Boy Scouts, Eagle Scouts. While they were proud of their accomplishments, I had to admit that I had pursued the decorations of scouting as an escape from an unhappy home. The recognition had felt good. But the accolade could not make up for the lack of what I needed. It was clearly my choice not to understand the good things I had at home, I said, and Boy Scouts gave me an easy out in more ways than one. I went to meetings regularly, did all the merit badge things I needed, and anxiously waited for the troop to take off on monthly or bimonthly overnights. A rainout was the ultimate disappointment. Every year from the age of eleven to eighteen, I had gone to summer camp in thick hardwood forest above the lazy Osage River. There I had learned that nature absent humans, no matter how unpredictable or scary it might be, had an order. Home, on the other hand, was arbitrary, explosive, and hurtful.

Like a lot of kids, I did a lot of growing up in Boy Scouts. But it wasn't maturing so much as doing what I thought were adult things. I had learned to smoke and drink in the church basement where we had scout meetings. I earned a lot of those merit badges while drunk or stoned, sometimes both.

"Every now and then," I said, "some priest would leave the door to the storage room unlocked. I was like a rat that gets a shot of cocaine pushing on the red button. I tried that door every week, and when it was open, it was like Christmas." I aped a rat pushing a button with its nose. "Yesss . . . ooooo . . . yesssss."

Life at the Academy seemed to suit Craig, even if he was glad to leave it to begin his military career. Craig said that he was glad that he was out of the academy and that he had taken the trip with his little brother. "After this, life's pretty set up," he said. "For the next four years, anyway." Craig seemed to tell Jeff what to do all the time. Jeff seemed to be humoring him. They were always on the edge of bickering. But theirs was a jokey, loving relationship, the kind that some people have and everyone else envies.

Hard, steady rain fell throughout the night. The next day threats of rain came and went, but it was cool and pleasant. Jeff and I walked down to a nearby stream to try a couple of flies on the trout there. We cast into fluffy riffles and rocky alleyways mostly absent of trout. But it was a joy all the same. Jeff talked about meeting his girlfriend four years before. His wallet picture showed her to be a lovely eighteen-year-old. He had dated only her, and she him. Such a good-looking boy with such a likable, energetic personality would have been a good catch for anyone. But his sights were set, his love found.

"We plan on marrying," he said. He picked the berries from a juniper at the side of the creek. We looked over the creek across the valley. The long ridges on the other side of the Gardiner River changed colors as clouds moved in front of the sun. "But we don't feel uncomfortable waiting a good, long time."

"Haven't you ever been tempted to try relationships with other women?" I said, casting into the shallows under a riffle.

"Not once."

"That's something not many of us have. I've never had it. Every relationship I get into, I want out of."

"Don't worry," he said. "It'll happen for you."

I laughed.

Despite all our efforts at communicating with them, the trout didn't have much to say. The creek was high and cold. After a while we couldn't find any good holes to put flies in and gave up.

Susan, a demure but confident young redhead, was talking with Craig when we returned. Since the campground was full, the hosts had put her, as a lone camper, in the site with me. She was on her way back to her home in New Hampshire after a stint as a Forest Service volunteer in Nevada. On her arrival home, she would be off next to take a Peace Corps position in Latin America. I found her intriguing. She was smart, tough, and had a lot going for her. She seemed very independent and knew what her next move was. I admired that. I had no doubt she would be a complete success someday.

We cooked our dinners and sat down to the table, laughing and joking, telling tales. We told about our travels, what we may have been looking for—which wasn't much except time to think, explore, see things. Susan told us of long hours, tedious work, and a recent citizen revolt against Forest Service management of land near Nye, Nevada.

"It's not a rich place," she said. "But there are rich ranchers around who have leased or bought all the prime land. What's left is tough to make a living from, and there's Forest Service land. Somehow some right-wingers picked up the cause and now everyone's convinced they can have something for nothing. The rich ranchers dodge the bullet, and the Forest Service got the worst of it."

Susan said that some ranchers had put cattle out on federal land they had not leased, others overgrazed lands in violation of leases, and still others broke lease agreements with the intention of tying disputes up in court and extending indefinitely the time they could graze their cattle almost cost-free.

"The farmers don't want to buy the land," she said, "and they didn't want to pay for leases or abide by lease agreements when they do. It was tough working out there, really heartbreaking. To go somewhere with my uniform shirt on and get the looks, hear the comments. I know stuff the Forest Service does that isn't right. But this—After a time, I couldn't go to a store or a café and feel safe. I'm glad to be out of there."

Our attention turned to the campfire. We joked, sang, and read passages from John Muir's slim and poetic pamphlet, *Yellowstone National Park*. My particular favorite was Muir's admonition to leave fear and indoor concerns behind: "Walk quietly in any direction and taste the freedom of the mountaineer. Camp out among the grass and gentians of glacier meadows, in craggy garden nooks full of nature's darlings. Climb the mountains and get their good tidings." Each of us had done just that in our own ways. In this we found ourselves bound, more than in just being relegated to the same campsite.

There came a call for beer, and Craig and I drove into Gardiner. We bought beer at a bar and lost all our pocket change in the gambling machines there. We drove back slowly, taking in the profiles of the trees and the ridges against the starry sky. There was no traffic. We stopped to listen to the river, a yawning rush in the distance, scattered with elk whistles. Craig's voice trailed off and we stood silently until the awareness that we had people waiting behind us moved us along.

Back at the campground, as my companions ran out of beer, we crawled into our tents and said good night, in voices that could have come from the closing scene of an episode of *The Waltons*.

A quiet serenity flowed through me, sweeping away the worry of the night before. Nothing would harm me here except fear. But even in those instances, I thought, everything would be all right. I had to allow every moment to envelope me as this one had. I smiled and remembered how I'd had just such flashes of calm while working in my tiny vegetable plot at home. If Yellowstone was a human-made garden, I thought, it was a damn fine one.

18

"That'll get you anywhere you want to go"

As I'd made my way across the plains, I'd felt as if I was swimming across the open ocean. Only when I arrived in Yellowstone did I understand that I had come ashore. The park was an enchanted island, a someplace else where I was able to connect myself to a larger world. I'd used its garden-like separateness to think about my daughter, what life might be like when I returned home, and the nature of my jagged emotions. It had been harder to see Roland drive away as anyone I'd met so far. It was even more difficult to confront the end of my time with my fellow campers. But a hundred people had entered and left my journey before them. All had acted as lenses into my own selfishness and immaturity. I was, in fact, a person experiencing the pain and joys of growing up.

Although I was thirty-two, a mature man in appearance, with adult responsibilities, I began to realize how inadequately I was prepared to deal with plain, ordinary, human difficulties. The morning

I left Yellowstone was the hardest. We had all been mostly silent as we moved around the campsite, afraid to face the end of our time together. We exchanged addresses, knowing full well but unwilling to admit that we would fade over time into incomplete memories. I sat in the campsite a while after everyone was gone, taking in its emptiness.

I walked out to the highway next to the Gardiner River. The ridge on the opposite side rose to clear sky. The air had an alluring odor of pine, dust, diesel, and river water. I was on my way again, and the disconnections and displacements I had experienced in Yellowstone would lead to new ones; some painful, some fulfilling, and all delicious. I was beginning to understand that good and bad were neither. Every moment, emotion, person, and event was neutral. Only I could make good or bad of it. Some people were malign, that was true. But I found they had mostly been unhappy. Regardless of the reasons for their discontent, I had begun to see in them what I had seen in myself before I started on my journey: feelings of being trapped, overwhelmed, or victimized. Even if their actions had been mean-spirited or just downright ugly, I had learned as much from them about myself and where I lived as I had from those who had been generous, kind, and open-hearted.

I spent the next few days with Darlene, a woman from Livingston, Montana, who worked as a cook for the Youth Conservation Corps, a National Parks Service program that employs teens to do conservation work in the parks. Like many other people, she used my presence as a reason to reexplore places she had not been for a while. We drove into the Madison Range, where deep, rocky valleys broke into the grasslands of the plains, which I was glad to see again. The mountains rose into smooth, rolling ridges, shattered from time to time by jagged plates. Towns built of wood and stone—Gallatin Gateway, Bozeman Hot Springs, and Big Sky—were tiny stops on a long ribbon of highway that followed the Gallatin River to the west edge of Yellowstone. Washed-out dirt roads joined the pavement from around draws and ravines. Vistas opened over ranges of sage-brush and up onto long, bare foothills that broke into mountains again. We stopped at turnouts to stare into the valleys and watch big trout splash in the river. We ate hamburgers in mom-and-pop diners and drank coffee from convenience stores. The days were cool and sunny and still. Independence Day passed with a sort of easy breath. We set up lawn chairs under the clotheslines in Darlene's small, shaggy backyard and watched fireworks until both of us were dopey with fatigue.

The onset of flu the next day put me in bed, addled with fever and aches. A few days later I took a bus to Three Forks, during which I slept soundly. When I awoke the fever had broken and I felt human for the first time in almost a week.

Still a little shaky, I stepped off the bus and into a phone booth outside the restaurant that doubled as a bus station. I called Barney Buzdikian, a friend of Kim Merchant, the man who had given me a horse ride down the Oregon Trail outside of Casper. Kim had told me that he would call Barney, and that I should contact Barney when I arrived in Three Forks. Barney answered the phone. He said hadn't heard from Kim, and hadn't heard of me.

"Who did you say you were?"

"Patrick Dobson. I'm a friend of Kim Merchant's."

"He's a good man."

"Sure is. But thank you anyway."

"Stay where you are, I'll be there in ten minutes." He hung up the phone before I could say anything else.

I stepped out and looked down the street. Three Forks was a sleepy town in the middle of a valley that stretched miles between mountains on the east and the west. Somewhere out there was the Missouri, a grand synthesis of three strong streams that led across the plains and through my town. I felt anticipation I had not felt before.

Barney was seventy-two, a kind man with gentle eyes and big

shoulders and hands. His daughter, Helen, was in the car with him. She wanted to be called Buzz. She was attractive, with dark curly hair and a smile that kept secrets.

Barney and Buzz lived in a respectable split-level house in a clean neighborhood of trim lawns and pruned trees. We ate a fine dinner of spaghetti, salad, garlic bread, and olives at a small kitchen table with matching vinyl-covered chairs. Buzz had cooked. She was in her mid thirties, recently divorced, confused, and attractive because of it. She had moved in with Barney, and he seemed to be irritated about it; Buzz's presence had upset his routine. But I suspected it wasn't as bad on him as he made out. He was more interested in seeing her settled and living with a good husband and family. Being in his house confirmed that she didn't have that. Plus it was only for a while, she said. She rubbed her father's shoulders.

"I'll be gone before you know it," she said.

"Oh, I'll know it," he said. He rolled his eyes.

I loved to see them together. While Buzz was perhaps a disappointment to her father, he still needed her around, even if he didn't say so—it was almost as if he enjoyed the annoyance. The way Barney and Buzz interacted revealed them to be two very loving people who would rather have had their relationship develop in a different way. But they liked what they had, and it was a damn sight more than many people. I thought about how I might be with Sydney if I lived long enough to be old, how I might be irritated by her and still want her in my life. I hoped that Syd and I would have a strong, open relationship, the kind that I had never had with my father or mother. Sitting there I realized that just thinking of Sydney and our relationship almost guaranteed that things would be different between her and me than it had been with my parents and me.

After dinner Barney and I drove over to Three Forks. At a park there, shelters and plaques with diagrams and stories of the Lewis and Clark Expedition stood on a small rise above the banks of the Missouri. The sun was setting and the whole plain was bathed in orange. Willows stood in tight knots under a few cottonwoods in a marshy wetland where the Gallatin and Jefferson came together (the Madison joins the Jefferson upstream) to form the Missouri. The Gallatin was the feistiest, if the smallest of the three. The Madison and Jefferson were of similar size and slower. I bathed my forehead and washed my hands in the river. The water felt good and cool on my face. I thought of the ripples I made joining the rest of the water that would flow through Kansas City weeks later.

We stood on a sandy beach strewn with small rocks. Barney smiled and beamed out over the rivers. It wasn't long, however, before clouds of mosquitoes descended and drove us slapping, dancing, and scratching back to the car. We drove around Three Forks and talked. Barney's grandparents had brought him to the United States from Armenia when he was a toddler. Aunts and uncles, brothers and sisters had joined him later. But before his parents could come, immigration law had changed, preventing their passage. He had only met his parents again in the 1960s when he was forty.

When we arrived back at his house, we talked trout. Kim had said that Barney had caught over forty thousand trout in the years he was counting. I asked him about it.

"Well," Barney said. He was sitting in an armchair. He folded his hands and looked down at his feet. "It's more like 41,380."

He had taken up fishing as a teenager between working part-time in diners and on ranches. After finishing high school in 1940, he had worked as a clerk and lineman for the Milwaukee Road in Three Forks, becoming the station agent there. To avoid boredom he began trout fishing every chance he could, up and down the rivers in Three Forks and in mountain streams and brooks to the west and south. Over the years he had fished isolated basins and twists of mountain ravines all over Montana. He fished bony little mountainside rivulets and beaver ponds where brook, brown, and rainbow trout grow to only five or six inches. He liked to fish, he said, where the fish were too small to attract many other anglers, the streams too narrow and rocky, the banks too broken with willow, the ground too boggy.

In 1980, when he was fifty seven, the Milwaukee Road went bankrupt and left Three Forks an empty freight depot and abandoned sidings.

"And then," he said, "I had no excuses—I could fish all the time."

Barney knew he had caught 41,380 trout because he had written down the size and weight of every one he had caught from 1954 to 1994, in pocket-sized books he'd received from the Montana Department of Fish and Game. He had turned the books in at the end of each year, and wildlife agents had recorded the information and sent them back to him. He kept the returned books in a desk in a small, windowless room in his basement.

We went downstairs, where it was quiet and still and cool. Barney sat at the wooden chair in the room and turned on the lamp at a small desk with a leather pad inlaid into the top. The finish around the edges had worn through and the blond wood was shiny from years of use. Affixed to one corner of the desk was a round magnifying glass on a movable arm. A small transistor radio stood on another corner. He opened the drawer under the top, where he kept his fly-tying supplies: various-sized hooks and hook vises, myriad yarns and flosses, tools, and glues. Other drawers held feathers of different birds, fur, and rooster hackles. Two of the bottom drawers were filled with his little logbooks, arranged in chronological order. It felt good to have the books in the desk, he said, "as my way of keeping track of myself." When he flipped through them, Barney said, he could tell who he was—by how, when, and where he had fished, what he kept and what he threw back.

"Too bad there aren't blanks in those books for the trout that got away," he said with a chortle. "Those books have no 'Trout Off' category."

Barney tied dry flies most of the time. But he would tie nymphs, minnows, and scuds to use when he knew he was headed into weather or to a stream where dry flies wouldn't work. "Trout sometimes won't rise, and no amount of skill put on a dry fly will make them," he said. "When the stream is high from winter melt or spring or fall rains, I tie nymphs and scuds, minnows and woolies." He held a Muddler Minnow up to the light. "I throw these guys far upstream to sink before they drift into the slow water behind rocks and riffles and into pools. There's time to wait, you see, to get a sense of what's around you. Then the fly sinks into a hole where the trout are waiting, and those little buggers snap you right back into fishing. It all comes together then, you and water and rocks and fish. There's no better feeling in the world than to feel like just another little piece of everything."

Occasionally, he said, he left his fly rod at home and went fishing with a spinning reel and can of live bait. "I'll put a worm or live minnow on a hook behind a casting bubble and sometimes pull trout in just for fun. But it's like fishing with dynamite."

Barney looked at his watch and apologized. "The Braves game's gonna start in a few minutes, and you can watch it with me if you want," he said. He leaned in his chair and pushed his hands on his thighs. "You know, I saw the Braves in Milwaukee back in 1967. I was there on railroad business. It was the only major-league game I've ever been to. Been a Braves fan ever since.

"Right now the *Atlanta* Braves are on their way to the World Series. I'm one of the few Braves fans in Three Forks, and probably in all of Montana. I watch all the team's games that come on the cable television."

Before he left, Barney showed me a few flies he was working on. He picked up a minuscule Adams and a Muddler Minnow on number-twenty hooks and rotated them in the light of the lamp.

"I like the look of these flies," he said. "They are damn near perfect." He was not complementing himself and his handiwork. He was just happy with the flies, knew what they could do, and what he could do with them. "You take them. You'll need them."

Barney laid twenty or so flies on the desktop. Neatly packing away his supplies, he went upstairs to watch the Braves game. Soon he was yelling at the television. I paged through his little books under the lamp at his desk. Sometimes they contained notes and comments about fish, streams, and weather, but also about personal events. The books chronicled the Braves' move to Atlanta, his wife's disposition through the years. They recorded her death, and Buzz's graduation from high school and her marriage. From his notes, I could see how work changed on the railroad. Barney's frustration with work, family, or life in general streamed from the lists of trout, as did his times of melancholy and lightheartedness.

I folded the flies into my fly box, tucked it into my pack, and went upstairs to watch part of the game with Barney. Buzz and I sat on a couch near the front window. Barney was animated in his armchair. I couldn't stay away from the secrets his fishing records revealed and went back downstairs to read more. I envied Barney's patience, his ability to count and keep track of how many trout he'd caught. He had routines, many of them, and they gave his life structure and form. I knew I could never have exactly what he had. For me, the routines I had formed gave life a structure that I really didn't fit into. I had the secure feeling that I would find my own new routines, my own life that let me live without regret. It would be a life much less selfish and self-absorbed than the one I had been living. I had a lot to learn and might not make it right off. But sitting there in Barney's chair I felt confident I had done the right thing in taking this trip, and that it was paying off. Upstairs, Barney became loud and excited during the closing melee of the game. I thought of him tying those flies and looking them over in the lamplight.

Barney insisted that he take me up the road to Helena the next day. It would mean the end of any more walking. But in many ways the walking part of the journey had been over since before I had made it to Jackson. It was disappointing. Walking seemed to put everything right. It translated earth into human. Its cadence regulated heart and lungs, and freed my mind to wander. I'd loved the long hikes in Yellowstone and had regretted taking the bus out of Livingston when I was sick. On the other hand, Barney was anxious to give me a ride and show me some things underway. And I liked his company.

Barney was a crappy driver, though. He took his time and pointed things out, driving all over the road in jerky accelerations. When we neared Helena he lost his way. We stopped for directions several times and Barney made nervous wrong turns. We drove into the old part of town, where many of the businesses were upscale, targeted at tourists and newly arrived wealth. Beyond these stretches, Helena was a tough place, with spreads of trailer homes and ramshackle houses.

We ended our time together at an outdoor goods store, where my canoe had been delivered. We stood in the back room of the store with our mouths dropped open. It was purple, grape purple, a fine, pretty boat with well-defined lines.

"Seems to me that'll get you anywhere you want to go," Barney said, running his hand down the gunwale and patting the side. "It's wide, so it will be stable. And it has just a little bit of a keel, which will keep you straight. I don't think there's much else in life a man can ask for."

Except not having to say goodbye to his friends. A man could ask for that in addition to stability and direction, I thought. When the time came, I could tell he was having a difficult go of it, just as I was. I hugged him and watched him drive away until I couldn't see him anymore.

Along Last Chance Gulch Street, old tourist hotels were perched above cast-iron storefronts.

The Park Hotel was on the second story of the building across the street. Jack McCabe sat behind a wooden counter at the top of a long flight of stairs. The stairs and the lobby were of lacquered pine, stained with age, but with a good feel. The furniture in the lobby around the counter was chrome and vinyl. The entire wall above the stairs was covered with a photograph mural of the Gates of the Wilderness, jagged narrows where the Missouri makes its last stand in the mountains before flowing out into the Great Plains. Wooden phone booths with glass panes flanked both sides of the stairwell. The place was church quiet.

"I would like a room for a couple of days," I said.

"Well, I'm glad to have you," he said. "It's eighteen a day. I don't have televisions, radios, or telephones in the rooms but I'll call on you in the morning if you know when you'd like to get up. I change the sheets and towels every two days, but if you want it every day, just let me know. Pay phones are there by the stairs. Do you know how long you'd like to stay?"

Jack was about sixty. He was bald and he had very sad blue eyes. But he was as neat as his lobby, both of which had seen more prosperous days.

"Not really," I said. "Probably four or five days. I have some business to do in town here before I take off again."

"Do you have a car?"

"No."

"Well, then, you won't have to worry about parking." He handed me the keys to room twelve. "Come around anytime if you have questions or just want to jaw."

"Are there many people here?" The place was so quiet, I had to ask.

"Not now. I have eighteen rooms. Some I let weekly. I only get filled up if people find me, and then only after the motels outside town are filled. I have thirty-three rooms altogether. But fifteen of them I don't use but to store things in."

"How long has this place been around?"

"I've had it now for forty years. It opened in 1933 at the bottom of the Depression. But rich people were always around, and people always traveled. It was high style in those days. Come around now, anytime."

I set my pack on the great swell of a bed that filled the small room, and pulled out my fly rod. I walked up Last Chance Gulch and into the mountains outside of Helena to tangle Barney's flies in pine branches above knuckly little pinecone-strewn gutters with hardly any water in them. I cast in good rhythm when I wasn't fetching my line out of branches, and soon lost myself in a kind of meditation that can only come from fly fishing, a kind of contemplation that the fish upset by actually biting on a fly. I think I began to understand what Barney had said about taking in water and rock and fish, and snapping from that mediation into fishing and out again. Soon I made the transitions without even noticing. The act of thinking and fishing—and the presences of water, rock, trees, and me—all became one. Besides pine trees and willows, I caught a couple of brook trout out of those tiny streams. I took a good look at them before setting them back in the water. I wondered if there was anything to be gained from pestering the wildlife.

When I tired of fishing, the sun was setting. I lit a small fire of pine twigs. I ran my fingers through the lucky stones I kept in my pocket and prayed that the Braves would win the Series.

"You'll get to the other side"

I HAD PUT off thinking about being on a large river by myself. Then I checked into the Park Hotel and it hit me. The road home was water. And not just any water but the same river that citizens of my town referred to as being a dirty trough. Growing up near the river, but not on it, I had absorbed an entire lifetime of horror stories: eddies and undertow, snags and sandbars, and logs and trees lying in wait to snatch people from boats. Newspapers carried articles about swimmers dragged under and washed up again, weeks later, bloated and decayed on rock jetties. Canoeists in Kansas City had had little experience with the Missouri. When I had fished around for information on the river before I left for Helena, those few I found to tell me about the river said it was big, dangerous, and dirty.

Fortunately for me, Helena had Gordon Longtree. I was wasting time in the Park Hotel and found I couldn't stand looking at the ceiling, alone with my fears. I had gone out and bought a newspaper from a vending machine near a row of storefronts, and was reading the headlines when a lanky, jovial man with long, straight, black hair, and bottomless eyes sidled up and mirrored my movements. At first it was irritating, but he smiled. That was the hook. He said his name was Gordon.

"You know, like a butler," he said. "Assiniboine. But I like when Indians get butler names. It makes us seem harmless."

"You mean you're not?" I said. I leaned up against the building and felt the heat in the stone.

"To white men I wanna seem harmless, you know." He pushed his hands into his jeans pockets. I thought I hadn't seen such a comfortable, laid-back person in weeks. "But I'm an Indian, and it makes me dangerous."

"What?" I said.

"I'm an Indian in a white man's city," he said. He was wearing a worn, button-up, cotton shirt with a red, zippered sweatshirt open at the front. "I get pulled over by the cops for smiling. If the cops are always after me, I must be dangerous. All those cops can't be wrong."

I was aching for a cup of coffee and asked him to join me. I ordered an espresso, Gordon a glass of water. Sitting a polished oak table, Gordon looked at my tiny cup of espresso and laughed.

"What's the deal?"

"Can't drink the stuff," he said. "Handle's too small."

"You drink coffee at all?"

"Nope. Just tea, the kind I get from the hills around here. I'll settle for water. It's hard to screw up water, unless you're a white man. Then, when it's no good anymore, you take the Indians'."

After a few minutes, Gordon seemed familiar. He had a great, toothy smile that shined from his dark, angular face. His long hair hung about his shoulders and down his back. He had grown up on the Fort Peck and Rocky Boys reservations in central Montana, tough but good places, he said, "fulla us Sioux up there. We're all over." His family was from there, but, like him, they lived outside the reservation much of the year. He still went back when his car worked, or when he could get a ride. But he didn't stay long. He had been caught by the lures of the city, he said, and though there wasn't much for Indians, "plenty of Indians live in Helena." And there was open land in the national forest near town. There he built prayer fires and smudged himself with sage and sweetgrass smoke.

"About this trip you're on," he said, "you don't seem like the Columbus type."

"What's that mean?"

"Columbus landed on Hispaniola and didn't realize it wasn't India." He leaned back in his chair, his hands on his thighs. "It's a damn island—still screwed up 'causa him. Man, he had a bad touch. He ran into it 'cause he didn't know how big the earth was. Took a bunch of Indians back to Spain with him, like they didn't have nothing better to do but be slaves. Claimed he discovered a new world. What exactly were the Indians doing there? I always wondered what happened to them Indians he stole."

"He was sort of a man of his time," I said.

He bent forward and folded his arms on the table. "Easy for you to say," he said. When he smiled, it seemed to go all the way into his eyes. "You white men been 'discovering' things a long time. It's sort of in your blood. White people come to a poor neighborhood here in Helena, discover it, and pretty soon, the place goes to pot."

"I still don't get it," I said.

"You don't seem to have discovered much on your trip."

"That's because none of it's new. I'm just seeing it for the first time. Except for what's inside. I suppose I'm discovering a lot there."

"Imagine if Columbus'd felt that way."

For the next few days, Gordon was a constant companion. He seemed to have all the time in the world. He had been evasive when asked what he did for a living. One afternoon we had just eaten fry bread and shredded meat, cornbread, and beans at a small, simple restaurant on the edge of town, and were headed out to his car, a rusty Mazda 626 with questionable brakes. He wanted to show me the capitol.

"I work sometimes but don't most times," he said, getting into the car.

"What do you do? How do you get by?"

"The beautiful thing about white men is they think money solves their problems. They took our land and gave us money. I get that money every month on the fifteenth, like clockwork." It was a funny term for him to use, since he said he existed on "Indian time," which he said meant anytime something was supposed to happen.

"So you pick your checks up every fifteenth?"

"I said the check arrived," he said. "I didn't say I picked it up. I said it comes to the mailbox on the fifteenth. Sometimes I go to the mailbox when I need money. Most times I don't. If I don't go for a while, it's like Christmas."

"Don't need money?"

"There's plenty of free stuff in Helena: soup kitchens, work and food at the Indian Center, clothes—whatever I need. That's where I meet my friends. I live off the fat of the land."

"Where do you stay?"

"People's basements. Sometimes they let me, sometimes they don't know. Especially when it's cold."

"How do you get away with that?"

"I get cold, you know. I'm a Plains Indian, man. Not an Eskimo."

We started from the parking lot. Pressure on the brake pedal conjured unearthly grinding and squealing. He drove slowly so he wouldn't have to stop in a hurry because he couldn't. He smiled all the time.

He called the car his "pony."

"It is a good pony," he said loudly over the engine. The car lacked a muffler. "Sometimes a young stallion." Then he put his hand up to his mouth as if he were whispering, "But mostly, an old nag that eats greenbacks. But it gets me places. Sometimes."

The next week I arranged one or two things for the river trip every morning, slept deeply every afternoon in a sort of depression I didn't understand. The one consistently good thing was meeting with Gordon whenever he showed up at the Park Hotel. We often walked down the line of homeless men who lined the street outside the mission and the Indian Center. He shook their hands, joked with them, and called them by name. In the afternoons, we took long rides around Helena, ate in small restaurants and grills. He knew most the people who owned the places at which we ate, and much of the time, when the food wasn't gratis, I paid. He had friends everywhere. Sometimes I would find myself with him around trash-can fires in alleyways, other times sitting in a well-to-do artist's or lawyer's living room, sipping iced tea. Invariably Gordon would leave late at night and disappear in his pony up Last Chance Gulch in a smoky sputter.

Gordon loved being alive. Until five years before, he said, he had been lost in drink and drugs, stealing to get by. But it all came to an end after one blackout too many. He woke one morning and understood that his whole life had revolved around dishonesty. Putting aside alcohol, he resolved to walk among people as a person, rather than as a drunken, angry thief who believed the world owed him something.

"I even had to change my name," he had told me one afternoon as we sat with some of his homeless buddies around a trash-can fire.

"You changed your name to Gordon?" I said, tossing my empty paper coffee cup into the flames.

"No," he said through his mischievous smile. "I changed it from 'Gordon Leaves His Car Running.'"

When I had first visited the sporting goods store with Barney to see if the canoe had arrived, I arranged a canoeing lesson with a local man named Reg. When the appointed day and time came, we met at the store and tied my boat to the top of his SUV. He was a beefy man, a whitewater canoeist from the local canoe club, with a muscle shirt and shorts that revealed fuzzy blond hair over the contours of smooth muscle. His hair was sun-bleached and his eyes green-blue.

"You've never been canoeing?" he said when we arrived at a medium-sized pond in the middle of a perfectly average city park. We were taking the boat down from the car. The sun was shining. Kids played on the swings and jungle gyms, a few joggers made circuits of the park, dodging sprinklers.

"Not seriously," I said, as we set the boat on the water off a small, sandy beach. The water that spilled into my sneakers was lukewarm. "Some drunken canoe trips a long time ago. I earned canoeing merit badge when I was a scout." I'd been drunk then, too.

"I see. Well—" He had the look of someone dealing with a hopeless case. He held his hands in front of him like a football coach. "Let me tell you first to stay away from sweepers. They're trees that have fallen into the river and water flows through the branches like through a strainer. You get caught in one of them, and that's bad. Second, watch for underwater hazards, anything that makes the water rise or ripple. Do you know if you have diversion dams to portage around?"

I shrugged. I didn't know what a diversion dam was.

"You'll be able to get maps and they'll show you. Don't go over a diversion dam; you go over and you can get caught for days just rolling around. That's bad."

"I suppose so," I said.

We stood on the beach. He demonstrated how to hold the paddle, how to get in and out of the canoe on shore and in the water. He instructed me to sit in the middle of the boat and demonstrated various paddle strokes, and I was off, zigzagging uncontrollably all over the tiny lake. I couldn't do a proper J-stroke. He told me to "pry," and I pried, nearly capsizing the canoe. We were there for about an hour. I got out my wallet to pay him for his time.

"You don't need to pay me," he said. "Usually I charge. But you have a lot to learn. I consider it saving a life."

"Have you ever been on the Missouri?" I said.

"No," he said.

"Do you know anything about what I'm in for?" I said.

"It's big, I know. And I know plenty of people who tried pieces of it. I wouldn't do any of it, though. Too dangerous." My shoulders sagged. This big, strong man would brave cataracts of whitewater but wouldn't put his boat on the river that would be my home for the next two months.

Through the week, my room had become a jumble of disorderly piles: coils of rope, dry bags, stove, sleeping bag, and other gear. On the desk were maps and papers. Against the bureau leaned paddles, life jacket, boots, and a small stack of clothes. I had no idea what I was doing. But I kept after it, one thing after another, day after day, until everything was packed into the dry bags—food in one, clothes and other gear in the other. They weren't heavy. My whole outfit weighed less than sixty pounds, including the life jacket and paddles.

Getting a ride fifteen miles to the river at Wolf Creek was an on-and-off proposition. Gordon's car wouldn't be able to make it, so I didn't ask him. A pair of young, do-rag-wearing boys I had talked into a ride flaked out at the last minute. Fortunately Gordon was standing next me when the younger of the two told me the bad news.

"Man, you shouldn't worry so much," Gordon said as they walked away.

"But goddamnit, this is kind of a big deal," I said. We stood on Last Chance Gulch outside the sporting goods store. The day was warm. Beads of sweat popped out on my head. Gordon's dark skin shined. "I have a boat and gear to get out to the river. These people in the store are getting sick of me. If it was just me, I'd walk. But I got the boat and all my shit."

"You have a dirty mouth," he said.

"What?"

"You have a dirty mouth and you worry too much," he said, looking out over the street with his hands in his pockets.

"Come on, Gordon. I'm stuck here. I don't know how I'm gonna get to the river."

"I could arrange something." He smiled that devious smile. His eyes turned into dark slits. I hadn't asked him to take me because none of the people he regularly hung around with had cars, and his pony wasn't up to the task.

"Really?"

"Sure," he said.

"Well, that would be great. Perfect. We've been together a whole week and you never said anything. How come you never brought this up when we were chasing all over looking for a ride?"

"You never asked," he said.

"You're kidding. You've got to be kidding."

"I thought about it but my pony won't carry your boat. And it doesn't have brakes. I am afraid it will get homesick if I go too far from town. That's out."

We stood there a few moments. I was fuming. A light, cool breeze blew down Last Chance Gulch. A pair of older women made their way past us on the sidewalk, and Gordon said hello to them.

"You still haven't asked," he said when they had passed. He didn't look at me.

I was exasperated. "Gordon, damn it."

"Uhp, watch your language."

I said in the calmest voice I could muster, "Would you try to find me a ride out to the river?"

"Yeah. Yeah, sure. I could do that." In that moment, I hated him.

He turned and walked around the corner and disappeared. I stood there in dejection. I had no idea when or if he would show up. My need to get going was not his, and it could be a few days before he arranged something. I had no way to get hold of him. He had no phone, so he would have to drive or walk to ask his friends.

I stood there another while, trying to ease my anxiety. I took in the street, the shadows lengthening as the sun slid behind the hills. Gordon drove up.

"It's all done," he yelled over the popping exhaust. "Rico will take us to the river."

"Who's Rico?" I said, leaning down to the passenger side window.

"He's a big man with a big car." He put his pony in gear, turned it off, and pulled the parking brake that didn't work. "He will take us tomorrow," Gordon said as he stood from the car and closed the door. "I don't know when. Let's walk down here. I want to do something for you."

We walked into a leather goods store two blocks away. He knew the man behind the counter, who wasn't friendly and didn't seem to like Gordon. The man cut a small piece of strong, soft leather and laid it on the counter. Gordon selected an opaque glass bead of turquoise blue from a case and held it up to the light.

"He didn't have these earlier in the week but got them in today," he said. "This will finish what I want to do for you."

"What's that?"

"Something special."

We walked back to Gordon's car, and he sputtered away again to wherever he went when he wasn't at my side.

I walked back to the motel and up the stairs. With a ride and with my gear ready to go, I felt only a sense of foreboding about the river. Since I had been in Helena, everyone—from the staff of the sporting goods store to Reg—had told me of the grave dangers I faced and how difficult it was ahead.

I didn't sleep well, thinking of my next day, possibly the first on the river. I wasn't sure that Gordon and Rico would show up. I stared at the shadows on the ceiling of my room. Finally I got up, took a book and my journal, and went to sit in the lobby in one of those chrome-and-vinyl chairs under the wall-long photo of the Gates of the Wilderness. Jack was there, reading a newspaper.

"What are you doing up?" I said. "It's late."

"It's early, you mean," he said. "I haven't slept right in years."

He rubbed his forehead with his stubby fingers. His skin was blotchy and soft, with a red tinge that can only come from drinking or high blood pressure. He looked as if he never went outside.

"Tough thing, what you're doing," he said, setting the newspaper aside. "If you don't mind my saying, I been watching you all week. You don't seem to be too worried."

"I'm scared shitless," I said. I settled into one of those chairs and kept settling. It was comfortable, and I knew it was going to be hard to get up again. "People have nothing but bad things to say about the river. Even the giant who gave me my canoe lesson had only bad things to say."

"You're giving everyone else too much credit," he said. He leaned on his elbows, arms crossed on the desk. "Of all the people who've said nasty things about it, have any of them done what you've done or are going to do?"

"I don't think so," I said. "A couple of them have gone fishing there."

"So none of them know, really," he said. He leaned back in his chair. "Listen, people look at me and see a tired old man who runs a fleabag. But this is a nice place, quiet and comfortable. It's clean. I sit here a lot and think about when I was young and the things I did. I'm tired and I'm old. But I have seen and done a lot things. Take the Gates of the Wilderness. It's a pretty famous place, lots of pictures in calendars and on walls, like mine here. I look at that picture of the Gates of the Wilderness every day and every night. The beauty of that place is not the way it looks in the picture, but the way I felt when I found that place on my own. I think of the times I was there whenever I look at this picture, and like I said, I look at it every day and every night.

"My point, son, you've seen things none of them'll ever see. When people tell you why you're gonna fail, they're really telling you about why they think they'd fail. They're telling you what they're afraid of, and why they won't do what you're doing. And they want to keep you from your task so they can feel better about themselves. I've watched you since you've been here. You call your girlfriend and your kid, and you tell them you are scared and tired. But you don't look it and you keep going on. You don't tell them the one thing I want you to tell me."

"What's that?" I asked.

"Have you ever thought about giving up and going home?"

"Not once."

"All right, then. It's time to trust that . . . inside."

The next morning I waited for Gordon in the Park Hotel lobby for two hours. I checked at the coffee shop and the Indian Center. No one had seen Gordon so I went back to the hotel to take a nap.

As soon as I fell to sleep, a worried churning mess, Gordon knocked on the door.

"White man," he said from the other side of the door. He had put on what he called his "movie Indian" voice. He made fun of movie Indians in old westerns, saying that most of them were white men anyway. "It is time to go, white man. Pony waits."

I was groggy, it was like a dream.

"White man. White man, heap bad medicine to make pony and Indian wait."

I stumbled out of the room, one dry bag on my shoulder, the other in my hands. I still had a couple of things on the bed, maps, water bottle, survival bag, and a few odds and ends.

"Is this all you're taking?" Gordon asked when he came into the room. He'd dropped his movie voice.

"Yep, this is it."

"Don't seem like much," he said, looking and gesturing at the bags. "This will keep you alive?"

"I hope so."

"You'd make a good Indian. I have this for you." He held up a small leather pouch on a thong and hung it around my neck. It had a fringe flap, and the turquoise blue bead set astride a little knot at the top.

"This is for that pocket of rocks you have," he said.

Gordon had noticed a few days before that every time I dug into my pocket, I pulled out a handful of small stones people had given me along my journey. They called them their lucky stones or rocks. They believed that I needed whatever they found in them for the road ahead. Some people had given them to me as parting gifts. Others had meant them to be mementos to remember them by. In all instances, the stones had reminded me of the givers and the things they had taught me. I liked those rocks and felt a certain responsibility to carry them. I even gained comfort from them when things had gotten rough.

"There's a reason people give you those rocks," Gordon said. "And a reason you keep them, but you don't know." His face became serious, his eyes deepened. "You keep them with you, though you tell me you don't know one way or the other about charms and totems. Charms're something people wear on bracelets. Totems're for poles. If those rocks weren't important to you every day, in a way deeper than a charm bracelet, you'd have given them to the mailman to take home or you'd've thrown them away."

He took a deep breath that was almost a sigh. "Those rocks are memories. People like to be remembered. But, more than that, they're prayers those people send with you. You keep the stones with you because you feel the strength of the prayers. This is a medicine bag. Put the rocks in there, close it tight, and keep them close to your heart."

The bag was cool against my chest. I had seen Gordon carrying a similar bag, often in a pocket or his hand. He was never without it. I didn't think I would wear it around my neck long, but I knew I would keep it with me.

Outside, in a giant rusted Ford with tired suspension, sat Rico. He was a big man, four hundred pounds big. The cigarette in his hand looked like a tiny, smoldering match. He wore sunglasses and a cowboy hat.

"Hey, Rico," I said. "I'm Patrick. Thanks for doing this for me." I looked at the top of the car, vinyl flaking off, trying to see where I would put the canoe.

"What's wrong, white boy?" he said. He lowered his glasses and smiled. "You act like you never seen a black man before. They got us where you come from, don't they?"

"I was just looking where we'd put the boat," I said.

"I'm just fuckin' with ya. We'll find a way to put that boat on. Let's ride."

We sputtered up to the back door of the sporting goods store. Gordon and I pulled the canoe out the door and tied it to the top of the car. Rico sat smoking behind the wheel, barking commands. Tied down to the bumpers, the canoe slung low over the windshield and back window. We took off in a great cloud of smoke.

"There's supposed to be a park next to the bridge at Wolf Creek," I said. "That's where we want to go." Gordon sat up front in the passenger seat. Rico held his right hand up over the seat, rubbing his thumb against his index and second fingers. I sat in the back seat and fished around in my wallet for a twenty-dollar bill.

"Know how much this hog drinks?" Rico said.

"It's right here," I said and held the bill over the seat.

"Ah, yes," he said, handing the bill to Gordon. "It's what makes the world go round 'n round. My man Gordon will take care of that for me. Hey, we got almost everyone here, a white boy, an Indian, and a black man. We find a Korean someplace we could be on a poster."

"They're cousins," Gordon said. "Almost is good enough. Besides, you know how ridiculous your pony looks. The canoe is purple."

"I don't give a shit one way or the other," Rico said. "If the Korean wants a ride, he gets one."

The Ford chugged and huffed and backfired up and down the hills toward Wolf Creek. Rico, like Gordon, was a jokester. He was good-natured but very much a tough guy. I asked him about being black in Helena.

"I'm from Chicago," he said. "So I come out here with all these rough and tough cowboys, and I like them. Most of them're good people. But most of them're pussies. They think because they live alone, they're tough. Hell, that ain't tough. Living with other people's tough. I respect all the hands-off, small-government stuff, though. Every fucker I know who got on welfare never got off 'cause the getting was good. It's become a way for you white guys to keep us under control."

"But many of these cowboy guys are on some kind of welfare," I said. "Cheap land, ag subsidies, highway building projects, something."

"Don't tell me," he said. "They whine more'an black folks in Chicago when someone wants to cut them off. But I say get the feds outta here. Get all this land into private ownership. Government keeps the land just so they can have control. Without the land, they got shit."

"Hey! Wait. Give it back to the Indians," Gordon said. "You Americans're real good about taking and giving what isn't yours."

The park was a wide meadow with a boat landing next to a bridge over the Missouri. The river was steel blue. It was smooth but for little ripples and eddies along the edges. Across the river was a grove of cottonwoods whose reflection on the river looked like an impressionist paintning.

"My god, it's beautiful," I said.

"Say, man, you gotta gun?" Rico said, turning to look over the seat at me.

"I want to meet people, not shoot them."

"Fuck, man. You'd never get all of me out there anyway. But if you did, I'd have a gun just to keep the crazy fuckers under control. And bears."

"There's no bears around here," Gordon said.

"Just in case one got a little stray," Rico said.

Gordon and I took the canoe off Rico's car. When the work was done, Rico emerged from the car. He was indeed a big man. His jeans and shirt were hand-made. We walked over to the river, which was not nearly as mirror-like as it had looked from the bridge. Heavy snowmelt and rain had filled the lake behind Holter Dam; the floodgates were open. The river had swollen to fill its banks and lapped over the grass at our feet.

"Sombitch, man," Rico said, lifting his sunglasses. "That's a hell of a thing. Not too many people'd get in there with it like this."

"But the river is a good thing," Gordon said. "It will take you where you wanna go."

"And damn quick," Rico said.

We sat down at a picnic table. Rico and I smoked. Cigarettes looked like toys in his fingers. My cigar smoke floated past Gordon's head. I looked at the water. It was strong, this river, clear and deep. I realized I really didn't know what I was getting myself into.

"You look kinda scared, fidgety-like," Gordon said.

"I'm frightened," I admitted.

"I wouldn't do it, but I ain't you," he said. "You'll be fine. Plus, you'll meet more Indians—Assiniboine—when you go through Fort Peck. That can't be all bad."

"I think you'll be all right, too," Rico said. "I have a feeling about you. Be scared. You gotta. But keep going. You'll get to the other side."

We sat a long time in silence. When it was time for them to leave, Rico took my hand in his catcher's mitt-sized fist. Gordon hugged me.

"Be a good white man," he said. "Be a good man."

They drove out of the park, leaving me alone, my canoe and bags stacked on the grass.

I sat at the picnic table watching the Missouri muscle by. Evening was falling and the river flowed deep, green, and smooth. The air smelled of water, fish, and wet stone. As I built a fire, I knew that another journey lay in front of me with its own lessons, insights, and people.

I reveled in the smell of the water and the fire, and watched the smoke curl into the evening. The journey so far had not been a vacation from life but a passage into it. In seeking escape from restlessness and fear, I'd found mentors who faced ordinary struggles and felt their honesty unfold in possibilities. They had taught me that fear of uncertainty, risk, and failure was our lot, but these had no place in governing a life. Instead fear was best faced, walked through, and used as motivation to move forward, look deeper, and to admit what I wanted to deny. I need not feel trapped or act out on my suffering. Life did not have to end painting a concrete floor. It could begin there.

The people I'd met were generous because they had so little. They did not have wealth and comfort depicted in magazine advertisements and television shows. Instead they were people of roads and trailer parks and convenience stores. Their lives were prosperous in spirit if not much else. Not flawless, they waved their country's flag with too much enthusiasm, as if a flag could give them the identity and belonging that their consumer society promised but failed to deliver. They prayed to a vengeful God to avoid the difficulties of thinking too deeply about the complexity and nuances of human relationships. They loved each other as individuals but despised abstracted, faceless crowds of which we all were a part. In all this they had showed me how to relish humanity—my own and others'—in all its mediocrity and beauty and ugliness, meanness and generosity, sadness and pain and joy.

Twilight played in colors across the river's surface. I smelled its green dampness. All the people I'd met were now a part of me. Underneath the immediate fear of the river, I trusted that the people of the vast grasslands ahead would take me home much in the same way they had gotten me here. I stared at the river until well after dark, feeling past and future flow together.

Forever alive, forever forward,
Stately, solemn, sad, withdrawn, baffled, mad, turbulent, feeble and
*   dissatisfied,*
Desperate, proud, fond, sick, accepted by men, rejected by men,
They go! they go! I know that they go, but I know not where they go,
But I know they go toward the best—toward something great.

WALT WHITMAN, "Song of the Open Road"